"EXPLOSIVE . . . A CORKER OF A THRILLER!"
—Associated Press

Siberia was heating up. Three Russians were found in the snow, sexually maimed and savagely slain. Rumors spread of orgies in official villas. Unrest seethed among the natives. A huge Soviet project was in jeopardy. And a freewheeling-and-dealing American millionaire was on the loose.

It was up to Militia Lieutenant Anna Kovina to find the murderer. But Anna was more than a dedicated police detective on the trail of a terrifying killer. She was also a woman on a path of dangerous desire . . . moving through a land primed to explode and toward a discovery that could destroy her. . . .

"Devastatingly different . . . chilling . . . full of surprises!"

—Pasadena Star News

"A brisk, entertaining cops 'n killers thriller . . . chilling in every sense!"

—New York Sunday News

EDWARD TOPOL knows whereof he writes. Before coming to America and becoming a best-selling novelist, he was a prominent writer in the Soviet Union.

D0206578

RED SNOW

EDWARD TOPOL

A SIGNET BOOK

NEW AMERICAN LIBRARY

I dedicate this book
to Sarah Dvorkina, my mother,
whose grave lies in the USSR,
and Sarah Adel Topol, my daughter,
who was born while I was writing the
final pages of the manuscript.

In my former Soviet life, I traveled so often to the Far North of the USSR on journalistic assignments that the living prototypes of this novel, and even the taste of bilberries with sugar, that rare dish you get only in Soviet restaurants above the Arctic Circle, live on in my dreams, dammit, as clearly as ever . . .

I reckon, therefore, that I dreamed all the events and characters in the novel, and any coincidences with actual reality up to and including the construction of the Siberia-Western Europe gas pipeline are simply part of a nightmare.

And the triple-edged arrow with the signal for revolt
has flown over our land, and all must go to the
battle: both valiant warrior and common man . . .

FROM A NENETS BALLAD

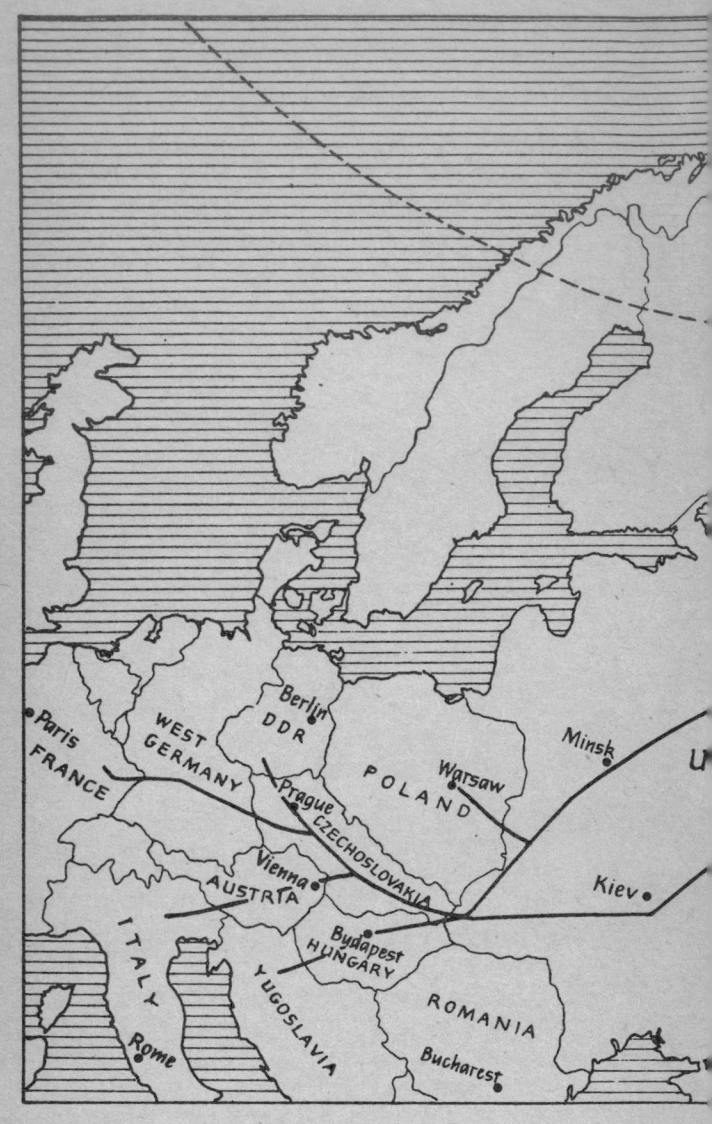

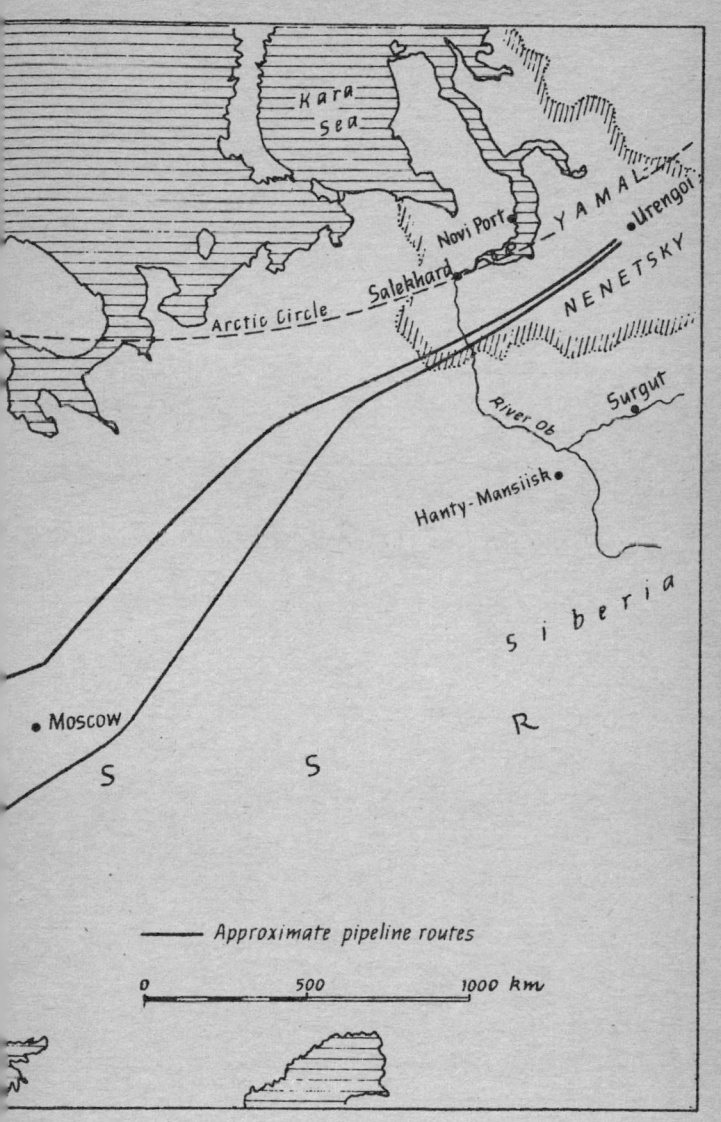

I

THREE CORPSES BEYOND THE ARCTIC CIRCLE

1

Part of a radio message to Militia Lieutenant Anna Kovina, Urengoi CID* investigator:

. . . NEAR YAKU-TUR SHIFT SETTLEMENT, THE NA-KED CORPSE OF VITALI VOROPAYEV, LEADER OF THE SEISMOGRAPHIC EXPEDITION, HAS BEEN DISCOVERED BY NENETS FISHERMEN. THE BODY BEARS MARKS OF SADISTIC VIOLENCE. AT THE SAME TIME NEAR THE RIVER JETTY IN SALEKHARD FISHERMEN HAVE FOUND THE BODY OF THE CHIEF CONSULTANT PHYSICIAN AT SALEKHARD DISTRICT HOSPITAL, OLEG HOTKO, MUTILATED IN SIMILAR FASHION. . . . THE LOCA-TIONS OF THE CRIMES COINCIDE WITH THE PROB-ABLE ROUTE OF ESCAPED PRISONERS FROM CAMP RS-549 . . .

Part of a government telegram to First Secretary Yamal-Nenets District Committee CPSU:†

THE SERIES OF MURDERS COMMITTED BY ESCAPEES FROM CAMP RS-549 THREATENS THE SECURITY OF

*Criminal Investigations Department
†Communist Party of the Soviet Union

THE OFFICIAL OPENING CEREMONY OF THE SIBERIA–
WESTERN EUROPE GAS PIPELINE. TAKE IMMEDIATE
MEASURES . . .

2

They escaped from the camp on the night of December 5, 1983, while the usual blizzard was raging across the polar tundra. Nobody ever did find out the exact time of the escape. Most likely, they intended to clear the camp compound by midnight, so as to put appreciable distance between them and the camp itself by morning. In any event, it happened on that night, when cosmic darkness shrouded the Yamal peninsula in the Soviet Arctic. A force-nine gale whipped up whirlwinds of powdered snow above the eternally frostbound tundra. There was no withstanding the biting storm even on the ground, never mind up on the watchtowers. Sheepskin jackets were no use; the wind chilled right through to the skin, took the breath away, slashed the eyeballs. The searchlights couldn't penetrate half a yard into the blizzard. It was on such a night that three convicts noiselessly left their barracks.

Getting out of a barracks of three hundred snoring prisoners on rough wooden bunks is not hard. The camp guards don't keep watch on every individual barracks; they stay on the towers along the wire fence. Besides, prisoners often leave their barracks in the middle of the night to sprint over to the latrine, a nasty little box of planks nesting above the permafrost on four timber posts.

In fine—that is, calm—weather, the soldiers on the

towers can easily see who ducks out of which barracks and runs where he should, and who decides to do his business there and then on the path trodden in the snow. For the fun of it, the soldiers blind the transgressors with their searchlights. In the morning the erring convicts could draw a spell in the stockade from the head of camp administration. Even in a camp above the Arctic Circle, hygiene must be observed!

But during a blizzard, no searchlight can penetrate the dancing snow. Three prisoners left their barracks and skirted the latrine. Thirty yards away was the camp fence, with coils of barbed wire along the top. The wire carried a powerful electric charge, and the slightest touch meant death. The convicts had no intention of touching the wire. On the contrary, they moved away from the fence and toward the highvoltage metal pylon that towered over the camp compound. This line, one of the dozens crossing the Yamal tundra in the last few years, supplied energy to a whole group of gas boreholes.

Helping each other up, the prisoners climbed the pylon. The storm could have plucked the daredevils off at any second, of course, and no one would even have heard their last cries over the howling of the wind. But they climbed to the top of the pylon, towering over the middle of the camp. In the pitch black, under the searing wind, they crawled out onto an arm of the pylon, a hundred and twenty feet up, and lobbed some X-shaped wooden spools, with metal clamps through the center, straight onto the thick high-tension cables. Clinging to the clamps, they literally rolled away through the air, out of the camp—over the fence with its barbed wire, six feet from the watchtower.

They were missed in the morning, if morning was the word for the same polar night, black and blinded by the unceasing blizzard. They were missed in the count at 6:30 during work allocation, while the camp guard was handing over the prisoners one by one to the outside escorts.

An alarm was raised, and the whole of camp security turned out. But there was no special panic: the head of camp security, an Ossetian named Orudjev, was renowned for the fact that in the twelve years he had served in guard units, not one runaway had escaped him or returned to the camp alive. On the contrary, Orudjev, a dashing, broad-chested major, with his hand-picked squad of crack troops, felt a surge of euphoria. In the first place, hunting down escapees was an excellent way of enlivening the monotony of service life. Second, for every runaway brought back to camp alive or dead, the successful hunters got ten days' home leave. And so an entire company of excited soldiers and NCOs with tracker dogs at once sped off in pursuit of the fugitives.

Despite the blizzard, the Alsatians were quick to find the spools discarded close by the next pylon beyond the camp compound; the manner in which the prisoners had contrived their escape was now clear. Beyond the spools, however, the dogs found nothing. The wind had obliterated any tracks and swept the tundra snow crust clean of their scent.

After five hours of battling the elements, which were becoming more brutal by the hour, the dogs had cut their paws to pieces on the rough ice; they were dropping, or, as policemen say, "they'd croaked." Major Orudjev had grown hoarse and exhausted his ample supply of Russian and Ossetian obscenities. Three soldiers had frostbitten feet, nine others had frostbitten cheeks and other poorly protected spots.

Shortly thereafter, two identical radio messages arrived in Urengoi, the center of the most extensive gas fields in the world and the dispatch point for the Siberia–Western Europe gas pipeline. One was to the local KGB, the second to us at the Urengoi CID.

ON THE NIGHT OF DECEMBER 6, THREE PRISONERS: CRIMINALS ZALOYEV AND SHIMANSKY AND POLITICAL TOLMACHOV BROKE OUT OF CAMP RS-549. BLIZZARDS HAVE OBLITERATED THE TRACKS OF FUGITIVES. ESSENTIAL TO INVOLVE SEARCH HELICOPTERS AND REINFORCE PATROLS ON SALEKHARD RAILWAY. CAMP COMMANDANT RS-549 SHVIRYOV, HEAD OF CAMP SECURITY ORUDJEV.

3

There could be no question of using search helicopters on the seventh or the eighth of December, however: the storm increased in ferocity to force sixteen and the temperature dropped to forty* below.

The deputy head of the Urengoi KGB Directorate, Major Gromov, rolled up in his Sno-Cat to pay the CID a visit. In preparation for the official opening of the Siberia–Western Europe gas pipeline in ten days, we investigators, like all employees in Urengoi, were engaged in a cleanup of our post and were painting floors and whitewashing walls. Gromov, a flamboyant man of forty with shrewd hazel eyes, strode purposefully along the corridor on the old newspapers we had put down. Without a word to anyone, he walked straight into the office of our chief, Major Zotov. He hadn't bothered to knock the snow off his calf-leather boots and left wet footmarks on the floor.

A visit from the KGB was nothing unusual: Zotov was an old arctic hand—one of the most experienced police detectives in Siberia. Naturally, we rank-and-file investigators heard nothing of what passed in the office: we kept on whitewashing, slapping the paint over the old dirty-brown walls until Gromov emerged

*Temperatures are Celsius.

ten minutes later. He looked reassured and was obviously no longer in a hurry.

"Greetings to the heroes of the paintbrush!" He bestowed an intent masculine stare on me and Katya, our typist.

"Hello then, Anechka." He spoke with a familiarity I had given him no pretext for in the four years I had worked in Urengoi. On the whole, relations between us in the militia and the KGB are pretty complicated; there's rivalry. They think they're the elite, the white bone and blue blood of national security; their pay and allowances are way above ours. But we know who does the basic everyday dirty work, looking after law and order in the country. Especially in Siberia, in the Yamal tundra, where the government has mobilized more than a million workers over the last few years—welders, fitters, drivers, and convicts to develop the gas fields and construct the Siberia-Western Europe gas pipeline. Along with them, naturally, came drifters and profiteers, prostitutes and other criminal elements from all over the country, every one of them after a fast arctic ruble. Drunken brawls and knife fights in restaurants and workingmen's hostels, murders over women, fistfights in dance halls with fatal consequences, poaching in the taiga, gang rapes, under the influence of liquor or not; add to that narcotics, unreported syphilis, prostitution, speculation in furs and fruit—that's the criminal dungheap we have to rake over day after day. The lily-white hands of the KGB, of course, keep well away.

But it was probably because I was wearing paint-splashed dungarees instead of my militia lieutenant's tunic that Gromov felt he could call me Anechka and run his masculine glance over my figure. I've no idea what scale Major Gromov uses in awarding points to women, but it looked as if I scored pretty highly, spattered dungarees and all. He came up to me.

"I've had good reports of your work. After the pipeline opens, we're having a New Year's party for KGB officers. Why not come along, I'll send you an invitation.''

Of course, everybody in the corridor froze in silence, watching how easily a KGB major could pick up CID Investigator Anna Kovina. As for me, I believe I blushed, a thing I hardly ever do.

"Thanks," I said, "I'm on duty over at the fitters' settlement on New Year's. There'll be a few knife fights, I expect, and other assorted entertainments. Why not come over here, don't bother about invitations.''

Other people turned away, smiling. Someone couldn't hold back a belly laugh; Katya fluttered her overpainted eyelids in alarm.

Gromov, however, rose to the occasion. He guffawed loudest of all, as his intelligent eyes flashed.

"You're on! I'll be over!" he said, giving me a mock salute and even clicking the heels of his calf-leather boots. "Permission to leave?"

"At ease. Off you go." The son of a bitch had wrung a smile out of me all the same!

Later, during the lunch hour, when all the investigators assembled in the common room and piled the sandwiches they'd brought from home on the table, and Katya had placed an enormous potbellied teapot on top of the samovar, the conversation turned to the escaped convicts.

As we listened to the howling storm outside and watched the street lamps shaking, somebody joked, "Actually, this is what the runaways are banking on: the blizzard will cover their tracks and no helicopters will be able to take off. And while we're sitting here swilling tea, they're crossing the tundra to Salekhard, jumping a moving train, and away to the 'mainland,' Russia.''

"I'll bet you those two criminals only took the political, Tolmachov, with them as a 'piglet,' '' said somebody else. This meant that the two criminal runaways had taken the third in case they got lost in the tundra and ran out of food.

"They just made one slip," announced old Zotov, briskly rubbing his left knee with a mixture of Tiger Balm and pure methylated spirits. Zotov's knee always ached during a blizzard; for this reason, whenever the weather was bad, he wore special fur trousers with a zipper down the side instead of a seam. Whatever the company, he would unzip his trousers practically to the hip, take out a bottle of his special rubbing compound, and, without the slightest embarrassment, set about treating his knee.

"Those prisoners had no weather forecast or my knee neither. I mean, if the weather was all right, they could get across the one hundred and forty kilometers of tundra from the camp to the railway; they wouldn't even need a piglet. They might get past the militia detachments on the railway. But! They escaped in eighteen degrees of frost and force-nine gale, not knowing that today it would get up to force sixteen and forty below! Toward night, it'll be knocking on for all of fifty. I can tell by my knee—that's better than any barometer. If I were them, I'd go back to the camp before it's too late."

We realized as well as Zotov did what the intensification of the storm signified for the escapees. Under local conditions, every unit of wind chill was equivalent to two degrees of frost. So, if a windchill factor of thirty-two was added to forty degrees of frost—well, no normal person could stand seventy below out on the open tundra. In any event, if it gets to fifty below, all working operations on the tundra are suspended, except for the drilling, of course. Even the Nentsi, the indigenous population of arctic Yamal, halt their dog and reindeer teams and lie down in the snow if they run into a storm like this one. They huddle the animals around them for warmth and call on the spirits of the tundra and Num, the god of the universe, to send a snowdrift swiftly over them.

But the escapees had no dogs, no reindeer, and no warm clothing. Above all, they couldn't wait out the storm under a snowdrift. Very likely that's what Zotov had told Gromov, to send Gromov away reassured.

"They would go trudging on through the blizzard, of course. As a rule, people always overestimate their strength, especially at the start, especially runaways," old man Zotov told us. "It's all right; as soon as the snow lifts, the helicopters are bound to spot their bodies; it's not the first time. Spoil the report though, bastards," he concluded, meaning that three frozen corpses in the taiga wouldn't look good on our report showing a sharp decrease in crime on the eve of the great event—the official opening of the Trans-Siberia gas pipeline.

On December 17 a government delegation from Moscow headed by practically everybody up to Andropov himself was due to fly in, along with a hundred or more guests of honor and foreign reporters. As a result there was a frantic rush across the whole territory—Salekhard, Surgut, Tarko-Sale, Nadym, and Medvezhe; gas reserves in the Yamal peninsula were somewhat less than in Urengoi, but could still be counted in billions of cubic meters. It was all hands on deck, a whirlwind of building activity, and the center of it all, our town of Urengoi, was being decked out like a bride: old buildings, such as our police station, were festooned with colorful posters, slogans, and exhortations, while fresh wooden planking was placed over the potholes in the roads. A new hotel, the Polar, rose up in the center of town. At the town party HQ, a rostrum was getting its finishing touches, and the Moscow architect in charge of all these operations had the brainstorm of deluging the town with not just electric and neon lighting but Roman candles as well! The idea was that at the very moment that an "ordinary" workingman, Boris Dunik, celebrated pipe welder and Hero of Socialist Labor, and Lenin laureate Rasim Salakhov, the geologist who had discovered Siberian oil and arctic gas, stood up on the rostrum together as a symbol of the harmony of labor and science and yanked open the valve sending Yamal gas from the Urengoi Compressor Station through to France, Germany, and other European countries, giant fireworks would erupt on all the taiga conifers around the town.

Before the celebrations, of course, we removed all the labor camps and, as in Moscow before the Olympics, got rid of just about all the drunks, drifters, prostitutes, people with criminal records, and similar undesirable elements from Urengoi and the other Yamal gas installations the government delegation and foreign journalists were due to visit. The town was so quiet that the local sobering-up station was temporarily converted into a public bathhouse, and we CID folk had it so easy we even found time to whitewash our building.

4

The storm died out on the morning of December 9. It had piled snow on the Urengoi streets so that boys were launching their sleds from second-floor windows. The entire population had turned out with wooden shovels to scrape the snow off porches and clear the roads and sidewalks.

I sank into snow up to my knees, even my waist, on my way to work. I was living in a hostel for young single specialists only seven blocks away from our directorate, but it took me more than half an hour to cover the first five. I could reach out and touch the tops of the street lamps. Somebody had taken the opportunity to decorate them with old children's dolls. Those little boys probably.

The center of the town, however—the square in front of party HQ and a few neighboring blocks of apartments—had already been cleared by bulldozers. Near our militia directorate, there were only "fifteen-day" men at work. These were men who had been sentenced to fifteen days for petty hooliganism or breaches of public disorder while drunk. They were wielding shovels in dilatory fashion; they were in no hurry to clear the path to the directorate.

But I was in a hurry. I was duty investigator for the day and was already twelve minutes late for work. I had barely got in, kicked the snow off my boots, and hung up my fur jacket when Katya said, "Hurry up. Zotov's waiting for you."

I adjusted my tunic and tapped on the door, prepared for a reprimand for being late.

"Comrade Major! Investigator Kovina, may I come in?" I said as cheerfully as I could, to disarm the old man with a brisk tone and smart appearance.

"Ah, Kovina," said Zotov. "You're always yelling I never give you anything 'exciting,' just routine jobs. Well, here's something 'exciting' all right. You're flying to Camp RS-549 and taking statements from the guard and the convicts in the runaways' hut."

"When did I ever yell, Comrade Major?" I asked, annoyed. "I'm not a fish wife, yelling . . ."

"All right, all right." Zotov waved it away.

"No, wait a minute! Of course, I get annoyed if you don't trust me to round up poachers in the taiga, just because I'm a woman, or help in stakeouts to pull in real criminals; you keep me on the 'everyday'—fights in workingmen's flophouses and thieving junkies and anti-Soviets. Those Leningrad students I caught reading Solzhenitsyn even called me the Urengoi Alsatian . . ."

"There you go getting wound up again," Zotov sighed. "The Alsatian's a pedigree breed; you should be pleased—"

"But I've never yelled and never complained," I interrupted, because it really was exasperating. "Five years I've been plowing through all this 'muck,' the preliminary work; even Major Gromov's heard of my successes. Anyway, it's not fair: as soon as any hot job comes up, you turn the investigation over to men, not me."

"Well I am giving you a hot job—you're going to Camp RS-549."

"What sort of a hot job is that?" I sneered. "Looking for frozen corpses!"

"I'm not sending you to look for frozen corpses,"

said Zotov. "The helicopter boys will find them without your help. Your job is to ferret around inside the camp; maybe the runaways had accomplices. While you're at it, get three or four sacks of sturgeon from Shviryov and Orudjev, they'll load it into the helicopter for the return flight. They swap the Nenets fishermen liquor for it. They won't be stingy about it. They're hardly in any position to be, are they? I'll get them on the radio."

I smiled sarcastically. So that's why Zotov had chosen me for this assignment! I was the only single person in our directorate. That meant that out of all the sturgeon loaded onto my helicopter in RS-549, Zotov would give me one or two fish and the rest would go to him. If he sent one of the married operatives, he'd have to give up a whole sackful, for the wife and kids. That the staff of RS-549 would load as much fish as I ordered was not in doubt. They'd had three men escape, and it was up to us in the CID to apportion responsibility for this "extraordinary occurrence."

Still, I was glad of the assignment. Drawing up a "Report on Infringement of Regulations for Security of Prisoners" was not interesting work, God knows, but it was better than whitening walls for the arrival of Moscow bigwigs, or poking around in students' suitcases. You never knew what you'd find there—Indian contraceptives with "whiskers" ("Have you tried them, Comrade Investigator? Fabulously exciting"), hashish, opium, marijuana ("Have you ever smoked it, Comrade Investigator? In bed, it's just ecstasy!"), or the routine Western detective novel with an anti-Soviet slant ("Have you read it, Comrade Investigator? One ought to know what our enemies write about us after all!").

In any event, at noon on December 9, when the road to Urengoi Airport had been cleared, the driver, Sergeant Krylov, or "Uncle Kolya" as we called him, took me there in the duty Volga. The helicopter squad had already excavated their Mi-8s from the snow. I boarded one and off we flew, northwest toward Camp RS-549. An enormous lustrous moon lit up the tundra. In the forty-degree chill, the whole fuselage was covered with hoarfrost while it stood on the ground; only the vibration of flight shook free the icy carapace and exposed the bright-red body of the Mi-8, the livery of polar aviation.

Immediately beyond Urengoi, the majestic panorama of the gas fields lay below—hundreds of drilling derricks and the enormous, almost extraterrestrial complex of the Main Compressor Station, a complete plant for the purification, cooling, and condensation of gas. We had built it during the American embargo on sharing mechanical and electronic know-how. Around the station gigantic spherical gas tanks glowed silver; the intertwining threads of dozens of pipelines, substations, fuel depots, temporary pipe pumps, the vast agglomeration of modern technology out on the tundra. The lights of electric and gas welding flickered at various points, earth movers and bulldozers swarmed, management Volgas scurried among KRAZ trucks and heavy-duty carriers on Caterpillar tracks. The storm had held up construction for three days, but the pipeline still had to open on the seventeenth. The top men in Moscow loathe having to wait; they'd promised that Europe would get Siberian gas by the New Year—and it would!

"Shit, it's beautiful! Just like Mars!" the pilot shouted to me and flew higher to take in the panorama in one sweep.

5

After about fifteen or twenty kilometers, the pipeline filaments began to snake away in all directions across the tundra. The tundra itself grew whiter; the farther we flew, the whiter and more lifeless it became. Now and then, at the edge of a bare, snow-filled plateau, the contours of some oil workers' settlement appeared, or a drilling derrick, the *choom** of a Nenets encampment, the frosted thread of a pipeline, or Nenets reindeer sleds racing across the tundra.

But the last traces of civilization soon vanished; we were flying northwest, deep into the wilderness. Only now, from the air, could the absolute madness of the runaways' decision be fully comprehended—to cross on foot this inhuman landscape, this endless, savage conglomeration of ice hummocks and snow, stretching to the horizon in every direction. Even in my rucksack, the bottle of vodka I had grabbed before starting had "separated out" into about two hundred grams of pure alcohol and a mat lump of ordinary ice. In other words, the temperature here was below minus forty. How would it be for a man down there in such a temperature, in a blizzard too, wearing a threadbare, state-issue convict's quilted jacket and canvas shoes? Of course he'd be frozen; it stood to reason.

*A dwelling made of reindeer hide, like a wigwam.

About two hours farther on, the icy field of the Ob estuary came into view and twenty kilometers or so beyond that, Camp RS-549, gray rectangles of barracks, sloppily repaired and strung around with barbed wire. Like the rest of the camps on the Yamal peninsula, RS-549 had been moved a month before so as to be farther from the itinerary of the guests of honor and foreign visitors at the official pipeline ceremony. Nobody was going to build a new camp here, of course; they just patched up one built under Stalin. From the south, through the camp, and on to the northwest, marched the notorious electric pylons. Two kilometers from the camp, the work zone could be seen—on the banks of a frozen tundra stream, the convicts were using crowbars to make holes in the permafrost, which rang under the blows, I knew, like metal. From above, the dark figures in their camp jackets looked like a flock of sheep scattered over the tundra, surrounded by the camp fires of shepherds and their dogs—the guards.

At first glance this might seem like idiocy. Why force people to cripple themselves hacking at the permafrost in temperatures of forty below? The clanging crowbar leaps back off the ice, frozen chips smack you in the face—even in windless weather a man gets worn out in half an hour working like that. But there's reason in the madness. The holes they make in the permafrost lay bare the top stratum of the tundra; the explosives men lay their charges in the holes and open up a layer of sand and gravel—valuable construction materials—under the ice. The howls about us using convict labor on the pipeline are a pack of Western lies. Who would let a prisoner get near a gas pipeline, or trust one to weld a pipe? But ancillary operations like digging out sand and gravel, clearing forests, building moorings, laying roadways across the swamps, that's hard labor convicts can do.

The helicopter passed over the work area and approached the camp. Hearing its noise, soldiers and the head of camp security, Major Orudjev, piled out of the guardroom. The helicopter landed alongside, let me disembark, and then headed off southwest to hunt for the bodies of the fugitives. In that direction, in Salekhard, the railway begins, so they could only have gone that way.

I got on with the routine, seeking personal details of the escapees, questioning the guards who had been on duty the night of the break. In his office Major Orudjev got three gray files bound with tape out of the safe—the fugitives' personal files. For a few minutes I examined the runaways' standard prison photographs. Timur Zaloyev, a Tartar recidivist with three terms for 217 house break-ins—a gloomy face with high cheekbones and narrow eyes. Gleb Shimansky, icon forger and dealer in Russian antiques—forty, tall, with a well-groomed face but a stubborn chin. Boris Tolmachov, a twenty-year-old dissident with a snub nose and light eyes—a mere boy. I noted the addresses of their relatives to be able to send official notification—if they wanted, they could come for the bodies when they were discovered that day or the next. Then came the interrogation of the camp security staff. The chief thing I wanted to get clear was where the wooden spools had come from that had helped the escapees fly over the fence on the electricity cables. The spools, which Orudjev also got from the safe, were clearly handmade and shaped like the letter X. Through the holes in the center of each, bent steel brackets had been inserted, rather like the handles on the subway. Maybe somebody had brought these things in, or sent them in a parcel?

"What do you mean, brought, sent?" Major Orudjev was indignant. "Do you think we don't check parcels? They made those rollers themselves, in the zone. We've got a mechanical workshop here in the camp. We repair Friendship electrical saws here, and other tools as well. This one, Boris Tolmachov, was a turner in the shop. He was the one who made the rollers.''

I walked over to the workshop. It was a rickety, unheated, temporary plank structure; the tundra wind blew through the chinks in the walls; the lathes stood directly on boards placed on the frozen ground; sundry pieces of metal, wooden billets, and machine components lay scattered around the floor—in contravention of regulations, incidentally. From these wooden strips, Tolmachov had made the rollers for his escape, and his own destruction. The thing that really stood out was that right over Tolmachov's own lathe hung the standard camp slogan: TO FREEDOM—WITH A CLEAR CONSCIENCE!

From the workshop, Major Orudjev led me through the compound to the officers' mess to have lunch. He had been walking behind me like a shadow, supposedly in the line of duty, but really because my fur trousers increased my backside to a size his Ossetian temperament found hard to bear. As we were passing the fateful high-voltage pylon, he gave it a hearty kick and said bitterly, "It's all Hudya Benokan's fault, Nenets bastard!''

I shot an astonished glance at the major. Hudya Benokan was a CID operative in Salekhard. He was the only Nenets investigator in the whole territory. How could he be blamed for three prisoners escaping from this camp?

6

I knew Hudya Benokan. I had been in my fifth year in the Juridical Faculty of Moscow University when a rumor went the rounds that some simple Nenets reindeer herder from the shores of the Arctic Circle had rolled up to join our faculty. By his own efforts, too! Not exempt on nationality grounds, not as part of the Yamal-Nenets area quota, not through influence, of course—where would an arctic Nenets get that?—but in open competition! Of course, he wasn't actually brought by reindeer, but he wore a *malitsa** instead of an overcoat. "Another suicide," I remember thinking at the time. In the four years I'd been at the university, there'd been nine cases of suicide among students from the arctic territories—Chukchi, Evenki, Nentsi, and Khanti. Eskimo boys and girls just can't handle the stress of a big city, and they take their own lives, odd as it may seem, always in the same way, by throwing themselves out of the windows of the skyscraper hostels on Lenin Hills.

"One more suicide," I thought when I heard of this wild "prodigy" coming to the university. And forgot

---

*The Nenets outer garment, an amply cut knee-length smock-shirt, put on over the head. It is stitched from reindeer skin with the fur outside. Mittens are sewn onto the sleeves. Sometimes the *malitsa* is decorated with patterns made out of young reindeer skins.

about him, of course. A few days later though, in the students' canteen, I noticed a boy with high cheekbones and narrow eyes, Japanese or Korean perhaps, staring fixedly at me. Half the university is composed of foreigners, but there are no Westerners on our faculty—why the hell should they study Soviet law when they have quite different systems of their own? Anyway, this boy wasn't a Japanese or Korean, he was Hudya Benokan, the "prodigy from Yamal." Pretty soon, my whole group, then the entire class, got to know that he had fallen for me. He would hang around in the canteen just when our class had their lunch break, or if there was a break between lectures. He sat as a rule in the farthest corner and drank tea—five, six, ten glasses—sweating in his new baggy Soviet suit and waiting till I appeared. Well, in the fifth year I was twenty-two and, without being overly modest, I must say that I was all right; a blue-eyed blonde with a braid down to the waist and a figure like Anouk Aimée's, a classy bit of goods. Anyway, I couldn't walk down the street without a Fiat or Volga homing in and the driver, some filmmaker or photographer, thirty or forty maybe, inviting me to go with him to Cinema House to a restricted screening of a Western film.

Still, when you're doing your law finals, there's no time for love affairs, or even a brief flirtation. I couldn't care less if some Eskimo-Nenets had worked out our group's schedule and hung around waiting for me, sweating out his tea and gazing at me gulping my cabbage soup or a cutlet that tasted like a mattress. Very soon he shifted his observation post from the canteen to the library; that really annoyed me. I couldn't possibly digest Soviet law or summarize *Fundamentals of Criminal Legislation* with the narrow gray eyes of this Nenets staring at me from the next desk. Well, could you?

It's true I only had to look back and he dropped his

cyes to his book right away, but that was just for as long as I was looking at him. In the end, I couldn't stand it. I got up and went over to him. Of course, he stopped looking at me and pretended he was reading Lenin, volume 33, *Dual Subordination Legalities*. I came right up to him and said, "Listen! What's the matter?" The whole library turned in our direction: everyone was looking at me—except him. That Nenets sat with his eyes glued on Lenin, as if he was deaf. Only his short neck turned purple above the collar of his Moscow-tailored suit. At that, I grabbed Lenin, volume 33, from under his eyes, slammed it down on his desk, and asked: "Well, how long do you intend to stare at me?"

The amazing thing was, he didn't budge or even look up at me. I stood over him, like a fool, expecting an answer, while he just sat stock-still looking at the table. I turned and left the library.

Next day he wasn't in the canteen or the reading room. Next day the same. And the next. Then somebody told me that he hadn't been seen at lectures for four days, or in the hostel; the dean had reported his disappearance to the police. To tell the truth, I was terrified and decided that this Nenets had committed suicide as well. For two days I walked around in a daze. Then the police came across Hudya in the woods beyond Izmailovo Park; he was sleeping on the ground under a pine tree, wrapped in his *malitsa*.

When a man sleeps out in the woods six days because of you, even if he is a Nenets, you can't ignore it and go on as if nothing had happened. Especially when you've got friends and acquaintances. Nobody said anything to me, of course, but they all looked at me as if I was a surgeon who'd taken out a patient's stomach when he had appendicitis. Anyway, when the police brought Hudya back to the hostel, I braced myself and set out for the men's zone.

It's an odd thing that the most prominent sight in

Moscow, the twenty-four-story skyscraper of the university students' hostel on the Lenin Hills, with the towers à la Russe that Stalin drew onto the original plan with his own hand and the spire with the star—that hostel is divided up inside into zones and blocks; just like a camp. I went past the porter by the elevator, went up to the fourth floor of Zone G, the law faculty, and headed along the corridor to Block 404. The blocks are living units with two separate rooms and two bunk beds in each, sharing a toilet and a shower. As I neared Number 404, which Hudya shared with some other Siberian national, I was expecting to see a gaunt, emaciated, unkempt individual whom it was my duty to release from love's thrall, in case he should up and throw himself out the window the following day. Of course, I had no intention of starting an affair with him, though I did have the idea of inviting him to the Saturday concert at our students' club.

Hudya opened the door for me. He was neither unkempt nor emaciated. He wasn't wearing his *malitsa* or any other article of Nenets national dress. He had on a T-shirt and navy-blue sports slacks. His narrow gray eyes looked at me calmly, without anxiety.

"Hi!" I said, somewhat at a loss. "Can I come in?"

He let me enter his room. It was clean, unlike the usual men's quarters, with their mess and photos of nude girls on the walls. Two bunks along the wall, a cupboard, a bookcase with legal books, a desk, and a table lamp—a totally spartan scene. A pile of books lay on the table, an open volume of *Fundamentals of Crime Classification,* and a summary. Next to it, a glass of strong tea, half-drunk.

"Some idiot said you slept on the floor," I said, just to break the ice. "I read somewhere that it's good for you. There was a famous ballerina who slept on the floor."

"Yes, I used to do that." He spoke in a low, even

38

voice. "I don't now, however. I make myself sleep in a bed."

"You make yourself?"

"Yes, we don't have beds in our tents; I'm not used to them. I'm training myself now, however."

"I see. . . ." I didn't know how to carry on the conversation. "Listen, I've got my old notes on that *Fundamentals*. Would you like them?"

"Thank you, however," he said. "But I have to read it all through myself and make notes."

"Why do you say *however* all the time?"

He smiled for the first time.

"It's a habit. Everybody talks like that in the North."

"Ah. Listen, I've got some tickets for the variety concert at our club, this Saturday. Do you want to come?"

He looked me straight in the eyes, and I suddenly understood that it was a case of the rabbit and the boa constrictor. His eyes held alarm, terror. But the very next second, he spoke, still in that even tone. "You must excuse me, however. I can't go to the concert. I'm behind in all my subjects, and there're a seminar and exams coming up."

"Really?" I was surprised. I hadn't expected a refusal at all! This Nenets refused me!

"Well," I brought out, with no idea of what to do next. "Well . . . as you like . . . I'll be off then."

I'd never been in such an idiotic and humiliating position in my life! He hadn't even invited me to sit down! I tried getting a bit of my dignity back as I was going out.

"And what were you doing in the woods?"

"I was curing myself," he replied coolly.

"What of?"

"Moscow and . . . and you, however."

I understood what he meant, but smiled. "I'm not infectious, am I?"

"No. But you . . ." He faltered, then looked me directly in the eyes.

"I came to Moscow to learn to be a criminal investigator, not to fall in love, however."

"Quite right; it's pointless anyway," I said vengefully. "Well, how did it go? Are you cured of me?"

He kept his eyes on mine. It was the fixed, protracted stare of a man who has resolved to endure any torture in silence.

I turned and went off down the corridor, deliberately swinging my hips a little and flung my braid over my shoulder as a crowning gesture.

He stood that as well. He sat it out for days on end in the library, but no longer on my account. If I came in, he would get up and move to another room. The winter exams were a month later, and I saw his name on the list of the Lenin grant winners—he'd got As in everything. I don't know if the professors made any allowance for his Nenets origins, but some well-wisher related to me how Hudya slaved away even when his brain was too tired to take in all that dull stuff the first-year students have to learn; he beat his head against the wall, insisting, "No! I will force you to work! Work, however!"

When he'd finished his exams, he went off into the woods again and slept in the snow for five days in his *malitsa*—getting rid of his tension.

A year later, when the work allocations were posted in the university and "Tyumen Province" stood beside my name, I had a formal reconciliation with Hudya; he came up to me in the canteen and said, "Hello. I found out you were going to work in our Tyumen Province. I'm very glad. It's just your sort of place. This'll come in handy, however!" He held out two books: *Russian-Nenets Dictionary* and *Nenets Fairy Tales and Legends*.

"Thank you," I said. "Maybe now you'll accept my old notes."

He smiled and shook his head. "I have to learn everything myself, however."

Four years had passed since then. Five months ago, in Urengoi, I had found out that Hudya Benokan had returned to Yamal, to Salekhard, with the "red" diploma of outstanding merit from Moscow University—and a two-year-old daughter. It's only about five hundred kilometers from Salekhard, the capital of Yamal, to Urengoi, but in those five months I had not seen Hudya once. He had become an investigator at the Salekhard CID, as I was at Urengoi. Police gossip, always faster than the telephone, reported that Hudya's daughter was by a pretty little Nenets girl who had gone to Moscow University through the influence of her father who was a member of the Tyumen Regional Party Committee. Hudya had married her when he was in his third year, but the girl had turned out to be a bit "free and easy" as the saying goes. She quickly went from hand to hand, or, more precisely, from bed to bed among Moscow artists, eager for any foreign exotica. A year later she quit the university, left her husband with a two-month-old child, and went off with the latest artist to a Black Sea resort; then the scent grew cold even for her own father. How Hudya raised his little girl at the university and lived and studied on his seventy-ruble-a-month Lenin grant, God only knows, but, somehow or other, he had turned up in Salekhard this summer and got a job at once as an investigator at the Salekhard Directorate. And now the head of camp security at RS-549, Major Orudjev, for some reason considered that Hudya was the man responsible for the convicts' escape.

7

I looked in amazement at Major Orudjev and blurted, "Hudya? How?"

"Very simple!" said Orudjev. "He was here about three weeks ago. The prisoners were still repairing their barracks; we'd just arrived here from Nadym. And this Hudya flew over from Salekhard to interrogate one of the convicts on some old business. So here he stands and in front of the prisoners blurts out to the camp commandant, 'Who was the prick who chose this as a campsite with the power lines going right through it? You could get clear of the compound along the cables from the pylon,' he says. 'They say the swan waits for spring and the convict waits for freedom!' And he cackled his head off, the bastard. The prisoners heard him and took the hint!"

I smiled. "That's not nice, Comrade Major. Don't try to shift the blame. You've permitted an escape, and now it turns out the CID even warned you about it. It looks as though you're going to need more than sturgeon to keep clear of us!"

Orudjev stared at me with his prominent dark eyes; he realized now that he shouldn't have mentioned Benokan and was wondering if I was pulling his leg or if I really did want more from him than sturgeon. In the midst of this unaccustomed mental exertion, the film of male lust faded from his dark eyes and they became really beautiful in their frame of bushy black brows, lightly powdered with the hoarfrost settling from his breath on the fur of his hat, on his mustache, his eyelashes.

"All right!" I took pity on him. "No damn point hanging around in the cold; my nose is ready to drop off."

When I talk to army or police officers, I try to adopt a rough tone right away to cool their overheated thoughts about me belonging to the opposite sex. But not always, of course. And Orudjev was nearer to the exception than the rule. A few minutes later, in the officers' mess, while a prisoner-cook served us salmon soup and sturgeon shashlik, Orudjev brought from his quarters a bottle of Armenian brandy and one of Tsimlyansky pink champagne (to drink cognac with pink champagne is considered the height of chic in the Arctic). Once more the transparent velvet of lust swam in his beautiful eyes, the powerful shoulders played under his uniform, while his chest thrust out so that it seemed the brass buttons on his uniform would fly off at any moment. Quite a hunk, I thought to myself, a champion goer at bedtime fences. He had already poured the cognac into cut-glass tumblers, mixed fifty-fifty with pink champagne.

"To the runaways, Anna Borisovna! May the arctic tundra feel like eiderdown to them! Otherwise, you would never have flown over to us."

I drained my glass in one pleasurable gulp. I'd got really frozen on the flight, in that repair shop, and around the camp. Right down to the bones, as the saying goes.

What happened afterward? Explanation means justification, and I don't need to do either. I'm single and my own woman. If I fancy a man, it is my choice and my right; I don't have to account to anyone. Orudjev and I drank the rest of the brandy and champagne and then, instead of waiting for the prisoners to finish digging up the tundra and continuing my work, I allowed Orudjev to talk me into staying the night in camp.

"What's the hurry then, Anna Borisovna?" said he, grinning slyly into his mustache. "They'll bring the convicts back around six. By the time they're counted, then supper and whatnot, it'll be eight. Interrogating prisoners after eight is forbidden in the regulations. Better to rest up after your journey, get your sleep. We've got a grand room by the guardhouse. And in the morning, I'll exempt all the prisoners in the run-aways' barracks from work; you can question them all day if you like. What do you say?"

Needless to say, I knew perfectly well what a night in camp would mean, parked next to the guardroom. Every camp has one; once a year every prisoner has the right to a visit from a close relative, and they're put up for three days in a room like this. If it's the convict's wife, he has the right to spend the night with her.

Naturally, there are no locks, and right next door you have a whole camp full of male prisoners; but I could sleep soundly—who would stick his nose into a guardhouse crammed with soldiers and guard dogs, clanking metal doors, and bars on the windows? Of course, any fool knows that for the head of camp security, Major Orudjev, no such obstacles existed. That evening, if polar nights have evenings, he sent the duty convict to light the Dutch stove. Then outside the window came the tramp of the column of prisoners returning from work. They were kept waiting at the camp gates for nearly an hour; the outside escort handed them over to the in-camp guards. The latter took over the column in ranks of six men, counting as they went: "First rank—forward! Remainder—stand fast! Second rank—forward! Remainder—stand fast! Third . . . !" Even the guard dogs whimpered from cold and impatience. At last all the prisoners had been allowed into the compound, the camp gates had clanged shut, the center pin had slammed home. The steel doors of the guardhouse stopped clattering; the dogs hushed their barking and whining; and only a lone polar wolf, whether from misery or cold, carried on howling somewhere far out on the tundra. The camp was settling down for the night.

I lay in bed, slowly dozing off and wondering when on earth friend Orudjev would appear. My legs began stretching of their own accord as desire grew, and my nipples hardened, making my breasts ache. This kept me awake, and in any case I don't like being wakened in the middle of the night, even for sex. Why interrupt one pleasure with another? Finally, at nine, when the guard had been dismissed, Major Orudjev opened my unlocked door without knocking. He didn't disappoint me, either. He carried me from the narrow camp bunk to a mattress on the floor so the creak of bedsprings wouldn't be audible in the guardroom. That mattress could tell a tale or two! But I was his equal in our joint labors. Well, hell, when you take off your tunic and holster, everything kept in check under your rough officer's uniform during the day suddenly bursts out of you with such frantic energy you don't need Indian contraceptives with exciting whiskers, or hashish, or imported marijuana! All you need is a man who can stand the assault for hours on end and not weaken. Orudjev was just the hammer—I'd made no mistake there.

At 5:00 A.M., an hour before camp reveille, Orudjev left, having lifted me and the mattress, with difficulty this time, back onto the bunk. I heard him promise to leave the convicts I needed for questioning on camp duty so that I could sleep in as long as I liked; no one would come and wake me. And I did sleep through reveille, the clang of the camp gates, the dogs barking, the tramp of the lines of prisoners leaving for work on the tundra. Half a day passed in sleep; to me it seemed like a minute. Anyway, when Orudjev came into my room again, perched on the edge of my bunk, and spoke insistently—"Anya! Anya, wake up!"—I had the greatest difficulty dragging myself into wakefulness. Hadn't he had enough? I saw his face bending over me and said, "No! Go away."

"Wake up! Read this!" He held out a radio message form. I opened my sticky eyelids and stared at the message.

TO MILITIA LIEUTENANT ANNA KOVINA, URENGOI CID INVESTIGATOR: THIRTY KILOMETERS FROM THE CAMP WHERE YOU ARE NOW, NEAR YAKU-TUR SHIFT SETTLEMENT, THE NAKED CORPSE OF VITALI VORO-PAYEV, LEADER OF THE SEISMOGRAPHIC EXPEDITION, HAS BEEN DISCOVERED BY NENETS FISHERMEN. THE BODY BEARS MARKS OF SADISTIC VIOLENCE: EARS AND SEXUAL ORGAN HAVE BEEN SEVERED. SEX ORGAN THRUST INTO VICTIM'S MOUTH. AT THE SAME TIME NEAR THE RIVER JETTY IN SALEKHARD FISHERMEN HAVE FOUND THE BODY OF THE CHIEF CONSULTANT PHYSICIAN AT SALEKHARD DISTRICT HOSPITAL, OLEG HOTKO, MUTILATED IN SIMILAR FASHION. CLOTHING OF MURDERED MEN HAS BEEN STOLEN. THE LOCATIONS OF THE CRIMES COINCIDE WITH THE PROBABLE ROUTE OF ESCAPED PRISONERS FROM CAMP RS-549 THROUGH YAKU-TUR TOWARD SALEKHARD RAILWAY. SINCE STORMS HAVE AGAIN DISRUPTED AIR TRANSPORTATION, IT IS IMPOSSIBLE TO SEND AN INVESTIGATOR AND FORENSIC MEDICAL EXPERT TO YAKU-TUR FROM URENGOI. LEAVE FOR YAKU-TUR IMMEDIATELY BY SNO-CAT TO EXAMINE THE CORPSE AND COLLECT EVIDENCE. ZOTOV.

I gradually revived as I read the message. This was it, the hot one! The escapees had survived the tundra by some miracle and, what's more, committed two murders, so *far* only two, but what murders! And nobody from Urengoi CID, none of the men, including Zotov, could get to Yaku-Tur because of this new blizzard. But I, Anna Kovina, the "domestic," the "spare wheel," I would be there in an hour—the first!

I scanned the message again swiftly; at the words "severed. Sex organ thrust into victim's mouth," I woke up completely. Of course, old man Zotov had no time for literary niceties, I knew. I understood even more than the message stated. If the railway was screened off by patrols and the escapees couldn't slip away to the "mainland," either they would hide out in Salekhard or they would circle around it on the tundra. How could members of the government and foreign visitors be received if there were three murderers loose in the territory! That was why Zotov was sending me over to Yaku-Tur "immediately by Sno-Cat."

Suddenly another idea occurred to me—what if the convicts had split up? Suppose only one or two had got as far as Salekhard, and somebody was still in Yaku-Tur, or close by?

I leapt out of bed and peered through the window. Outside there was no moon, no stars, no silvery-blue tundra sheen. The usual blizzard covered everything. Powdery snow flailed the window; the barbed wire of the camp fence was creaking and through it could be heard the nervous barking of dogs and the crunch of snow beneath the feet of lines of prisoners. I glanced at Orudjev, amazed.

"I can't have slept to the end of the shift? The clock only says eleven."

"Fifty below, work suspended," he explained.

So, they were bringing the prisoners in from the tundra; for them the storm meant rest, whereas for me it meant the first real hot job, an actual crime, a chance to prove that the Urengoi Alsatian was good for more than sniffing out anti-Soviet trash. Terrific! I wouldn't miss this chance! Like Jews, women investigators, all women specialists in fact, working in so-called male professions, have to demonstrate that they are not only as good as, but actually better than, men. Only then are men forced to recognize us as more or less equal.

Woolen stockings, men's underpants, sweater, tunic, fur flying suit, leather belt, holster, pistol, felt boots, sheepskin jacket, fur hat with earmuffs—as I hastily got dressed, I did some thinking. The fugitives needed clothing, papers, and money. That's why they had stripped and robbed their victims. But there were three of them and so far only two corpses. That meant someone else might be lying out on the tundra pretty soon. If they hadn't made use of their "piglet," of course, on the journey . . .

"Well, what are you gawking at me for?" I said to Orudjev. "Get the Sno-Cat ready!"

"It's ready and waiting." He nodded toward the window. "I'm going as well. There could be a trail for the dogs to follow."

I had no time to wonder if this was just an excuse to go with me in the hope of another passionate night, or if he really was itching to get hold of the runaways. In any case he could think as well as I and in a hectic affair like hunting down escapees there couldn't be a better partner. And, after all, if fortune was to smile on us—well, we could celebrate with another night.

I stuck the three gray folders containing the personal details of the escapees into my rucksack and followed Orudjev on the run. The blizzard burned my face like a razor and cut off my breath. The Sno-Cat, engines roaring, stood only two steps from the guardhouse and I vaulted easily over the Caterpillar track—it wasn't the first time, was it?—and into the cabin. Apart from the driver, there were four gallant sergeants. All displayed their highly polished Merit Guard badges under their casually unbuttoned sheepskin jackets. They made no effort to hide dreamy smiles as they contemplated ten days' leave for taking even one escapee, and stroked the full-grown Alsatians at their knees.

8

I wasn't the only one thinking at that time of the link between the official openings of the gas pipeline and the escaped prisoners. A few hours later someone a bit higher up sounded the alarm. This is the full text of the government telegram with which I began this narrative:

> SALEKHARD, TO FIRST SECRETARY YAMAL-NENETS DISTRICT COMMITTEE CPSU, COMRADE PYOTR TUSYADA
> COPIES:
> TO HEAD OF DIRECTORATE YAMAL-NENETS KGB
>   MAJOR V. SHATUNOV
> TO HEAD OF DIRECTORATE YAMAL-NENETS MILITIA,
>   COLONEL N. SINI
>   MILITARY COMMANDER SALEKHARD GARRISON
>   SOVIET ARMY, COLONEL S. BURYATKO
>
> THE SERIES OF MURDERS COMMITTED BY ESCAPEES FROM CAMP RS-549 THREATENS THE SECURITY OF THE OFFICIAL OPENING CEREMONY OF THE SIBERIA–WESTERN EUROPE GAS PIPELINE.
>
> TAKE IMMEDIATE MEASURES TO APPREHEND OR ELIMINATE. MAXIMUM TIME LIMIT FOR EXECUTION OF THIS PARTY INSTRUCTION—24 HOURS. EVERY EX-

RED SNOW

TRA HOUR MURDERERS REMAIN AT LIBERTY WILL BE YOUR PERSONAL PARTY RESPONSIBILITY.

FIRST SECRETARY TYUMEN PROVINCE COMMITTEE CPSU
MEMBER OF CENTRAL COMMITTEE CPSU
V. BOGOMYATOV
TYUMEN, 10 DECEMBER 1983
18:30 HOURS

9

While our Sno-Cat ground along the ice of a frozen river, battering its way into the snowstorm and night, Orudjev, I, and the four sergeants were all busy wondering: Why such a savage and barbaric method of murder? All right, they were killed for their clothing, money, and papers, that was understandable. But why cut off their ears and the rest of it? The first explanation that occurred to me was revenge. But why should the escapees revenge themselves on this Voropayev or Hotko, people they'd never seen in their lives? That left sadism, clinical maniacal sadism. But the twenty-year-old dissident, Boris Tolmachov, was doing time, according to his file, for "reading and distributing Solzhenitsyn's books among Moscow University students." And Gleb Shimansky, the icon faker, had graduated from the Moscow Art Institute in 1965 as a specialist easel painter; he had been represented in Moscow and international exhibitions. Neither of them seemed likely sadistic murderers.

"That Tartar!" Orudjev confidently asserted. "The Tartar, that bastard Zaloyev, I know their little ways! Never mind! If I get him, I swear by my father, I'll cut his off! No! I won't lay a finger on him—he'll do it himself, he'll cut the lot off himself, I swear by my mother's grave!"

"It's not his style, though," I said. "Two hundred

and seventeen burglaries, never used a weapon once. We were taught at the institute that criminals never change their trademark. Robbing a shop in Yaku-Tur is more his style.''

''What for?'' One of the sergeants grinned. ''Rice and stew? What they need is papers, identity cards.''

''But people don't get their ears and members cut off for that.''

''At the institute! Trademark!'' said one of the sergeants, bobbing up as we went over a hummock. ''We've got an architect in the camp. He was going off on a job, so he fitted his wife's vagina with a lock, a real iron lock. Of course, she turned up her toes after three days—blood poisoning. Did you learn that at the institute? And he was an engineer with higher education, an architect. The tundra does things to people. This Tolmachov, maybe he accepted the thieves' code, now he wants to be a *pakhan.* ''*

''Balls!'' said Orudjev, contemptuous. ''I'll bet a case of cognac on it: it's the Tartar, Zaloyev! Blood of Genghis Khan; shit, it's their trademark. If we could just get to Salekhard; he's there near Salekhard, skulking around. How could they get to Salekhard in a blizzard like that? Fucking hell!''

''*Kekliki, Kekliki,* Comrade Major! Shall I stop?'' shouted the driver.

Sure enough, in front of the vehicle, blinded by the headlights, white clumps of arctic partridges, known locally as *kekliki,* could be seen pressing themselves into the ground. When danger threatens the stupid birds freeze where they are, trying to make their white plumage blend in with the whiteness of the tundra. Even from as close as a couple of yards, they look just like clumps of snow. In fine weather, when there are no blizzards, all the drivers in the North, whatever the trip, come home with a sackful of *kekliki*—they kill

*Leader of a gang of thieves.

them with sticks, and the sharpest catch them with their bare hands. There's nothing tastier in the whole world than these game birds. But now . . .

"Drive on! Drive on!" Orudjev ordered savagely. The driver stepped on the gas.

10

The trembling lights of the wagon town of Yaku-Tur swam up out of the blizzard unexpectedly close. In each of the wagons, positioned in long rows above the icebound river, a light was burning. On the edge of the settlement, the siren of an electricity substation hooted heartrendingly; the door of a trading post banged in the wind. I had been in shift settlements like this often enough. In the heat of the last few years, while the arctic gas fields were being developed and the government was signing contracts for the delivery of Urengoi gas to Western Europe, the Soviet Arctic began to languish for lack of qualified drillers, welders, fitters. These specialists are held in higher esteem than engineers, and a fast ruble isn't enough to entice them to the tundra. You have to throw in a fully furnished apartment, kindergarten, a school for the older ones, and even a cinema for the wife. But there was just no time to build cities with central heating, hospitals, theaters, and kindergartens! The reserves of the Urengoi gas fields exceed 7.5 trillion cubic meters, an ocean of gas; and in January 1984 it had to be flooding into Europe. With a deadline like that, there's no way you can build settlements with all the modern conveniences.

So the authorities introduced a different system of working, by shifts. For the past five years, planes had been ferrying work teams to the Yamal tundra from all the oil and gas areas of the country to work fifteen-day shifts. From Azerbaijan, Tataria, Bashkiria, Moldavia, workers fly in to shift settlements like Yaku-Tur. They get a night's rest, then, in the morning, out to the tundra drilling installations or pipe-welding sites, for fifteen days and nights. Out there, it's a sixteen-hour working day, canned food heated over a Primus for dinner, and a short sleep in a railcar, in your clothes. Then back to work again, till the arrival of the next fifteen-day shift. Every shift worker gets paid a fortune, eight hundred to nine hundred rubles a month—that's five times my salary.

It's still worth it to the state, though—it means they don't have to build towns and settlements with civilized amenities on the tundra. The main thing is, more and more drilling tubes driving down into the permafrost like nails, and thousands of tons of clay mortar to cork up the gas and prevent its eruption before the opening of the pipeline. All so that the pipeline can roll onward, across swamps and fens, taiga and tundra, across the rivers and mountains of Siberia and Europe, ever onward to the West. Money meant nothing to the government—money was paper—pay the toiling men in thousands, so long as from January 1984 onward, our country supplied Europe annually some 40 billion cubic meters of gas and earned \$10 billion a year!

True, after fifteen days of work on the open tundra, scoured by the icy wind, when the mortar and hydrochloric acid eat into your body, when your soul and liver are frozen through, even an impeccable Communist needs more than a bottle of vodka to console him and can't stay faithful to his wife or girlfriend pining away somewhere in Moldavia. Women are worth a fortune in the shift settlements, even Nenets girls in their filthy tents or prostitutes too worn out for the Black Sea resorts. And where there are vodka and women, you get knife fights, and where there are knife fights, that's where we are, of course, the militia, the CID.

Yaku-Tur was a typical shift settlement of the privileged type, so to speak: nearby, about a kilometer and a half away, stood a Nenets fish farm called Road to Communism. There the workers could always lay their hands on *stroganina*,* made from pink and white salmon, which goes well with vodka and Nenets girls. That was why several of the railcar porches had stocks of frozen fish stacked up like firewood.

Our Sno-Cat rolled up to a railcar with a sign outside:

OFFICE OF YAKU-TUR SEISMOGRAPHIC RESEARCH
EXPEDITION

Next to the sign, a red poster hung on the wall:

LET'S GIVE THE COUNTRY
ANOTHER BILLION CUBIC METERS
OF YAMAL GAS!

Nearby two tracked vehicles and a KRAZ snuffled, their engines still running. There were no drivers in them. In these parts drivers don't turn off truck engines in the winter; otherwise, they'd have to warm them up with fires to get them started again.

Orudjev threw open the metal door, and the fury of the icy wind once more stung our faces. It was a mere ten yards from the Sno-Cat to the railcar, but to cover it you had to lean forward into the wind; you felt naked in that wind; face, neck, knees froze instantly. I again thought fleetingly of the escaping convicts—how

---

*Freshly frozen raw fish, thinly sliced. Stroganina made of sturgeon, pink and white salmon, and a dash of pomegranate sauce is a fantastic snack with vodka.

could they make 140 kilometers from the camp to Salekhard in a blizzard like this?

Orudjev literally tore open the carriage door, so powerful was the pressure of that frenzied wind, and allowed me inside. Beyond the first, outer door was a second, padded with thick felt for warmth; ragged singing by hoarse masculine voices could be heard behind it:

> *I remember the port in Vanino.*
> *The ship horn's mournful sound.*
> *I remember we walked up the gangplank*
> *To a cold, empty steerage cell.*

I opened the felted door, and we found ourselves in reviving warmth and dense cigarette smoke, underscored by the sharp smell of liquor. In this tiny room-cum-office, it seemed the entire leadership of the Yaku-Tur Seismographic Research Expedition—some twelve men and three women—sat behind a plank table. They were all obviously drunk. There were already about ten empty bottles with white and green labels POTABLE SPIRIT, 96 PROOF alongside cut-glass tumblers with cigarette ends floating in them and slices of greasy pink salmon, long thawed, lying on a copy of the *Tyumen Pravda*. My sweeping glance automatically noted that patches of dirty grease had disfigured the portrait of Andropov.

Our appearance cut short the song. The entire company turned in our direction, their liquor-laden bodies drunkenly swaying. A shortish fellow with pale, swimming eyes detached himself from his seat and strode forward to meet us. It was clearly taking all his willpower to stay upright.

"W-What can I do for you, c-comrades?"

"Name?" I said, feeling disgust.

"M-Mine? M-Malofeyev."

"Your job?"

"M-Mine? Er . . . er . . . deputy manager in charge of c-commissariat. W-Would you take a seat?" He swayed, but leaned an arm against somebody's shoulder.

"I'm an investigator from Urengoi CID, Anna Kovina. We've come about Voropayev's murder. Where's the body?"

"Perhaps you'd care . . . for a swig of vodka first. Must be cold?" Somebody said from the table, "Drink to his soul, eh?"

I realized now that this party was actually a wake for the murdered manager. Judging by the number of empty bottles on the table, it had been going on for quite a while, probably since morning.

"I said 'Where's the body?' " I repeated coldly.

"What do you mean, b-body?" Malofeyev tottered. "I-It's in the coffin, where on earth sh-should it be? Outside, b-behind the office . . ."

"It's got to go to Kiev, by air. That's where his family is," someone added.

Orudjev turned to me and asked, "Where will you examine it? Shall I have it brought in here?"

I was desperate not to go out into the icy blizzard again, but I couldn't examine the body in here, of course, not on the table in front of this drunken crew.

11

To Urengoi, Head of Urengoi CID Directorate Major Zotov

In accordance with your directive, today December 10, 1983, at Yaku-Tur settlement, I carried out an external examination of the corpse of the former chief of the Yaku-Tur Seismographic Research Expedition, Voropayev, and questioned his subordinates. In addition, together with the head of security at Camp RS-549, Major Orudjev, and using tracker dogs, a detailed search was made of the scene of the incident despite blizzard conditions. As a result of the said investigations, the following has been established:

Early on the morning of December 6, Vitali Voropayev, aged 37, nationality Russian, was returning to the Yaku-Tur settlement from visiting his Nenets cohabitant, Savana Pyrerko, about a kilometer and a half away at the Nenets encampment near the state fish farm Road to Communism. During questioning, Pyrerko (aged 19) stated that Voropayev had disappeared from her tent while she was asleep, i.e., approximately between 5:00 and 8:00 on the morning of December 7. She was able to give details of clothing taken from Voropayev by the murderers. Hat of young reindeer fur, light brown; canvas jacket with wolf fur, with canvas hood; dark-blue dungarees, fur; flying boots, dog fur, black trim.

Additional questioning of the local population established that Citizeness Savana Pyrerko, nominally a member of the fish unit at the state farm Road to Communism, lives on income from prostitution, cohabiting with workmen and engineer-technical staff of the Yaku-Tur shift settlement. A search of her tent revealed about three thousand (3,000) rubles in cash and, in the vicinity of the tent, several cases of empty glass containers of liquor, vodka, and eau de cologne.

Since the sale of spirits to the Nenets population is forbidden by law, there can be no doubt that liquor was brought in quantity by the clients of the said Savana Pyrerko, who visited her both singly and in groups.

I will fill in the details. The body of the murdered Voropayev was discovered early in the morning of December 10, 1983, by a local inhabitant, Yakhano Tokho, a foreman at the Nenets fish unit Road to Communism. The corpse was about two hundred yards from Pyrerko's tent. So Voropayev, visiting Savana Pyrerko on the night of December 5–6, was absent from work four days, which must naturally have caused concern among his subordinates. Voropayev's deputy, however, Rodion Malofeyev, and others of his staff stated that since all exploration work has been suspended between December 6 and 9, owing to the severe blizzard, they did not want to disturb their leader, Voropayev, whom they supposed to be staying with Savana Pyrerko.

The Nenets, Yakhano Tokho, aged 63, testified that this morning, December 10 (he cannot state the exact time, since he does not wear a watch, but by my calculations about 6:30–7:00 A.M.), he took his dog team out of the encampment and headed toward Yaku-Tur to buy tobacco, flour, and tea. On the way the dogs halted near a snowdrift, squatted in the snow, and began howling, while the lead dog started scratching away at the snow with its forepaws. Jumping off the sled, Yakhano Tokho dug into the drift and discovered the body of Voropayev. The corpse, in Tokho's words, was completely naked and frozen stiff; the sliced-off ears were frozen to the chest. In the groin a frozen crust of blood surrounded the severed *khote.**

Convinced that this was a punishment for debauchery inflicted by "the tundra spirits at the behest of the great god of the tundra," Num, Tokho left the body untouched and raced his sled into Yaku-Tur to report his find to Voropayev's deputy, Rodion Malofeyev. He, together with his driver, Malyshko, and other assistants, set out into the tundra along the trail left by Tokho's dogs (the old man was terrified of the tundra spirits and refused to go with them), where they picked up Voropayev's body.

My external examination of the body showed no signs of decay, owing to the forty-degree frost. The bodily injuries, the severed ears and sex organ, had been carried out with a sharp, cold weapon. The same weapon was apparently responsible for the fatal blow to the heart. Voropayev's wrists and shoulders show clear bruising, which may testify to the victim's attempts to defend himself.

In my opinion, Voropayev left Savana Pyrerko's tent early on the morning of December 6, intending to return to work. The blizzard did not stop him, since the night before he and Pyrerko had drunk between them three bottles of pure alcohol. Two hundred yards from the tent, Voropayev encountered his murderer or murderers, evidently the prisoners who had escaped that night from Camp RS-549.

---

*Male sexual organ (Nenets).

To determine the time of Voropayev's death beyond any doubt, however, and the exact sequence of events connected with his execution, an expert in forensic medicine must be sent to Yaku-Tur.

As regards the scene of the incident, I have to record that no trace of the criminal or criminals has been discovered.

I await your further instructions.
Lieutenant of Militia, Investigator Anna Kovina
Yaku-Tur Settlement
10 December 1983

I reckoned my work rate had put me one up on the best investigators at our Urengoi CID. Within a few hours of my arrival at Yaku-Tur and the fish farm, I had gathered practically every scrap of information on Voropayev's murder—in a snowstorm, what's more, when I had to take statements not only from drunken Russians but from Nentsi as well, in their black tents, reeking of dog.

The brief reply to my radio message did not come from my chief, Zotov, however.

TO: YAKU-TUR, DEPUTY LEADER SEISMOGRAPHIC RE-
SEARCH EXPEDITION R. MALOFEYEV
ORGANIZE IMMEDIATE DEPARTURE OF URENGOI CID
INVESTIGATOR ANNA KOVINA TO SALEKHARD KGB
WITH ALL PERSONAL DOCUMENTS RELATING TO ES-
CAPED CRIMINALS AND BODY OF VOROPAYEV. INFORM
KOVINA THAT PHOTOGRAPHS OF ESCAPEES IN THEIR
PAPERS ABSOLUTELY NECESSARY IN PURSUIT AND
ARREST OF CRIMINALS.
TO ENSURE SAFE PASSAGE IN THE BLIZZARD CONDI-
TIONS, SEND NO FEWER THAN THREE SNO-CATS WITH
MOST EXPERIENCED DRIVERS. REPORT IMMEDIATELY
ON COMPLETION.

CHIEF OF SALEKHARD KGB
DIRECTORATE
MAJOR SHATUNOV

12

I took the summons to Salekhard, capital of the Yamal-Nenets District, as a fateful sign, whereas Orudjev reacted like a working dog hearing the command "Go fetch!" He settled into the driver's seat of the leading Sno-Cat, and three tank engines revving up at full blast drowned out the roar of the snowstorm.

Orudjev drove the Sno-Cat by compass reckoning—straight ahead across the ice hummocks, through the sparse tundra scrub, across frozen bogs and gullies. Because of the appalling shaking, Voropayev's coffin broke open in the first hour, and the frozen corpse fell out onto the floor.

"Stop!" I yelled at Orudjev. "Stop! You're spoiling my corpse. It's got to be medically examined! Stop!"

But Orudjev drove on without a pause. He didn't give a damn for forensic medicine or any such criminological refinements. Over there in Salekhard or close by, he might find his escaped criminals and restore his unsullied reputation in the guard service.

Meanwhile, I almost wept with exasperation. Voropayev's murdered body was of unique value to forensic science since it had been frozen instantly on the tundra, like the fish the Nentsi catch under the ice in winter. Once drawn out of the water, one touch of the forty- or fifty-degree frost, and the fish freezes in a fraction of a second; even the water has no time to drip off its slimy back. So Voropayev had frozen on the tundra, except that, in his case, instead of water around the gaping mouth with the *khote* thrust down the throat, there was a border of scarlet blood. The same icy loops of blood lay around the severed ears and in the groin around the excised *khote*. At the same time there were no traces of decay; the corpse had lain four days on the tundra as if in a refrigerator; the bruises on shoulders and wrists were ideally visible.

But now the jolting of the Sno-Cat was rolling the body around the floor. Driving the dogs away, and with the help of two sergeants, I somehow crammed the corpse back into the coffin and strapped it down with our belts. The frozen body rumbled about in the coffin, and I regretted not having wrapped it up in a jacket, but there was no opening the coffin again; it was all I could do to hang on to a metal stanchion.

I probably survived that journey without being sick only because I'd eaten nothing since the previous day and so had nothing to vomit. Six times we overturned, skidding down the bank of a stream or the lip of a tundra gully.

Four steel hawsers snapped while two of the Sno-Cats were putting the third back on its tracks after yet another capsize. During these operations the tundra heard Russian, Ossetian, and Ukrainian curses, the likes of which I had never heard in all my years in the militia.

After three hours of this mad journey, the engine of one vehicle overheated and began smoking, and an hour later the track of a second broke apart. We abandoned them on the tundra and, all in one Sno-Cat, rolled into the dark streets of Salekhard. The treads clanked along the frozen log roadway, and the vehicle drew up outside the building of the local directorate of the KGB. I crawled out of the cabin only half-alive, with frozen cheeks and stiff, unbending legs. My back, shoulders, and knees ached from the knocks they had received. However, I was still able to help the soldiers drag the whimpering dogs out of the vehicle, along with Voropayev's coffin.

"Leave that!" Orudjev pushed me away. "Let's see Shatunov!"

In Shatunov's office sat about fifteen men—the entire Salekhard staff working on the detection of the runaways. Hudya Benokan was among them. Orudjev and I, swaying from exhaustion, halted in the doorway; I had the personal files of the prisoners in my hands. Major Shatunov, a fifty-year-old Siberian with a strong, weather-beaten face and the white eyelashes of an albino, glanced at me approvingly.

"You got through, then?" He nodded to someone. "Give her a chair; she'll fall over in a minute."

Everyone burst out laughing. It's always the same, damn them; do work three men couldn't manage and all they can do is snigger.

Somebody got me a chair, took the files from me, and placed them in front of Shatunov. I sat down and began to feel that the warmth was making me fall apart; a hiccup came to my throat. Hudya gave me a glass of strong tea. He had altered a lot over four years. Before, at the university, he had been a buttoned-up Nenets with the artless face of a reindeer herdsman. But now something adult, harsh, and weary had appeared on that face. No wonder, I thought. I just couldn't imagine how he got through his exams and papers at the University Law Faculty and looked after a babe in arms in the hostel at the same time. When I had been there, I'd been overworked even without a baby to think of.

Shatunov, meanwhile, without raising his eyes from the prisoners' personal files, asked Orudjev, "Was it you who let these prisoners escape from the camp?"

"It was, Comrade Major," said Orudjev, coming to attention.

"You'll be reduced to the ranks," rasped Shatunov, still without looking at him. He tore the sheets of photographs from each folder and gave them to one of his assistants. "Get these copied right away and distributed to all concerned. I want posters with the murderers' pictures on every post within two hours!"

"Permission to wipe out guilt, Comrade Major," said Orudjev.

Only now did Shatunov lift his eyes.

"How do you propose going about that?"

Orudjev's fancy white sheepskin was wet with snow, his face and hands a mass of bruises from banging against the windshield; his right ear was frostbitten, and a dark stubble had sprouted on his unshaven cheeks. It was clear it was taking all his strength to stay on his feet. However, he spoke firmly, even brusquely, "I'll get those bastards if I have to dig up the tundra!"

"Very well, go ahead and try," replied Shatunov and glanced in my direction. My hiccups were audible throughout the office.

He frowned, irritated. "See her to a hotel," he told Hudya.

Hudya came over and made as if to help me rise, but I shoved his arm away and stood up on my own. That was all I needed—Hudya Benokan of all people to be a nanny to me. The most exasperating part though—I could have cried!—was that after a whole hectic day spent on a "hot job," after all my efforts in Yaku-Tur and that crazy drive to Salekhard, now came these idiotic, nonstop hiccups. With tears in my eyes, I shot out of the office. The door to the street was open for the soldiers to carry in Voropayev's coffin. I couldn't stir for people. Why is it when somebody falls over or has the hiccups everybody thinks it's so funny? Even Hudya! He brought me a whole decanter of water. "Drink up, however, it'll help," he said. "Let's be off to the hotel."

I rounded on him in a pause between hiccups and said, hatefully, "Listen! Piss off, will you! Hic!"

He shrugged and went back to Shatunov's office.

13

TYUMEN

TO: FIRST SECRETARY TYUMEN PROVINCE COMMITTEE CPSU, COMRADE BOGOMYATOV

IN REPLY TO YOUR EXPRESS TELEGRAM RE ARREST OF PRISONERS ESCAPED FROM CAMP RS-549, WE REPORT: IN SALEKHARD, ENTIRE AVAILABLE COMPLEMENT OF LOCAL KGB, POLICE MILITIA, AND MILITARY GARRISON NOW MOBILIZED IN HUNT FOR CRIMINAL-MURDERERS. SPECIAL OPERATIONS STAFF HAS BEEN ESTABLISHED FOR THEIR APPREHENSION. A CAREFUL SEARCH BEING CARRIED OUT OF ALL BUILDINGS IN TOWN, LABYTNANGI RAILWAY STATION, AND NEARBY SETTLEMENTS. AIRPORT BLOCKADED, RAILWAY BEING PATROLLED. DESPITE BLIZZARD, URENGOI CID INVESTIGATOR ANNA KOVINA HAS DELIVERED PHOTOGRAPHS OF ESCAPEES FROM CAMP RS-549. PHOTOGRAPHS HAVE BEEN COPIED AND DISTRIBUTED TO ALL PATROLS. AT VERY FIRST SIGN OF IMPROVEMENT IN WEATHER CONDITIONS, AIRCRAFT WILL BE USED TO SEARCH SURROUNDING TUNDRA.

CONFIDENT THAT YOUR PARTY INSTRUCTION RE APPREHENSION OR ELIMINATION OF MURDERERS OF HEAD OF YAKU-TUR SEISMOGRAPHIC EXPLORATION TEAM VOROPAYEV AND SENIOR CONSULTANT SALEK-

HARD DISTRICT HOSPITAL HOTKO IS A MATTER OF HOURS.

FIRST SECRETARY YAMAL-NENETS DISTRICT COMMIT-
TEE CPSU PYOTR TUSYADA
CHIEF OF OPERATIONAL STAFF MAJOR STATE SECU-
RITY SHATUNOV

SALEKHARD, 10 DECEMBER 1983

14

Only a few minutes remained of the time limit set by the first secretary of the Tyumen Province Party Committee, Bogomyatov; it was 6:30 P.M. on December 11. We, that is, virtually the whole operational staff working on the murder hunt, were sitting in the office of Pyotr Tusyada, first secretary of the Yamal-Nenets Party District Committee.

In anticipation of the arrival of the government delegation and foreign guests for the pipeline opening, the Soviet furniture had been replaced by Swedish furniture, the walls had been faced with Karelian birch, and an enormous relief map of the Yamal-Nenets National District, with green derricks marking the gas fields and red threads indicating pipelines, had been hung. Little figures of reindeer, arctic foxes, and fish were used to show the other resources of the Nenets tundra—reindeer ranches, fish-processing plants, farms where fur-bearing animals were raised. The map convincingly demonstrated that this wild arctic territory, one and a half times the size of France, really was a unique repository of "blue gold" (gas), "soft gold" (fur), and "red gold" (salmon).

And the titular master of this whole territory, Pyotr Tusyada, a Nenets who had been appointed by Moscow six months before especially to demonstrate to foreign visitors the advancement of minority personnel to posts of responsibility, indeed had something to exhibit: the Nentsi of several exemplary fur-breeding establishments and collective farms had been hastily transferred from reindeer-skin tents into European-type settlements; the Nenets song and dance ensemble Northern Lights had learned French, German, and Czech folk songs; and even the children of the local school had worked up a concert program in four languages.

At this moment, however, Tusyada was in no mood for French songs. A squat, thickset man of about thirty-six, he had been merely a manager of a Nenets fur farm before his promotion. He sat heavily in his leather armchair and slowly, after the fashion of his forebears, rocked his whole body backward and forward in time with his round, almost neckless head. His narrow eyes were open, but it was doubtful that he saw us. It seemed as if for the first time in the six months of his dizzying party career, he desperately wished himself back on the tundra with his reindeer and arctic foxes. That went for the rest of the company too; at that moment we all wanted to be as far away as possible from the red telephone on the table, the direct line to the Tyumen Province Party Committee.

All the extraordinary measures for the detection of the escaped criminals had yielded no results. The blizzard had abated somewhat toward morning, and since then two polar aviation helicopters had been circling over Salekhard pinpointing every car, Sno-Cat, even Nenets sled that left the town, but without result. The soldiers of the local garrison had combed every dwelling, every warehouse and hut, every habitable and uninhabitable corner, including the barges frozen into the Ob, all in vain. All over the town the wind shredded and tore at hastily slapped up posters bearing the portraits of the fugitives and the caption WANTED CRIMINALS. On the railway soldiers not only searched every carriage, they escorted the trains almost as far as the Urals. Sno-Cats quartered the surrounding tundra with a similar lack of result, visiting all Nenets encampments within a radius of fifty kilometers. The Nentsi greeted the soldiers with open derision. ''The Russians are looking for spirits, however. How can you find a spirit, however?''

In some unimaginable fashion the rumor that the tundra spirits had put to death two Russian officials had spread rapidly across the Yamal peninsula. The Nenets bush telegraph at once adorned the facts with an incredible explanation: when the Russians had arrived in the tundra three hundred years ago to rob the Nentsi of their fur and fish, the tundra spirits had held their peace; they had slept beneath the earth. But when the Russians began drilling the Nenets earth to seize the last riches of the Nentsi—oil and gas—the spirits awoke. However, the Russians did not release them from beneath the earth; the Russians blocked the holes in the earth with clay. Now, because of the opening of the pipeline, the Russians had begun to unplug the boreholes. The tundra spirits had burst forth and begun to take revenge on the Russians for having, they said, ripped the tundra apart with their iron machines, destroyed the reindeer pastures so there was now nowhere a Nenets could graze his reindeer. The Russians had killed the rivers, polluted them with gas, hydrochloric acid, and oil. They had brought ''bad'' diseases to the tundra—syphilis, gonorrhea, tuberculosis . . .

Of course, nobody on the operations staff gave any consideration to these rumors. We were concerned about something else—where on earth could the three escapees have got to? No spirits broke out of RS-549! Nearly five days had passed since they had absconded. They needed food, warmth, shelter, and yet along their entire route from the camp to Salekhard, a route marked by two corpses, there wasn't a single burglarized shop, no campfire, nothing. And in Salekhard itself, not a single burglary, not a trace of any criminal on the run. After Voropayev had been killed in Yaku-Tur and Hotko in Salekhard, the fugitives had simply been swallowed up. Or had they slipped past the railway patrols in some mysterious fashion and rolled away to "the mainland"?

Anyway, everybody gathered in Tusyada's office was depressed. It was at that moment that the door burst open and Orudjev propelled two little Nenets boys, wearing ragged reindeer *malitsas*, into the office. Everybody turned toward Orudjev, questioning and a little hopeful.

"Well?" said Shatunov impatiently.

"They'll speak for themselves, little shits!"

Orudjev jerked the boys roughly by the shoulder. His previous dash and polish had disappeared completely. A day and night of sleepless roaming around Salekhard had stiffened his face; his cheeks had fallen in.

The boys said nothing, glancing at us with narrow, malevolent little eyes.

"Well, out with it!" Shatunov demanded of Orudjev.

"I caught them red-handed," reported Orudjev, "writing in charcoal, little buggers, on the Lenin monument: 'Russians—get out of the tundra!' "

"And that's all?" asked Shatunov.

"That's all, Comrade Major. They'd started writing something about spirits . . ."

"Get lost," said Shatunov softly.

"What?" Orudjev thought he must have misheard.

"I said—get lost!" Shatunov's voice broke as he shouted, "Just fuck off!"

While all this was going on, nobody had noticed that the chief of the district militia, Colonel Sini, had hurried into the office. Although Sini had the rank of colonel and Shatunov was only a major, Shatunov, as chief of operations and the KGB representative, acted as top man while the colonel simply tried to preserve his independence. Without looking at anyone, he went straight up to Tusyada's desk and placed before him a typed sheet of paper.

Tusyada read it without speaking, glanced briefly at Colonel Sini, then lowered his eyes back to the paper. He rose and walked heavily on his short legs over to a wall cupboard, which he opened. Hanging there were a *malitsa* and other items of Nenets national dress. Tusyada removed his dark jacket with its supreme Soviet deputy's badge, his tie, and white shirt.

We watched him in amazement. Was he going to strip completely?

Meanwhile, he was calmly putting a *yagushka* next to his bare skin; this garment was a shirt of reindeer hide with the fur inside. He then slipped off his fashionable shoes and, without rolling up his trousers, drew on some *ichigi* (fur stockings) and, on top of them, high reindeer boots, *kisi*, and pulled them above the knee by the laces. After this he neatly slipped into his *malitsa,* with its all-enveloping hood and sleeves. And so, without a word, he walked out of the office, pausing only in a gesture of paternal authority to lay hold of the two Nenets boys by the hood and take them with him.

"What's happened?" Shatunov looked at Colonel Sini, then leaned across Tusyada's table and took the typewritten sheet. He had not finished reading it when outside the window, illuminated by the bright street lamps, Tusyada hailed a passing Nenets reindeer sled, took his seat, and departed.

The clock on the wall showed 18:30. The red telephone on Tusyada's desk came to life with a soft, muffled ring. Nobody picked it up. The white sheet with its typewritten text passed from hand to hand to the accompaniment of the evenly spaced ringing of the phone. This is what was typed on that paper:

REPORT

To: Chief of Yamal-Nencts Directorate of Militia,
Colonel N. Sini

While carrying out routine patrol of Poluisky region of Salekhard, today, December 11, at 18 hrs. 10 minutes, duty patrol of three men under Militia Sergeant Orlov noticed that the wicket gate of the cottage belonging to R. Ryazanov, chief geologist of Yamal Oil and Gas Exploration Trust, was open. Upon entering the cottage yard, the patrol discovered in the snow near the sauna the frozen naked corpse of Comrade Ryazanov with marks of brutal violation—ears and sex organ cut off. The severed sex organ was in the victim's mouth. Clothing and documents of the murdered man have disappeared. One meter from the corpse on the snow was discovered a mitten with a Camp RS-549 tag and the initials *T.Z.* written on the lining with a chemical pencil, which may prove the mitten belongs to one of the three criminals from Camp RS-549, namely Timur Zaloyev. . . .

While we were reading this, Shatunov was conversing with Colonel Sini in staccato phrases.

"Is the area cordoned off?"

"We're doing it now."

"How many investigators at the scene of the crime?"

"From our Urengoi CID, Kovrov's just gone out there with Benokan and the dog handler Telichkin."

"How many dogs?"

"Three."

"OK. Mitten to Major Orudjev for identification. Nothing's to be touched in Ryazanov's house till I get there." Having made these arrangements, Shatunov at last lifted the phone.

"Yes, Comrade Bogomyatov. . . . No, Tusyada's gone out, this is Major Shatunov. . . . No, unfortu-

nately not caught yet, but they are in Salekhard. . . .
I know because a third body's just been found. It's the
chief geologist of Yamal Oil and Gas, Ryazanov . . .''

Even from the impenetrable face of Shatunov, it was
clear that the party terminology being used at the other
end of the line was weighty and coarse. Shatunov could
only get a word in now and again.

''No, they won't get away. . . . I understand, but
now they won't get away . . .''

At last he had heard everything Bogomyatov had to
say to him. He replied curtly, ''Very good, sir,'' re-
placed the phone, and turned to us.

''They've given us an extension till tomorrow morn-
ing. But if we don't get them . . . Well, you don't need
me to tell you. Now, all investigators follow me, to
the scene of the crime.'' He admonished the rest, who
had risen noisily to their feet, ''There's nothing for the
rest of you to do over there; go and join the police
cordon!''

15

Meanwhile, what a few hours before had seemed a delirium of wild superstition unworthy of serious attention, had turned, as soon as Ryazanov's body had been discovered, into something close to mass hysteria. Yes indeed, three murders in two days. And what killings! *Khore* stuffed down the throat and all. Well a mob's a mob, no matter how much you teach them atheism and materialism. That the mitten found at Ryazanov's cottage confirmed the murders as the work of the runaway convicts, not tundra spirits, nobody in Salekhard wanted to hear. "The tundra spirits are punishing the Russians," was on everybody's lips. And the streets of Salekhard went dead. In their houses the Russians barricaded doors and windows. Lights were on in the workingmen's hostels—the single men were packing their suitcases. Run! Run from the tundra! In Labytnangi, a settlement on the west bank of the Ob, there was a stampede at the railway station. Shift workers stormed the ticket office; those without tickets broke through the police cordon around the cars on the platform and the Salekhard-Moscow train had to be delayed for three hours.

In the crush and fighting over tickets, a number of people were injured; about thirty were arrested for disorderly behavior and obstructing the police. Even that didn't help. A drunk climbed onto the garbage can next to the ticket office laughing hysterically and yelling out over the heads of the sweating mob: "Been out shagging on the tundra? You running away from your sons? Who's grabbed sables off the Nentsi for a fifth? Is it your balls you're protecting? Ha-ha-haah! Which one of you tipped oil in the river? Eh? Who's been banging little Nentsi girls? Now you're scared for your balls, you cunt busters! Who brought syphilis into the tundra, I ask you!"

"Shut your mouth, shitface! What about you?" Someone yelled at him from the crowd.

"Truth hurts, eh?" responded the drunk carefully. "Pity Jack London's not about. He could have described you lot, builders of Communism, tundra prick swingers!"

"I'll slice your ears off myself!" Someone darted toward him.

"Hoboes!" cried the drunk gaily. "What about me, then? I'm not denying anything. I've been whoring out there as well! I was a naughty boy as well! Just let him that is without sin cast the first stone! What? Nobody? Well, I'm going to atone—to the tundra spirits, fuck it!"

He fell or jumped off the can and dived through the crowd onto the station platform. He drew out of his jacket a thick wad of notes—a year's pay most likely—and began flinging them to the tundra wind. "All of it! The lot! Keep it, tundra!" he shouted. "Well now, who's brave enough to damn well give back what he looted?"

He was arrested on the spot, of course, but even in the police station, he turned out all his pockets, threw his last small change on the floor, and went on acting the goat. "What's the matter? I earned them here, I've thrown them away here! I've got the right! My balls mean more to me! I demand you write on the charge sheet: 'Driller Trofimov redeemed his balls from the spirits of the Nentsi!' "

The next morning not a single Russian family let its children go to school, and the majority of the town's Russian population did not turn up for work. It was like Moscow in 1971, when the police couldn't lay hands on the sadist-murderer Idonesyan, who killed a child a day.

Of course, nobody on the Operations Staff gave any credence to these "tundra spirits" or any such superstitions, but to keep the madness from spreading across the territory, Shatunov ordered that Salekhard and Labytnangi be sealed off: all mail was halted, no private calls to other towns were allowed, the airport was closed for outbound flights, and train schedules were suspended.

Shatunov called this action "psychological quarantine."

16

On the steep bank of the river Polui, a tributary of the Ob, Ryazanov's cottage had been cordoned off by the police militia; the yard was lit up by car headlights and searchlights positioned in the cottage windows. The cottage itself was in a modern little development where the local elite lived; Salekhard residents had dubbed the place "Laureateville" since nearly all the local leading lights were state-prize laureates and the like. Major Orudjev had been toiling for three hours already in the yard alongside Sergeant Telichkin, the Salekhard police dog handler. Orudjev took Zaloyev's mitten, found near Ryazanov's body, out of its cellophane bag and gave it to the dog to sniff. Then he described a wide circle with his arm and said softly, "Seek, Titan. Trace."

Titan, a sinewy gray championship dog, knew his job. Lowering his muzzle to the snow, he moved around the yard in ever-narrowing circles until he returned to the spot where the patrol had found the mitten several hours before. At this point, he squatted down, yawned, and gave every indication that the search was over.

The same thing happened with the other dogs.

We were all crowded together at the doors and windows of the cottage watching Orudjev and Telichkin's vain efforts to find the faintest trace of Zaloyev's presence. It should be said that we investigators had got nowhere either. Hudya and his colleague from the Salekhard CID, the criminal law expert Kovrov, had literally crawled on hands and knees around Ryazanov's cottage and the sauna building before reporting to Shatunov.

"That's it. You can go inside now. There are no prints or traces except for those of Ryazanov and his driver."

Shatunov glared at them so savagely that the expert amplified, or rather, added in self-justification, "Nobody's lived in the cottage for a month. Everything's covered with dust. So fingerprints and other traces would be obvious. Ryazanov's prints are in the kitchen, on the refrigerator, on a bottle of cognac, a coat hook, and the radiator. His driver's prints are on two of Ryazanov's suitcases. That's the lot."

Shatunov sighed and went into the cottage; the rest trailed along behind him, myself among them.

I had never been in a millionaire's villa before; I'd only seen them in films. I'd only known about government dachas by hearsay. Now I was seeing with my own eyes what real luxury meant. Perhaps it's worth mentioning a few more details about Laureateville. Elite villages like this exist in every development area of national importance—Bratsk, Ust-Ilin, the Viluisk hydroelectric project, and up here in the North at Urengoi, Surgut, and Tayezhni. I don't know who pays for the buildings in places like Bratsk, but up here they're obviously built out of resources released by the "shift method of developing the tundra": instead of going for apartment buildings, schools, and hospitals in Yaku-Tur and similar workingmen's settlements, all scarce building materials came here to Laureateville.

A special team of architects directed the building, adapting each cottage to the personal tastes of its future occupant. At the same time two camps' worth of convicts laid out the streets and terraces, planted birches and pines from the taiga, and constructed yacht-club moorings down by the Polui, a secluded swimming pool, two tennis courts. Each cottage was fitted out with a sauna, fireplaces, and similar Western-style comforts. Once ensconced, the owners began competing over their furnishings: washable Finnish wallpaper that looks like leather, Swedish furniture, polar-bear skins, even ancient Nenets idols adorned the interiors of these villas.

Ryazanov's cottage was one of them—an enormous polar-bear skin covered the parquet floor of the living room. Light-colored furniture matched the rug, while over by the fireplace stood three low stools with legs of walrus ivory; on closer inspection, these were revealed to be the cores of walrus penises. (Because walruses mate in subarctic temperatures, nature has actually equipped their penises with bones.) No doubt at another time these penis legs would have given rise to ribald comment, but we were in no mood for humor. The "comparative findings of the forensic medical examination" on all three corpses had arrived from the hospital.

"All three deaths," Shatunov read, "came about as the result of a precisely delivered blow by a sharp piercing/cutting instrument in the neighborhood of the heart. A fact meriting attention is that in all three cases the depth of penetration is approximately the same, from fourteen point five centimeters to sixteen centimeters, which points to the same hand being responsible for all three wounds. . . . The nature of the cuts where the ears and sexual organs of the victims have been removed is likewise identical. This allows us to state that all the wounds were caused by the same sharp-edged instrument, most probably a knife. . . . After comparative microscopic analysis of the wounds and cuts and study of the dynamics of the infliction of body injuries, the examination concludes that the murderer possesses average strength and uses the right hand in a characteristic fashion—each slash is made by one abrupt blow from bottom to top, as indicated by the upward and outward direction of the slash lines where ears and sex organs have been severed.''

"That Tartar way!'' commented Shatunov by way of conclusion.

"And Nenets!'' I couldn't help saying. "Nentsi butcher meat like that, I've seen them. They put one end of a fresh reindeer liver in their mouth and cut it with a knife from underneath.''

"So you're saying it's Nentsi who are doing the killing?'' Hudya Benokan interposed, as if I'd insulted the whole Nenets people with my suspicion.

"Don't fight over it,'' said Kovrov soothingly. "Neither Nentsi nor their spirits wear prison mittens.''

"Exactly,'' Shatunov went on reading the medical report. "As a result of the extraordinary fast freezing of the corpses due to the low temperature of their surroundings, it is not possible to determine the exact time of death of Voropayev and Hotko by bacteriological analysis. As regards Ryazanov, the exceptional weight of the deceased (one hundred forty kilograms with height one meter sixty-seven centimeters), together with a thick layer of fat in the abdominal area, partially retarded the freezing process. The autopsy has revealed unfrozen remains of food in stomach and intestine; this enables the moment of the attack to be fixed at from three to three and a half hours prior to the discovery of the corpse.

"The Examination Team would draw attention to the fact that there are no bruises or scratches on the bodies of Hotko and Ryazanov, while the preliminary external examination of Voropayev's body by Investigator A. Kovina revealed scratches and bruises in the area of the right shoulder and the wrists, which may point to Voropayev's struggle for life. Unfortunately, inappropriate transportation of Voropayev's body from

Yaku-Tur to Salekhard led to additional injury to the body and hindered the work of the team in determining the nature and location of injuries sustained while alive.''

Shatunov glanced at me with his white eyes.

I shrugged. ''You don't get bruised wrists in a coffin.''

''OK,'' said Shatunov and read on to the end of the report. ''The autopsy revealed a high alcohol level in Voropayev's blood. No traces of alcohol were found in Hotko. Signatures. That's it. Cretins!'' said Shatunov without a pause, flinging the report onto the kitchen table. ''It seems two sober chaps—Ryazanov and Hotko—quietly let their penises and ears get cut off. Voropayev, drunk as a skunk, did put up some resistance. What does that tell us? Who the fuck knows. Right, Kovina, while those pricks are messing about with the dogs, tell us what you've got.''

He gazed around the kitchen and looked questioningly at Benokan and Kovrov.

''Can we sit down here? Have you checked the chairs?''

''Now we really are offended.'' Kovrov grinned. ''You can even drink the cognac in that bottle—I've got all the fingerprints on film.''

Shatunov sat down at the table and poured himself half a glass of brandy, downed it in a gulp, grunted, took a sniff at his fist, and gave me an interrogative glance. ''Well? Make your report.''

I wouldn't have minded a drink either, but it didn't occur to him to offer, though I'd been hanging around in the cold as long as he had.

I spoke. ''Ryazanov got into this business straight off the ship, so to speak. He only got back from vacation today; he'd been at a government sanatorium on the Black Sea. His wife and daughter stayed in Moscow to celebrate New Year's. He hurried back here for the pipeline opening; he even brought a whole suitcase of whiskey and cognac. Judging by the stamps on the labels, they're from the gas industry minister's special supply."

Shatunov didn't care for my informal tone and interrupted. "Keep it short! Stick to essentials."

I got the record of my interrogation of Ryazanov's driver out of my briefcase and began to read. "Ryazanov's chauffeur stated: 'At two o'clock in the afternoon, I met Comrade Ryazanov at the Labytnangi Railway Station. While we were crossing the frozen Ob from the left bank to the right, I told Comrade Ryazanov about the escape of the prisoners and the two murders. Comrade Ryazanov knew both Voropayev and Hotko well and was extremely upset. The "tundra spirits" business just made him laugh. "That's all we need, spirits cutting your balls off for a bit of humping" was what Comrade Ryazanov said. "Anyway, these Nentsi should be grateful for so-called debauchery: if it hadn't been for Russian sperm, they'd have died out two hundred years ago!" ' "

"True enough." Shatunov grinned. "You've seen the children the Nentsi wives have got now? Nearly taller than me. Fair lads, real Russkies." Here he recollected that Hudya Benokan, the Nenets, was standing next to him, and said, "Hmm . . . Just, er, strike those words about debauchery out of the record, will you?"

I nodded and continued reading. " 'At approximately three fifteen, we drove up to Ryazanov's house in Laureateville. I took his two suitcases out of the trunk of the Volga and brought them into the cottage after Comrade Ryazanov. The path from the gate to the porch had been cleared, the yard as well.' "

"Who cleared the path and yard?" asked Shatunov abruptly.

"I've checked. The caretaker swept both out at eleven that morning. He does it every morning for all the cottages. Shall I go on?"

"Yes, go on."

" 'Comrade Ryazanov opened the cottage door with his key and went in; I carried the two suitcases after him. Comrade Ryazanov took his things off and hung his sheepskin up on some reindeer antlers in the hallway. It was cold in the cottage, unheated, so Comrade Ryazanov put his old sheepskin jacket on and turned on the central heating. I asked him if he needed me for anything else and whether he wanted the car that day. He said he was tired from the journey and was going to stoke up the sauna, have a bit of a steam, then go to bed. "Come for me at seven in the morning as usual," he said, and I drove away. I noticed nothing suspicious in the house. When I went out to the car, the street was empty. I saw lights in the nearby cottages, but everything was quiet.' Signature. Date," I added and placed the record in the briefcase.

"There's more, Comrade Major. The sheepskin jacket the driver mentioned has vanished along with the rest of the things Ryazanov was wearing when he was killed. The picture begins to look like this: after dismissing the driver, Ryazanov opened that bottle of cognac over there; he drank fifty to eighty grams straight from the bottle and went out to stoke up the sauna. He did do that; it's still warm. Then he came back into the yard, where the murderer met him seven yards from the sauna. This was between three thirty and four in the afternoon—that is, in total darkness. I made the rounds of the neighboring cottages where Ryazanov's chauffeur had seen lights. The ones to right and left of Ryazanov's are about a hundred seventy yards away. If Ryazanov had shouted loudly for help, he would have been heard. Both the men in those cottages were at work; the women say they heard nothing. Now I've got a question: does a man shout out when his, excuse me, sex organs are cut off, or are his vocal cords so constricted by pain and fear that he can't make a sound?"

"Don't know," said Shatunov gloomily. "I've never had anything cut off me yet. But if we don't find that Tartar by morning, I'll be able to answer the question tomorrow. They missed the main thing: What came first? Was it the knife thrust to the heart and then the severing of ears and penis, or the other way around?" He rose, looked out the window, and shouted to Orudjev and Telichkin, "Well? How long are you going to be with those dogs?"

Neither Orudjev nor Telichkin replied; both were watching intently as the last dog, called Carter, nosed about. For some reason, every militia unit has dogs named after American presidents or English prime ministers. Probably it gives the soldiers a bit of pleasure ordering American or English leaders around. "Carter, sit!" or "Thatcher, go get it!" On this occasion, however, Carter played a truly imperialist, anti-Soviet joke on Orudjev: not only did he fail to find anything like all the other dogs, but when he reached the spot where Ryazanov's corpse and Zaloyev's mitten had been discovered, he suddenly raised his hind leg and demonstratively pissed on the scene of the crime.

Any other time we would probably have fallen over laughing; now we all kept quiet, except, of course, Shatunov.

"Your dog?" he asked Orudjev, through the window.

"Yes," Orudjev brought out in a low crushed voice.

"The abattoir—boil him down for soap! And you as well. OK, take the dogs away; let's have the investigators examine the yard." Here Shatunov turned to Hudya and the rest. "All snow in the yard must be gone through! With magnifying glasses!"

The sound of a helicopter drowned out his words. We stared into the dark sky. The aircraft was heading straight for Ryazanov's cottage using a powerful searchlight to find a landing place. At about sixty feet above the cottage, however, it hovered indecisively, then turned away toward the street and came down on the snowy roadway. A small figure detached itself from the helicopter, and I recognized it as my Urengoi chief, Zotov. Bending to the earth, he moved away from the aircraft, waving to the pilot to swing away. Two minutes later he was walking into Ryazanov's cottage, scraping his felt boots.

"Here we are," he said, addressing Shatunov and shaking powdery snow from his fur jacket. "Flown in from Urengoi to lend a hand. What have you got here? Any tea going?"

"Kovina, can you make tea?" asked Shatunov. "A Pinkerton man from the sky, that's all I needed." With that he went out into the yard to supervise the work of the investigators, who had replaced the dogs in scouring every inch of Ryazanov's yard, actually using magnifying glasses.

I put the kettle on the electric stove, and while it was heating up briefly told Zotov all I knew.

While he listened Zotov took off his felt boots, undid the zipper on the left side of his fur trousers, and started rubbing his troublesome knee with that foulsmelling ointment of his. Afterward he took a few calm sips of tea, lit his pipe, and took a look around the cottage. He went outside, stamped around near the sauna, then came back in.

I called the hospital and learned from the doctors that they were unable to answer Shatunov's question. They mumbled something about needing a specialist's opinion on vocal cords to determine whether the victims cried out before they were killed. There was no such specialist in Salekhard; he would have to be summoned from the district center, Tyumen.

"Well now," said Zotov, when I had put down the phone, "did you fetch Voropayev's clothes from Yaku-Tur?"

"You know they took all his clothes, stole them. What could I bring?"

"The rest of his stuff, from his flat, did you bring any?"

"What for?"

"Did you or didn't you?"

"No, of course not."

"You're a fool then," said Zotov and turned to Shatunov as he came in from the yard.

"Before you started tormenting those dogs with Zaloyev's mitten, you should have put your brain in gear. If the murderer took the clothes off Voropayev and Hotko, he wasn't going to take them to market and sell them, was he? He put them on to keep himself warm, didn't he? Flying boots first of all. Now think: three made the break, but only one of them, according to the medical evidence, actually did the killing. The first victim was Voropayev. Well, the killer would be first in line for the clothes, right? Therefore, that murderer came here in Voropayev's boots, yes? And what have you given the dogs to sniff? Zaloyev's mitten. There's no scent of Zaloyev's boots around here; he threw them away long, long ago in the tundra."

My heart went cold. What a plain, simple idea it was. And I, like an idiot, hadn't fetched a scrap of Voropayev's clothing, not even a handkerchief. There was no way I could avoid a dressing down from Shatunov now. There he was, looking at me now with his pale KGB eyes.

"Don't panic now, Anna." Zotov grinned and slipped his hand into his jacket. "Why do you think I flew in from Urengoi? I made a stop in Yaku-Tur; it was practically on the way. And look . . ." With these words Zotov pulled out a cellophane bag. He opened it and cautiously shook out onto the table a quantity of crumpled male underwear—pants and shirts.

"All Voropayev's and all unwashed," said old man Zotov with pride. "Even I can smell the sweat on them. But before you start tormenting those dogs again, you should get another lot like this from Hotko's flat. The murderer might just have put on Hotko's boots, hell knows.''

I went up to Zotov and gave him a smacking kiss on the cheek. Whether or not the dogs got on the scent from Voropayev's underpants, Zotov had saved me from disgrace.

17

Zotov's idea brought no results. Orudjev and Telichkin toiled away with the dogs for another three hours, giving them now Voropayev's, now Hotko's underwear, taken from his house in Laureateville, to sniff. But the dogs turned up no leads.

"Zaloyev didn't get out of here by air, did he?" fumed Shatunov toward morning. "He was walking around here on his feet. He didn't fly, dammit!"

"There's only one explanation," said old Zotov, sitting by the fireplace puffing on his dead pipe. "It wasn't Zaloyev. His glove was left here on purpose."

"Oh, of course. It was the tundra spirits who did it." Shatunov smiled caustically. "The tundra spirits cut Ryazanov's ears and balls off and dropped Zaloyev's glove in the yard!"

"If it was Zaloyev, his behavior was illogical. Ryazanov was alone in the cottage and alone in the sauna. Any murderer prefers to do the job inside, so that everything's nice and quiet and nobody sees. In that case, we would only have found out about the murder at seven in the morning, when the driver came for Ryazanov. But instead of doing everything on the quiet, instead of getting Ryazanov's fine sheepskin coat and any other stuff, he kills him in the open, takes an old jacket, and leaves a mitten at the scene of the crime for everyone to see. Like a challenge to a duel."

"That's what drives me wild; he's toying with us, the son of a bitch," said Shatunov. "The only thing I don't get is why?"

"He wants to show it's him, Zaloyev, doing the killing and not the tundra spirits," said Hudya. "That will help us quell the panic."

"But why?" Shatunov repeated. "Why bring it on himself?"

Hudya shrugged. "Fame, however. There are such things as psychopaths. Hinckley, for example. Shot the president of America. For the publicity, the fame. Zaloyev could be one of those. Doesn't want to give the glory to our Nenets spirits, however."

"However, however," Shatunov mocked him. "However, that break happened with your help. You're a know-it-all, aren't you? Hinckley."

"It was me, however, who warned the camp commandant that a break like that was theoretically possible. Three weeks beforehand, however," said Benokan, offended.

"Theoretically," snarled Shatunov, since there was no getting around that. It was the truth: an ordinary police investigator, a Nenets at that, had warned the authorities at Camp RS-549, hand-picked KGB officers, that the high-tension cables could be used for an escape attempt, and they hadn't taken a bit of notice.

"There is one point," I said. "We don't know why he's only killing higher-ups. At the moment, it looks like a string of coincidences . . ."

"Get on with it!" said Shatunov irritably. "Is this an idea, or are you talking for talking's sake?"

"It's an idea," I said. "Three got away. To get out of Salekhard they needed three sets of clothes and three sets of documents. One of the runaways had been an artist and icon faker. It would have been easy for him to take out the names of Voropayev, Hotko, and Ryazanov and insert three different ones. Now they actually have three sets of clothes and documents.

They've got no reason to hang around in Salekhard any longer. Even if this Zaloyev is crazy like Hinckley, the other two must be trying to slip out of Salekhard on faked passports. And they'll be doing it now, today.''

"Good thinking," said Shatunov. "But the airport and railway are closed as it is, and the winter roads are being patrolled.''

"There are other ways out of Salekhard in winter," Kovrov remarked. "The tundra's frozen solid now.''

"There are helicopters over the town," said Colonel Sini. "Not a mouse has got out of Salekhard tonight. Kovina's right, though: there's no damn reason for them to sit tight in town while we check every house. They've got to get out of here, and they'll try today. The only thing is, how? You can't crawl across the tundra—''

"Ech!" sighed Shatunov. "If I only had a couple of thousand soldiers—I'd turn Salekhard into a rattrap! What can these villains do, though? Pinch a Sno-Cat? Don't make me laugh! We'd pick them off from the air like *kekliki!*''

"Or they—you," said Zotov suddenly.

We turned to him in amazement.

"Anybody know if there were any firearms here in Ryazanov's cottage?'' Zotov asked.

Shatunov screwed up his eyes, assimilating this new tack of Zotov's.

Meanwhile, Zotov continued, "As my investigatress, Anna Kovina, found out in Yaku-Tur, Voropayev had a pistol with him when he went whoring with his Nenka in the encampment. That pistol disappeared along with his clothes. The question is now: Was Hotko carrying a weapon when they killed him?''

I hadn't found out anything about Voropayev's pistol in Yaku-Tur, that was another of my slipups, but Zotov was covering for me again. He certainly hadn't wasted his time going to Yaku-Tur! Any one of us knew there was a tacit instruction going back thirty years to Stalin's time that all leaders of tundra and taiga expeditions, as well as all party chiefs, from regional committee secretaries upward, were entitled to carry a personal firearm. In both cases it was in case workers rioted. Nobody has countermanded the order up to now, but today they only give pistols out to the KGB, and even then on a strictly limited basis. So Voropayev, as the leader of an arctic expedition, had a right to his pistol. Why the devil didn't I think of that in Yaku-Tur? I wondered if Dr. Hotko had had a pistol. If so, it was illegal.

"Hotko's pistol was removed by me from his apartment and handed in to the KGB," said Hudya coolly. "Which doesn't rule out the possibility of his having another one. Hotko's firearm was held illegally; even his wife didn't know about it. According to her, Hotko went out fishing with spinners and a drill to bore holes in the ice. Three hours later the fishermen found him naked by the river; he hadn't started fishing."

"Ryazanov had a rifle and a pistol," said Shatunov. "I went wild-reindeer hunting with him myself last year."

"No such weapons were discovered during the search of the cottage," said Hudya. "No rifle, no pistol, no cartridges, no money."

"Ye-e-s," drawled Shatunov. "That's spirits for you! That means the villains have now got two pistols and a rifle, minimum. It could be quite a story arresting them! All right! If it's war, it's war . . . but where's the battle going to be? The sooner the better."

"I think we can now give a material explanation for the mystical fact that only higher-ups have been killed," Zotov observed calmly. "Spirits, spirits, the revenge of the tundra! All the criminals needed were arms and money. The top brass have got both." Pleased with himself, Zotov got out his jar of smelly cream again.

But at that moment the echo of a deafening explosion rolled over Laureateville. We exchanged bewildered glances. Shatunov stretched out his hand to the phone, but it preempted him by ringing first. He picked it up. The longer he listened, the darker his face grew. Then he flung the phone from him and barked, "The balloon's gone up! To your cars, philosophers! There's been an explosion at the Yamal Gas Trust."

18

We raced along the empty streets of a darkened Salekhard toward the city center and the headquarters of the Yamal Gas Trust, which stood on a street named after the Nenets national hero, Vauli Piettomin. In the jolting Sno-Cat no one spoke; we were amazed at the nerve of the criminals—three savage murders and now an explosion in the main Yamal gas trust. The first thing that occurred to me was that they had blown up the trust to divert the KGB, police militia, and duty helicopters to the town center while they nipped out of Salekhard. Apparently everybody had the same idea: Shatunov leaned out of his Volga and started waving his cap at the helicopter that was following us. "The tundra! The tundra, fuck it!" he shouted.

The pilot seemed to hear him; the helicopter banked and headed for the outskirts.

We rolled up to the Yamal Gas building at about the same time as the ambulances and fire trucks. One look was enough to tell us what had happened. The explosion had been at the entrance to the building, not inside. Fragments of a forty-ton Hurricane dump truck were burning brightly in the roadway. Some little Nenets boys were dancing about and warming themselves by the fire, while the Hurricane's driver, a skinny middle-aged man, tried to chase them away with his fur hat.

The office workers inside, those who had steeled themselves to come to work that day, were terrified. They peered timidly out of the shattered windows of the four-story building and made no attempt even to catch the papers and drawings being carried out by the wind.

Naturally, we questioned the Hurricane driver on the spot. He began explaining that he was innocent; he had stopped in at the trust offices on his way to work, just for a minute, about some meat coupons because his wife had given birth to twins a month ago and they weren't giving him any meat coupons for twins because, they said, the babies didn't need any meat, they were still on the breast . . . Anyway, he went on describing how he had gone up to the first floor to the accounts office, "and then e-everything shook—look, I got cut on the cheek, maybe it was the gas tank exploding—lucky I was empty, if I'd had a load on . . ." In the meantime Shatunov was shouting into the phone to the airport chief: "All aircraft scramble! I don't need permission from Moscow aviation authority, I'm the KGB. I order you to get those planes up! Or would you rather take the escapees' place in camp?" At that very moment there came a second blast.

Ten blocks away, by the main entrance to the headquarters of another trust, Northern Pipe Laying, the director's official car had been blown up. This explosion was somewhat less severe than the first: only the ground-floor windows of the building had been blown out. In the car trunk, however, there had been six boxes of oranges and one of Heineken beer, which the trust director had obtained from the senior management special distribution warehouse. The oranges and aluminum beer cans lay strewn all over the dark, snow-covered road.

"The bastards have bribed somebody to plant explosives, to keep us busy while they slip out of town,"

Colonel Sini perceived belatedly as they got out of the car in front of Northern Pipe Laying.

"They got hold of money from the victims . . ."

"Yes . . . ," said Major Shatunov, pensively gazing at the remains of the Volga, "but this isn't fun and games cutting off people's dicks. This is sabotage. And it's got a political smell about it." He turned to me.

"That escapee Tolmachov's a political?"

I nodded.

19

After the two explosions Salekhard was numbed.

People waited, holding their breath, for the next act of sabotage. If there had been air-raid shelters in the town, I believe the entire population would have camped out in them. In permafrost, though, you can't even dig a grave, never mind a bomb shelter, so people stayed at home with doors and windows barricaded, waiting for the next explosion or the next murder. The radio called on the population to keep calm, but nobody listened to the radio. A lot of people reckoned that the next blast would be at the power station or the water department and started laying in supplies of water and retrieving candles and old primus stoves from storage.

Meanwhile, we sat by telephones and radios in the local KGB building, waiting for a message from the helicopter pilots on where the escapees were trying to break the militia cordon or what else they were up to in town.

But all was quiet.

After an hour of this, the nerves (and stomachs) of the people in the hostels could hold out no longer. Hard workers and vagrants alike had been sitting starving since morning; they were afraid to venture out to the diner. By about ten in the morning, they had drunk up all their stocks of liquor on empty stomachs.

There's never any food in the rooms of workingmen's hostels, but half-drunk bottles of vodka and liquor can always be found. Now, emboldened by liquor, with hunting rifles in hand, vagrants and workers began to dribble out singly and in groups toward the diner-restaurant Wave. (By day the place is open from seven on as a workingmen's café; after seven in the evening, it's a restaurant—that is, the prices go up and vodka is sold.)

The Wave was closed, of course; none of the cooks had come out to work. The workers, about sixty in number, smashed the lock off the café door, entered, and set up a self-service system, starting, of course, with the stocks of vodka.

One hour later the whole drunken crowd of them, fearless in the face of tundra spirits or the devil himself, laid siege to the small, one-story KGB post. They smashed the panes in the barred windows and tried to unhinge the entrance doors, bawling, "Give us a train! Shatunov, give us a train, bastard! An express! To Moscow! Otherwise, we'll rip your balls off!" Someone let fly with a sporting rifle at the window of Shatunov's office.

We lay on the floor and shoved the heavy steel security safes over to the windows with our feet; Shatunov was shouting into the telephone to the chief of the town fire brigade.

"All fire engines over here! We'll turn the hoses on these pricks!"

A few minutes later, amid the roar of the crowd, the obscenities, the tinkle of broken glass and rifle shots, we heard the saving howl of the fire engines and the rumble of the three armored personnel carriers from the local military garrison. In another couple of minutes, it was possible to look out the shattered windows: the mob had dispersed, fleeing from the water lashing at them in powerful jets from the water cannon. Those who lingered were knocked off their feet and couldn't run away—at forty below the water froze instantly and converted their clothing into icy armor, while their wet fur or felt boots froze them to the road-way.

"That's more like it!" Shatunov hissed through his teeth as he rose, brushing off the dust and glass splinters. "This isn't fucking Poland!"

Through the window he shouted an order to the soldiers who were busy hauling the frozen workmen off to the Black Maria.

"Leave them! Let them lie on the ice. They'll sober up fast enough, fuck them. Then they'll show a bit of respect for Soviet authority!"

He immediately seized the phone and dialed the airport chief's number. "Agapov! Whatever happens in the town, even if—I don't know—even if they blow up the party committee, keep all aircraft flying! Got me? Not a mouse to creep out of town! What! Out of fuel! Nothing to do with me—get it from the emergency reserves."

While radio messages about these events were being sent to Tyumen and Moscow and the first response received from Bogomyatov, the secretary of the Tyumen Province Party, we swept out the KGB offices and boarded up the smashed panes with plywood and display placards saying: KGB—SHIELD AND SWORD OF SOVIET POWER. Only then, an hour later, did Shatunov allow the soldiers and ambulance attendants to pick the freezing people up off the road. There was no point now in taking them off to the remand cell in military headquarters or the prison. They were badly frostbitten and were taken straight to the hospital.

20

EXPRESS TELEGRAM
Urgent, by
government phototelegraph

MOSCOW, KREMLIN, CENTRAL COMMITTEE CPSU

FORCES OF THE SALEKHARD KGB, POLICE MILITIA, AND MILITARY GARRISON UNABLE TO STEM DISORDERS AND PREVENT POSSIBLE ANTI-RUSSIAN ACTIONS BY NENETS POPULATION. TO GUARANTEE SECURITY OF OFFICIAL OPENING OF GAS PIPELINE SIBERIA—WESTERN EUROPE, THE COMMANDER OF THE SIBERIAN MILITARY DISTRICT, COLONEL POPOV, HAS, AT MY REQUEST, ASKED THE SOVIET ARMY GENERAL STAFF TO PERMIT HIM TO TRANSFER PARATROOP DIVISION OCTOBER REVOLUTION TO SALEKHARD.

I REQUEST COOPERATION IN SECURING IMMEDIATE PERMISSION OF GENERAL STAFF FOR THIS OPERATION.

AT THE SAME TIME I CONSIDER IT APPROPRIATE TO RAISE THE QUESTION OF POSTPONEMENT OF OFFICIAL CEREMONY IN URENGOI FOR OPENING OF SIBERIA—WESTERN EUROPE PIPELINE.

RED SNOW

FIRST SECRETARY TYUMEN PROVINCE COMMITTEE
CPSU
CANDIDATE-MEMBER OF CENTRAL COMMITTEE CPSU
V. BOGOMYATOV
TYUMEN, 12 DECEMBER 1983
12:30 LOCAL TIME

II

A TRAP IN UDMURTIA

21

Central Committee of the Communist Party of the Soviet Union
Member of the Politburo Central Committee CPSU
  Konstantin Ustinovich Chernenko
Urgent
Secret
Special Delivery

To: Minister of Defense USSR
  Marshal Ustinov—one copy
To: President of KGB USSR
  Army General Chebrikov—one copy

I am forwarding to you a copy of the letter from First Secretary Tyumen Province Committee Comrade Bogomyatov. I support his request regarding the urgent transfer of forces to the Yamal-Nenets District. Order must be restored in Salekhard within 24 hours. There can be no talk of postponing the opening of the pipeline.

I request the KGB to take effective measures to prevent the leakage of any information to the West about disturbances in the Arctic.

Further details at the meeting with Comrade Andropov.

K. Chernenko
12 December 1983
9:00 Moscow time

22

The clock on the Spassky Tower of the Kremlin showed 9:35. The black bullet-proof *Chaika* with its government escort softly rolled out from the Kremlin through the Trotsky gates on the bridge and drove on to Kuntsevo, a Moscow suburb, where the Kremlin Hospital occupied Stalin's former dacha. A heavy, wet snow was falling. It was the time of the thaw in Moscow, just before the Christmas frosts.

Konstantin Chernenko always felt lousy in damp weather. With his emphysema, it was hard enough to breathe in dry weather; only the upper half of his lungs took in any air, but in this . . . And he was fed up with this morning ritual—for three months now he'd been going to the Kremlin Hospital almost every day for a conference with the dying Andropov. A man who had been head of the KGB for fifteen years and with a stroke of the pen or a wave of the hand had consigned thousands to the next world at home and abroad, Andropov refused to believe in the inevitable reality of his own imminent death. Paralyzed, his face gray and pinched, there he lay on the second floor of the Kremlin Hospital looking down on Moscow with his washed-out eyes; and every morning, just after the medical procedures, he would hold meetings of the Politburo or a conference with the State Planning Department or with Gromyko or other ministers. In fucking charge! He'd even ordered the annual session of the USSR Supreme Soviet to take place on December 28, the last day of the working year!—hoping, no doubt, he would be up on the rostrum making his speech. Fat chance you getting up anywhere, asshole. Communists don't believe in God, but there is one now! You brought two heart attacks on Brezhnev and sent him to his grave, but you're in a bed yourself just one year later!

Chernenko's limousine drove on down the central restricted lane of the Kutuzov prospect, then passed the Gates of Triumph and, a few minutes later, turned onto the road, closed to public traffic, toward the checkpoint of the Kremlin Hospital. A long line of government limousines and black Volgas were parked in the hospital's courtyard. Of course they're all here, thought Chernenko, even though I'm twenty minutes early myself. There's Ustinov's car, Gromyko's; closest of all to the hospital entrance was the limousine belonging to Andropov's favorite, that upstart Gorbachev. Got here first, the son of a bitch! Maybe he camps out here at night?

The bodyguard opened the door and assisted Chernenko out of the car. He conducted him by the elbow through a corridor of guards and up to the hospital door. The warm vestibule was packed with security men. Somebody took Chernenko's coat with the astrakhan collar and his fur hat. Chernenko feebly wriggled his shoulders, planning at least to take a deeper breath, and at once caught a faint whiff of tobacco. Assholes, some security man had been smoking again before his arrival. But finding out who . . . Coughing, Chernenko surveyed the respectful poker faces of the escort, shook his head reproachfully, and passed on into the elevator.

On the second floor, in a spacious hall with potted palms for decoration and a Persian carpet on the floor, all of them were sitting: Ustinov, Gromyko, the new

KGB chief Chebrikov, the new Internal Affairs minister Fedorchuk, Tikhonov, the president of the Council of Ministers, and Gorbachev, young looking enough to be out of place here. While waiting for the meeting to begin, they hadn't been wasting time; next to each stood a doctor—or even two. They were measuring Ustinov's and Tikhonov's blood pressure, and Gromyko was having his head massaged. Fedorchuk was swallowing some tablets, and the octogenarians, Politburo members Ponomaryov and Kuznetsov, were simply asleep. Next to these portly patriarchs of the Kremlin power structure (Kuznetsov had been in the Politburo back in Stalin's time, 1952), the fifty-year-old Mikhail Gorbachev looked like a merc lad. He was the only one without a doctor. Bent over a thick notepad, he was writing something quickly and underlining it with sharp strokes. He's playing Lenin, the little shit, thought Chernenko wearily. He gazed once more at the whole Kremlin senate and shook his head in despair.

"Good God, the geriatric ward! . . . Morning all."

His bodyguard helped him sink into an armchair between Ustinov and Chebrikov. Two doctors with pronounced Jewish features hastened over to him. One was holding the blood pressure apparatus, the other gently took him by the wrist, ready to take his pulse.

"Fuck off!" Chernenko withdrew his arm.

"We have to check pulse and blood pressure, Konstantin Ustinovich," the doctor said softly, as if to a naughty child.

"If you have to, check your own," said Chernenko, gasping.

"Konstantin Ustinovich!" said the doctor reproachfully.

"Oh, all right, here." Chernenko gave him his arm. "Do they check Reagan every morning as well, motherfucker? We're the same damn age, and they shot that Hollywood dog pointblank, punctured his lung, he laughs it off, the fucker! He goes out horseback riding, the bastard.''

''He doesn't smoke, and you shouldn't smoke, Konstantin Ustinovich. Categorically,'' said the doctor. ''You're smoking on the sly, I can tell by your breathing. With your emphysema . . .''

Chernenko didn't bother listening to the tedious medical rigmarole. He turned to Ustinov. ''You got my *tsedulya** about the Nentsi?''

Ustinov nodded. ''I've already given the order . . . to GHQ . . .''

Chernenko turned to Chebrikov, noticing that Gorbachev was still scribbling away on his pad.

''Every measure will be taken at our end,'' Chebrikov hastened to say. ''There's only one small point, Konstantin Ustinovich. Actually, I wanted to ask your opinion . . .''

''Well . . .''

''An hour before your order banning the entry of foreigners into Siberia, an American called Siegfried Shertz took a flight for Urengoi. . . . You know him . . .''

''Who is he?'' asked Ustinov.

''He's the middleman between our External Trade Agency and the West European banks. A broker, in other words. Five years ago he helped us get Western loans for the building of the pipeline. Not for nothing, of course. Leonid Ilyich gave him two and a half percent commission on the deal.''

Chernenko knew this Shertz. He was a crafty animal who had conned Brezhnev into giving him 2.5 percent while the pipeline was still at the talking stage. It seemed Brezhnev's son, Yuri, the deputy minister for external trade, had introduced Shertz to Brezhnev and recommended him as an outstanding broker—he knew Russian perfectly, had even been born in Russia to a

*Note (Ukrainian).

family of Volga Germans, though he'd left the USSR as a boy. He was a German by blood and an American businessman—nobody could be better as an intermediary between the USSR and the German banks. Later on, when the West German and French banks agreed to finance the pipeline construction, Brezhnev lit up: "Eighteen billion dollars they're giving—that's fucking fantastic! Maybe not all at once, but never mind. We'll build the pipeline into Europe at their expense, and as soon as the French, Dutch, or Germans start raising hell, we'll just up and turn off the tap; they'll be left without gas and all their industries will be crippled! Or we could raise the price, blackmail . . ."

"Right!" said Gorbachev loudly all of a sudden to the whole assembly, as he placed a fat full stop on his notepad. "The question of the Salekhard disturbances has several aspects. First: on December seventeenth, when the pipeline completion protocol is due to be signed, the European banks must pay us the second half of the credit, that is, nine billion dollars." Here, he turned to Tikhonov. "Right?"

Tikhonov nodded.

"Recently, there have been complications in getting these credits," continued Gorbachev, glancing at his pad, "in particular, because of the KGB allowing rumors to filter out to the West that political prisoners were being used on the construction work. Comrade Andropov did not punish anyone at that time; you know very well he covers up for the security organs. But if the West finds out about the Salekhard disturbances now, you can be sure their newspapers will blow it up into hell knows what. Especially if they find out that troops have been sent in.

"You need have no doubts about the reaction of the European banks either—they'll latch onto any excuse not to pay us. And that's not all!" Gorbachev raised an admonitory hand. "The second aspect. I recall that the previous leadership had plans to build the pipeline into Europe with French and German money and then hold economic control over half of Europe. But the French and Germans aren't idiots. They financed pipelines from Algeria and Norway at the same time, and now it's not clear who's blackmailing whom. If we don't give them Siberian gas today, they'll go over to Algerian tomorrow and Norwegian the day after. And they'll be able to dictate *our* gas prices. Right?'' He turned again to Tikhonov.

Tikhonov nodded once more.

''And finally, the third aspect. As you well know, Comrade Andropov wishes to announce the completion of the gas pipeline ahead of schedule to the Supreme Soviet. I therefore suggest that the army general staff should not only send the paratroop division to the Arctic, they should also assume control of the entire Salekhard situation.''

Chernenko looked at Gromyko, Ustinov, Tikhonov, and the other members of the Kremlin old guard. Nothing could be read in those half-listening, half-dozing faces, but he well knew what lay behind the heavy wrinkled features. Fear. If Gorbachev took Andropov's place tomorrow, he'd swamp everybody with his businesslike calculations and sling the whole geriatric ward off the Politburo and onto their pensions. He'd managed to reach the very top of the Kremlin power structure in such a short time, the bastard. In a few years he had got himself to where Chernenko had spent his whole life climbing. All because he exploited the fact that we are old and ailing, son of a bitch. He sat down there in the Stavropol Regional Party Committee like any ordinary provincial secretary and showed no particular talent for anything. The collective farms in his region were in just as much of a mess as those in the rest of the country—the harvest, when it exists, rots in the fields because the farm workers couldn't give a shit about it—they'd rather try to grow a few more tomatoes on their private plots to sell on the black market.

He'd never have risen from the position of a party pawn to the Politburo if the leadership hadn't been suffering from all sorts of geriatric ailments, and hadn't gone to recuperate in the Stavropol region, where the main resorts—*Mineralnyye Vody* (Mineral Waters), *Kislovodsk* (Sour Waters), *Zheleznovodsk* (Iron Waters)—are located. It is the place for the government elite's best sanatoriums and Kremlin dachas. So it stands to reason that Gorbachev, in the role of the hospitable host, often met the visiting party bosses, who came to convalesce or simply on vacation. He not only flooded their dachas and sanatoriums with the best food products, the freshest fruit and vegetables, but around the sanatoriums, he established an entire area of exemplary collective farms, which supplied them with milk, meat, apples, grapes, crab, fish. These farms were given much more fertilizer than any of the others. They had the best equipment and the best agronomists to guarantee, as it were, sustenance for the Kremlin visitors.

But the second aim of this cunning Gorbachev was quite another story: when Brezhnev, Andropov, Romanov, Grishin, Gromyko, Ustinov et al. walked in the countryside around their dachas—or at least drove through it on their way from the airport—they would see what an outstanding leader Gorbachev was. And they took the bait! Even he, himself, Chernenko, voted in the Politburo for the nomination of Gorbachev as the minister of agriculture. Who could have known then that Andropov and Gromyko were moving their pawn into a controlling position in the Politburo? And now foreign journalists were sniffing all around Moscow like bloodhounds for clues as to who was the most likely heir to Andropov's power. Chernenko, Romanov, Grishin, or Gorbachev? Fuck him! For now, anyway, there was a majority in the Politburo from the old school. That bald Gorbachev with the devil's mark on his skull can't get any further. We are smart enough to realize that any young general secretary would drive us old men out.

"Apart from the fact that the army must take the situation in Salekhard under its control," continued Gorbachev, while they were waiting for Andropov to appear in the lobby, "apart from that, the KGB must ensure a hundred percent secrecy about all events taking place in the Yamal-Nenets region. And having put a decisive end to the disturbances, we must immediately open the pipeline. This opening must be celebrated by the whole country as proof of the triumph of our system."

Chernenko smiled. The son of a bitch had said nothing new. All that had to be done had been done already; orders were already issued. Without all these speeches and paragraphs, of course, quietly, without fuss.

Gorbachev clearly expected some discussion of his points, but Chernenko turned to Chebrikov and asked quietly, "Well, what about Siegfried Shertz?"

"He was supposed to be going to the pipeline opening in Urengoi with the gas industry minister, Dynkov," said Chebrikov. "But Dynkov got the flu yesterday, so Shertz flew off on his own."

"Did Dynkov get in touch with you about his health?" Gorbachev asked the doctors.

"No," answered one of the medical men.

"I see!" Gorbachev smiled ironically. "He's got flu like I've got labor pains. He's just scared to leave Moscow in case he loses his ministerial portfolio. For some reason, everybody's convinced that Comrade Andropov is about to depart from us at any moment and government personnel will change immediately. Meanwhile, the doctors couldn't be more optimistic, isn't that right?"

"Absolutely! Absolutely!" The senior Kremlin

Hospital consultant hastened to his support. "The hemoglobin levels in Comrade Andropov's blood have returned to normal . . ."

You're a crafty one, Gorbachev. My, but you're crafty, thought Chernenko. Just giving us the hint that we'll all keep our places if you take Andropov's place. Just you wait, though; we're a little bit craftier than you . . .

Paying no heed to the consultant's report on Andropov's state of health, Chernenko asked Chebrikov, "Are there any foreigners up there in Urengoi, generally speaking?"

"Luckily, no. There were some Frenchmen and Germans, installing the computers and electronics at the compressor station, but they finished about a week ago. They'll be skiing in Switzerland now. . . . There's just this Shertz on his way there. Do you want the aircraft returned to Moscow, or should he be put down somewhere in the Urals? If he's in Moscow, he'll mess around trying to get on another flight, I think, whereas in the Urals . . ."

"Yes, put him down in the Urals," Chernenko agreed.

"Very good, Konstantin Ustinovich." Chebrikov rose hurriedly and walked over to the elevator.

"And as for . . ."—Chernenko chewed his lip, savoring the spoke he was about to put in Gorbachev's wheel—"Comrade Andropov's health, well, we all have faith in our doctors. Nevertheless . . . they'll hardly permit Yuri Vladimirovich to fly to Urengoi for the pipeline opening. Or me either—an old man, emphysema, it's damn cold up there, as well. So all things considered . . . why don't you go to Urengoi as the head of the government delegation, eh?" And Chernenko for the very first time looked Gorbachev directly in the eye. His gaze was pure, gentle, and benign. "You are the youngest of us . . ."

Gorbachev got the point, all right, but smiled as if nothing was out of the way.

"Of course I'll go. If Comrade Andropov sends me."

He suddenly rose, looking down the length of the corridor.

There, the doctors were carefully wheeling a bed with an intravenous unit along the parquet. On the bed, under a sheet, lay Andropov.

Gorbachev spoke quickly and softly. "Comrades, please rise. Here is Yuri Vladimirovich."

23

NO SMOKING! FASTEN YOUR SEAT BELTS! the display flashed. Siegfried Shertz glanced out his window, and his stomach became aware at the same instant that the plane was descending sharply. What the hell? They were three hours' flying time from Tyumen, surely.

Beyond the glass the sun was dazzling; below the aircraft lay Russia, white and snowbound with an occasional bare Ural peak and a frosty gray stubble of taiga. Siegfried was in no mood to appreciate the scenery. What were these blasted Russians up to? Maybe some drunken mechanic had made an error, perhaps the fuel tank had depressurized and they were about to blow up! Or the navigation systems had failed like in that Korean airliner? Or all the pilots were drunk; he'd seen the captain at the airport: red nose, an obvious drinker—and now he was just diving the aircraft into the deck!

Siegfried knew he had acrophobia and was probably panicking over nothing; on the other hand, why were they going down so suddenly? Why hadn't there been an announcement? Why didn't that bitch of a stewardess come when he called? Two years before, thank God, the Soviet classless society had decided to introduce first- and second-class seating. Not on Siegfried's account, of course; it was for their own top men, so they wouldn't have to fly in the same cabin as their people. Brezhnev's son, Yuri, used to laugh. "We are the servants of the people, and servants should travel separately from their masters!"

Never mind first or second class, insolence was classless here. He'd been pressing the button for three minutes and no stewardess had appeared. And if she wouldn't answer the only first-class passenger on board, that meant she hadn't time for any passengers; the flyers were drunk! Jesus, do something! Why the hell had he gone on alone when his Moscow secretary-lover, Tanya, and the minister, Dynkov, came down with flu? Wasn't the flu a warning to him not to fly?

Why did he have this stupid habit of always trying to outwit fate? That summer he'd gone into the Bermuda Triangle, even though practically all the yachtsmen of Palm Beach had warned him about the storm-force winds and the strength of the Gulf Stream in that region. But he'd gone! Naturally, he had to demonstrate his audacity to his Siberian visitors, Bogomyatov, Salakhov, and Ryazanov. He had brought them from Moscow to Florida at his own expense and organized a cruise for them around the Caribbean aboard his yacht *Dreamboat*. And naturally, thirty miles off the Bahamas, his engine had started smoking and the navigational computer had gone wrong. At least then something depended on him, he could fight for life himself, and he did bring *Dreamboat* to port— on one engine! But what could be done here? What the hell was the opening of the gas pipeline to him and all the millions he would get out of the "project of the century" if now, at this moment, they were falling, falling, falling! . . . in the middle of Russia, in the taiga, the Siberian snows.

"Attention, all passengers! Owing to weather conditions in Siberia, Tyumen Airport is closed. Our aircraft will land in Izhevsk, the capital of the Udmurt Autonomous Republic. The temperature outside the aircraft is minus twenty-four degrees Celsius. Passengers are requested to remain in their seats until the aircraft has stopped. Additional flight information will be announced by radio in the airport terminal building.''

So that was it! Siegfried breathed again. Tyumen was closed, so they'd landed in Izhevsk, wherever that was. Still, dammit, they could have said earlier! These Russians always made such a botch of everything. It wasn't a country, it was a sort of gigantic safari; nobody gave a damn for anything, the people were so resentful that if you got on a bus or a subway wearing a sheepskin coat, they looked ready to smash your face in. To them, a sheepskin coat was a mark of class distinction; it meant you were either a lousy intellectual or a black marketeer asking for it—and that was in Moscow. Imagine what went on here in, what did she say? Udmurtia. . . . Ah, there she was, the stewardess, fat-assed bitch! Turned up at last, and with a miserable look on her face too.

''What's the matter?'' she asked.

Well! He'd called her up there, in the air, and now she appeared when they were rolling along the runway, with a bad-tempered ''what's the matter?''

''How long will we be stuck here?'' he asked in Russian. He had been eight years old before his parents had managed to get out of the USSR. With a German sense of thrift, they had not allowed him to forget his Russian, and they had been right; in the years of détente, his translation firm, very small at the time, had made its first million. Now, in perfect Russian, he asked this stewardess, ''Is Tyumen likely to be closed for long?''

''It'll be announced over there.'' The stewardess, fat-assed insolence and all, nodded outside the plane and walked off. Bitch! If his Russian had contained the merest hint of a foreign accent, she would have been more polite. Russian women adore foreigners; he'd made use of that fact more than once, but he wasn't going to mangle his beautiful Russian on account of this idiot.

"Passengers are requested to leave the aircraft. Do not forget your personal belongings," said a man's voice over the intercom. Immediately, the searing frost and powdery needles of snow wafted in the open door of the plane.

Siegfried donned his sheepskin, tied his fur hat on securely, and settled his scarf around his throat. He was a seasoned traveler on Aeroflot; in his years of working with the Russians, he'd done plenty of flying around the USSR. If Siberia is closed off because of the weather, he thought, I can imagine the number of passengers who've dropped out of the skies on Izhevsk. They would be conducted across the bone-hard airfield on foot; there'd be no room to breathe in the airport buildings, there'd be children yelling, people sleeping on sacks and suitcases, and some drunk puking continuously in the toilet. No, one should never fly on Aeroflot internal flights on one's own—without Dynkov, Bogomyatov, or some other member of the government.

"Mr. Siegfried Shertz?" A voice spoke in English as soon as he stepped off the gangway.

"Yes . . . ," he replied in astonishment to a rather colorless thirty-year-old blonde in a dark-gray provincial overcoat and felt boots.

"I'm your interpreter from Intourist, Vera Kolesova. Please." She indicated a black Volga standing nearby.

"I didn't request any interpreter."

"I know. But as a foreign tourist first class, you are entitled to an interpreter and special service in the event of forced landing. After you." She inclined her head toward the car again.

Siegfried smiled to himself. It looked as if the KGB worked to a standard pattern throughout the USSR. They'd also palmed Tanya off on him in Moscow as an interpreter—he, the boss of the largest translation firm in the world, translating tons of technical documents from scores of languages into Russian and vice versa! Still, you had to admire the KGB's efficiency—even when an aircraft had to land totally unexpectedly, they kept their eye on you. If only their agriculture worked like the KGB!

Already eyeing this Vera Kolesova as his private property (mm—yes, definitely not Raquel Welch, still, what do you expect in Udmurtia?), Siegfried smiled wryly as he got into the car.

"Does your Intourist happen to know how long Tyumen is going to be closed?"

"Yes," Kolesova replied, getting into the front seat next to the driver. "Three days, according to the forecast. There are blizzards all over Tyumen Province."

Siegfried was aghast. These Siberian blizzards sometimes lasted a week. What about the pipeline opening?

"What if I get a train? How long is it by train from here to Tyumen?" he asked as he watched the Volga come up to the freight compartment where men were unloading the passengers' baggage.

"Three days just the same," said Kolesova, "but if the snowstorm intensifies, the train would get stuck as well."

The prospect of being stuck in a train under a Siberian snowdrift was not attractive. Fucking Japanese god, as they say in Russia. Of course, Dynkov's and Tanya's flu had been a sign to him to stay put. Now it was a case of sitting three days in this crappy Izhevsk, where the maximum in the way of amusement was this "interpreter." Of course, she didn't have syphilis, you could count absolutely on the KGB for that, but her English was terrible and she had two gold crowns in her mouth. Still, if she was undressed . . . Hell, in Russia you could sometimes come across an Aphrodite in canvas boots and quilted jacket with a metal crown on her front teeth!

Siegfried glimpsed his suitcase in the loader's hands and pointed it out to the driver.

One minute later the Volga was heading out of the airport past the one-story lounge, which bore an enormous portrait of Lenin on the pediment. Lenin's face was somewhat moon shaped in this portrait, and Siegfried recalled that in every Soviet town he had been in Lenin looked different: in Georgia, he looked like a Georgian; in Salekhard, like a Nenets; in Tashkent, he resembled an Uzbek. Here, it would seem, moon-faced Udmurts resided. So it would have been better if the KGB had saddled him with some Udmurt girl instead of this Kolesova. It would have been a bit exotic at least. Maybe I'll put in an order, he thought, recalling one of his earliest adventures in Salekhard.

The Volga skirted the airport buildings and shot out onto the main road, hemmed in by huge snowdrifts. Above the drifts towered the supports of stereotype posters—exhortations to raise productivity and improve labor discipline. It was hard to imagine, thought Siegfried, that in a country plastered with slogans like this from Leningrad to Vladivostok general enthusiasm for work was not in evidence; what did prevail was an obsession with sex and alcohol. Even Siegfried had become infected with it, whether he liked it or not. The Russians just couldn't understand business without vodka and women. Even when Yuri Brezhnev had brought Siegfried out to the dacha to see his dad it had been true. He'd said, "Father, here's the man we've been looking for. He was born here, knows Russian, German, and English, and he's an American citizen. Talented businessman, head of the Globus translation firm. Ideal candidate for middleman between us and the European banks in getting a loan to construct the gas pipeline." That very evening they had got as drunk as skunks and Brezhnev had said, with alcoholic generosity, "If you can screw a loan out of the European banks, you're on two percent commission." "Two and a half, Leonid Ilyich," Siegfried had said cautiously. "Up you! Two and a half!"

The car entered Izhevsk, a snowbound provincial city of one- and two-story houses with peeling paint.

"Where are we going?" Siegfried inquired.

"The Izhevsk Hotel," Kolesova said.

Meanwhile, at Izhevsk Airport, twenty minutes after Siegfried Shertz had departed, a radio announcement rang out: "Passengers for flight Moscow-Tyumen-Urengoi. Please board the aircraft."

All the passengers, blaspheming but overjoyed, returned to the plane. All, that is, except the sole first-class passenger, the middleman between the West European banks and Soviet Extrade, Mr. Siegfried Shertz.

The black Volga drew to a halt before the entrance of the Izhevsk Hotel.

24

General Chebrikov's instructions to entertain Mr. Siegfried Shertz in Izhevsk for three days placed Colonel Khanov, chief of the Udmurt Autonomous Republic KGB, in a near-impossible situation. "He's got to be entertained so that he forgets about Urengoi for three days and nights. Think of something in the Intourist line and make it snappy—the plane's landing in Izhevsk in thirty minutes. Report on action taken in two hours."

Khanov didn't waste time explaining to Chebrikov that there was no Intourist in Izhevsk, a city closed to foreigners. Orders are orders. They couldn't very well take Shertz to the Udmurt theater; the local populace didn't go to that! No excursions around the Izhevsk motorcycle factory either. He would notice that the nationally famous IZH motorbikes were only a sideline of the giant tank factory.

Khanov said, "Very good, sir," and replaced the red receiver—the direct departmental link with Moscow. At once he picked up the local phone and dialed the foreign languages department of the teacher-training institute. He couldn't delegate an order from the KGB president; he would deal with this Shertz himself. "Khanov speaking," he said, aware of the effect of his name on Udmurt citizens. "Vera Kolesova, urgent!"

Eight years before, while Kolesova had been a student at the institute, she had angrily condemned "certain students" who "had sunk to the level of reading scum like Solzhenitsyn and Orwell behind closed doors." The next morning in Khanov's office, Kolesova had named those students; Khanov had encouraged her political vigilance and included her in the Udmurt youth delegation that traveled in the Friendship Train around the fraternal countries of Eastern Europe. At this point Kolesova had realized the advantages that a close working relationship with Colonel Khanov might bring. She had become his main informer in the institute and as a consequence been taken on as a postgraduate after completing her degree. In her turn, she had repaid Khanov, not just with official denunciations, but with sexual favors. In exchange for these, she had remained on the staff as a teacher and was on the point of becoming assistant professor.

"Hello!" came Kolesova's breathless voice on the line.

"Go outside, I'll pick you up shortly."

"But I've got a lecture!" Kolesova was indignant, thinking Khanov was having one of his periodic lustful fits. That did happen with him; sometimes he just couldn't wait.

That wasn't it now, however.

"No time to talk; this is business! Out you come!" he said.

A few minutes later he was briefing Kolesova before her trip to the airport. "It's an order from Moscow, you realize. The president of the KGB in person."

"I won't sleep with a German," announced Kolesova emphatically. "I'm warning you right now; both my grandfathers were killed in the war. So I can be a guide but I'm not going to sleep with this German."

"Hold on, what German? He's an American."

"If he's called Shertz *and* Siegfried, he's a German.

What's written in his passport doesn't interest me. I'm not sleeping with him.''

Khanov scratched his head, perplexed. As a rule, Kolesova's strong political principles appealed to him, but . . .

''All right,'' he said. ''Take him around the town, show him the center, then go to the hotel.''

''And then?'' Kolesova broke in with a sneer. ''Once we're at the hotel, how am I going to entertain him? I repeat: I won't sleep with him!''

Khanov regarded unflappability as his main character feature. ''In the hotel, in the restaurant, you will introduce him to me. As if by chance. Say I'm the director of the nature reserve in Zataika.''

Kolesova started in astonishment. Zataika was 120 kilometers from Izhevsk, deep in the forest. It was one of the dachas belonging to the USSR Council of Ministers and was famous for its elk hunting and other pleasures, both legal and clandestine. Although nobody visited the dacha except Moscow ministers and Khanov himself, rumors circulated in Izhevsk about incredible orgies there. Kolesova therefore was intrigued into asking, ''Are you taking him to Zataika?''

''If he agrees to go,'' responded Khanov. He thought, And if he doesn't, I can't really think what to do with him. Chebrikov expects my report in two hours.

25

For two hours Khanov and Kolesova had been driving him somewhere to the back of beyond, deep into the snowbound taiga. Siegfried, enveloped in his sheepskin, was half-dozing in the back of the car; the farther they traveled, the less he understood why the KGB should all of a sudden be so obligingly protective—an interpreter, a nature reserve, an elk hunt! Of course, given the Russian mania for keeping everything secret, which extended to the mechanism of copying machines and the prices on the New York Stock Exchange, it was quite possible that this Khanov would regard an Udmurt toilet-paper factory as a strategic supersecret if its smoke could be seen from his hotel window. Khanov and Kolesova were driving him farther and farther from Izhevsk, and tomorrow they'd be drawing a bead on an aurochs or an elk. Surely it couldn't be because Siegfried, heaven forbid, might work out from the color of the smoke what chemical poison they made at the factory along with the toilet paper?

That Kolesova was no part of Intourist and Khanov was no nature reserve director Siegfried had realized from the first minute. One look at the military carriage of the moon-faced Udmurt, his jacket, all buttons fastened, like a uniform, his gray tie tight against the collar of his white nylon shirt, his black typical-army shoes; there could be no mistake: a Gee Bee, and no less than a major, that was for sure.

But it was just because Siegfried had recognized Khanov as a KGB officer that he had agreed almost without hesitation to go elk hunting with him at Zataika. He had long ago gotten used to falling in with the KGB's little whims, having realized once and for all that what was convenient for them was ultimately convenient and advantageous to him as well. Did he regret accepting Tanya as his so-called interpreter six years ago, even though it had been obvious from the start that she was an interpreter the way he was a soloist at the Bolshoi Theater? But it was more convenient for *them* to follow his every move in Moscow and the Black Sea resorts through Tanya's eyes, and through her hands to fix the timetable of his working day. So what? Tanya had become not only his unpaid secretary but his beautiful unpaid lover. And what a lover! What a pity rotten old Moscow kept suffering from epidemics of Hong Kong, Afghan, hell knows what kind of flu! Otherwise, Tanya would be with him on this elk hunt.

Siegfried stirred, opened his eyes, and looked out the window.

"Beautiful, isn't it?"

It certainly was. Along the roadside the luxuriant branching taiga was covered in powdery snow; on the left a frozen brook sparkled in the sunshine, the snow just as pure; a bright ruddy sun fled through the gaps between the pine trees as they tried to keep pace with the Volga. But why do Russians believe that such beauty exists only in Russia! Any forest near Munich or in Vermont looks as fine.

Around the next bend of the rutted roadway, Siegfried glimpsed Zataika; on the high bank of the river was a patch of fenced off forest. Beyond the fence was a two-story house with a smoking chimney. A Gazik pickup truck stood by the front steps. A female figure quickly ran across from the house to a small structure on the very edge of the river, which also had a smoking stove pipe.

"What's this? Are they stoking up the sauna?" asked Siegfried, reviving.

"Hmm . . ." drawled Khanov vaguely. "Sauna, yes . . ."

He didn't care for people anticipating events. General Chebrikov had approved his actions; now the main thing was to carry it all out as planned. Some cheery surprises awaited Mr. Shertz. Udmurtia would not disgrace itself in the eyes of America.

26

There was more food on the table than could possibly be eaten. An ample dish held mountains of hot curd dumplings, and another displayed baked carp; beyond were fish and caviar pasties, meat and cabbage pie, little mushrooms marinated and salted, fresh vegetable salad, a Russian salad, and lots of other pies and bits and pieces to which Siegfried, familiar as he was with Russian cuisine, couldn't put a name. There was so much drink on the table that ten couldn't put it away, much less the three present. There were cognac and vodka and champagne, wines galore, and the plain white bottles Siegfried recognized from his trips to Urengoi: POTABLE SPIRIT 96 PROOF.

The most remarkable feature of Zataika was not the food or drink, however; it was three sprightly, round-faced, black-eyed Udmurt lasses—the cooks and waitresses. Their eyes were so openly lascivious that Siegfried realized at once it wasn't just deer hunting that was in store for him. The movement with which one of them relieved Siegfried of his sheepskin was more pornographic than her cotton shift, which reached just below her ass and showed she hadn't a stitch on underneath. A brothel in Udmurtia, thought Siegfried to himself. He smiled. The KGB could read his mind! He'd hardly had time to think and lo! three Udmurt girlies. True, they were a good deal older than those little Nenets birds that time in Salekhard . . .

"Well, now! A nature reserve indeed! But what have I done to deserve a license?" he said, smiling at Khanov, as if proposing a practical talk, one businessman to another.

"Ha . . . yes, hum." Khanov smiled into his dark mustache and in his usual temporizing way said, "Let's eat just now . . ."

"Take your places! Sit down!" The three little waitresses fussed around them, placing chairs for Siegfried, Khanov, and Kolesova. Their youthful Udmurt flesh swelled their abbreviated smocks so powerfully it seemed the buttons at their breasts would fly off at any moment like pistol shots.

Gazing at these openly whorish girls, Kolesova was again reminded of the vague rumors of Zataika orgies and felt intrigued and excited. Meanwhile, she kept her eyes studiously averted from Siegfried, as if embarrassed at the equivocal situation. At this point, however, Khanov filled her glass, not with wine or brandy, or even vodka, but with pure alcohol from the bottle labeled POTABLE SPIRIT 96 PROOF, and Kolesova seized the wineglass by the stem, as if taking a spear in her hand. All her self-consciousness evaporated. A veritable warrior-maiden now sat next to Siegfried; she gripped the glass like a scepter. She's an alcoholic, that's all, thought Siegfried suddenly.

"Well now," Kolesova turned toward him. "Shall we try you on spirit, Comrade Shertz?"

Her eyes and her voice, which had grown suddenly hoarse, held a challenge.

"Vera!" A sharp cry from Khanov, like a whiplash, checked her. He added in a milder tone, clearly for his guest's benefit, "Mr. Shertz isn't used to spirit. We'll all start with the vodka, eh?"

"I'll start on the eatables," said Siegfried emphatically. He'd learned a lot of Russian habits over six years, but he did not like the Russian tendency to get drunk even before supper, almost before touching the food.

"Now you men, let's get on with it." Kolesova grinned. Once she had a glass of spirit in her hand, she feared neither devil nor Khanov. "You're not telling me you can't down a glass of spirit to the historic Russian-German-Udmurt friendship? And, as they say, 'Great Germany! Conquered half the world during the war!' God, what a pity we've got no schnapps!"

Siegfried was furious. So this idiot woman had some historical claims on Germany, had she? She needed putting in her place. He had never attached any significance to his nationality. Born in Russia, German by blood, and American by passport, he regarded himself as a citizen of the world, a businessman outside racial and political prejudices; even his business was international. If you got tangled up in political games, racial barriers, and whatnot, bang went your profits. But this . . .

He reached for the bottle of spirit and, with everyone watching, calmly poured himself a full glass; he then clicked his lighter and brought the flame to the liquid, first in his own glass, then in Kolesova's. Both glasses spurted blue flames, which crackled in the silence. Now I'll teach you something, bitch, thought Siegfried, smiling grimly to himself as he gazed directly into Kolesova's astonished eyes.

"I would like to say a few words," he said, raising his flaming glass. "I have been conducting business with the Soviet Union for over ten years. As president of my own firm, I could have sent a vice president or some other subordinate to Russia. But I always come here myself. And do you know why? Because a trip to Russia is always an adventure! And the best thing about these adventures is—Russian women. They are always a puzzle one dies to solve! I want to drink to you,

Vera, and, in your person, to all Russian women. I trust you won't refuse to drink to that?''

So saying, he lifted the blazing glass to his mouth and serenely drank the contents. He had learned this trick when he first got to know Ryazanov, the chief geologist of the Salekhard Yamal Oil and Gas Trust. Ryazanov was a fat bon vivant, greatly addicted to little Nenets girls. What you have to do as you bring the burning glass to your mouth is breathe through your nose onto the flame; that extinguishes it just before it gets to your lips.

The Udmurt waitresses burst into applause, but Kolesova did not risk drinking the stuff; instead, she gave Siegfried an ecstatic kiss on the cheek.

"Bravo!" said she. "Where did you learn to speak Russian so well?"

"I was born in Saratov, on the Volga," said Siegfried.

"So, you're one of us really!" She blew out the flame in her glass and downed what was left of the liquor in one gulp. Thus she abandoned her historical claims to Germany. Meanwhile, Siegfried was thinking, there it is—the unique capacity Russian women have for adapting themselves to men. German, Swedish, French, and especially English or American women remain themselves with any man, and retain their internal autonomy, like Tibetan ladies in China. But Russian women are above feminism.

In less than twenty minutes the bottle of pure alcohol had been finished off in toasts to Russian-German-American-Udmurt friendship, peace throughout the world, women in general, and every lady present individually. Kolesova put an Abba tape on the cassette deck and insisted on Siegfried drinking to *Brüderschaft* with her. Pure surrealism, thought Siegfried, smiling wryly. Here we are in the Siberian taiga, an American businessman drinking pure alcohol with KGB operatives and Udmurt whores to Swedish music. How true it was, every trip to Russia was an adventure!

He bent over to Khanov and inquired softly, "Listen, Khanov, don't give me any more of that shit about being a wildlife supervisor. Just tell me honestly—what's going on? Why am I getting all this in Udmurtia?"

Khanov, however, only smiled into his little black mustache. "I think we'll all go to the sauna now," he said. "The girls can give us a wash . . ."

27

The log bathhouse stood by the river, and the red light of the setting sun illuminated the whole company as they slung on their coats and ran with a bottle of vodka and brandy each along the snowy path from the dacha.

Inside the sauna, in the dark changing room, there were wooden benches, and on these cases of Zhigulyovsky beer. Warmed by the liquor, the excellent food, and the mischievous glances of the black-eyed Udmurt girls, Siegfried felt no embarrassment as he undressed along with the others. It was the usual way of a brothel; only the ritual was different here, which was what made it interesting.

Quickly throwing off his clothes, Siegfried strode after Khanov into the steam room. It wasn't a dry steam room as in ordinary saunas. On the contrary, one of the ''waitresses'' was splashing jugs of water and beer onto hot sizzling stones; the air was heavy with fragrant white steam. Siegfried promptly climbed onto the upper bench after Khanov and felt he was getting drunk, but in a cheerful boisterous fashion. Anyway, thought Siegfried, on the upper bench of a steam room, one does tend to view the world from a different angle. It was fun, for instance, to watch the frisky Vera Kolesova, instinctively rather than consciously, covering her breasts and gingerish pubic bush with her hands as she came in, and then forget her self-consciousness completely!

Soon, everything got pretty confused anyhow. There was giggling and shrieking on the lower benches as the girls lashed each other with birch twigs soaked in beer, stoked up the heat, and then rushed out into the changing room for gulps of cold beer. Four female figures, with rounded hips and bottoms and wobbling pear-shaped breasts, swam out of the curtain of steam, then vanished into it again, only to reappear somewhere else with more giggles and shrieks. Then, after conspiratorial whispers, they climbed to the upper benches and dragged Khanov and Siegfried down. They laid them face down on the benches below and began lashing their backs with birch twigs, wetting the leafy branches from time to time in a bucket of cold beer.

From the chastisement of these branches, tingling but not at all painful, somehow burning and relaxing at the same time, Siegfried's body seemed to grow lighter, while from the scent of birch leaves, beer, and female hands running across his damp body, his head spun in a delightful floating fashion. While he was yielding to this ecstasy, hovering above the world in body and spirit, hands turned him over onto his back and the burning-icy birch twigs flailed their trembling leaves against his chest, shoulders, belly, and legs, as a result of which Siegfried felt an extraordinarily sharp and powerful surge of sexual desire. Without opening his eyes, just by listening to the voices and laughter around him, he realized that they had achieved the same with Khanov.

What followed was like a merry-go-round: three raven-haired Udmurt amazons and one Russian blonde straddled the men in turn, not staying on each longer than a minute, but managing in that minute to exhibit individuality of temperament and experience. From this whirl of sensation, Siegfried's soul had ascended into outer space, while his body emitted sighs mixed with groans. Then Vera Kolesova knelt down and washed his penis, now trembling in anticipation, using the potable spirit; with a ritual solemnity in her severe blue eyes, she slowly bent her head to this now pure and sterile flesh and began to suck it in. . . . Siegfried, as he fainted away, distinctly felt his body winging its way upward in pursuit of his soaring soul.

Two hours later Siegfried and Khanov continued their meal at the bountiful table. The waitresses had brought a suckling pig baked whole. Siegfried felt he could eat an entire boar.

"Not a rustle out in the garden now," he suddenly began singing, as if the popular Soviet tune had just been born inside him. "Quiet till the dawn's early light . . ."

"If you only knew, how I dream of you, and those wonderful Moscow nights." Khanov, the waitresses, and Kolesova joined in.

And they sang on and on that evening, sang and drank, and sang again, as if no sin lay between them, nor, as *Pravda* would say, "the fierce struggle of two ideologies."

When Khanov was seeing Siegfried to his room, Siegfried addressed him with drunken docility. "You know, old pal, even if you are a Gee Bee and took shots of me fucking around in the bathhouse so's you can blackmail me, I don't care. It was fabulous, damn me if it wasn't."

Khanov merely smiled wordlessly into his mustache—he'd taken no photos and had no intention of blackmailing Siegfried. He had honestly tried to amuse him, and the next day they really were going elk hunting. In the evening there'd be another feast and the usual orgy, and so it would go on until the signal from Moscow released Siegfried from his happy confinement. Everything had gone according to plan, and

Khanov had already taken a fancy to this gregarious American, much as a scientist becomes attached to his experimental animal.

Left alone in his room, Siegfried pulled his pajamas out of his case, along with a small, powerful Grundig transistor. Every night before he went to sleep, wherever he was in the world, Siegfried had to hear the share prices in New York, London, and Hamburg as well as the rest of the political and economic news. Otherwise, he couldn't get to sleep. As he lay down, he switched on the radio and at once got the voice of a Russian announcer: "And now here's the weather forecast. Over the whole territory of Siberia, from the Urals to Irkutsk, the weather has been fine, with no wind, for the second day running. Temperatures today, Sverdlovsk, minus twenty-seven; Tyumen, minus thirty-two; Urengoi, minus thirty-seven; and Salekhard, thirty-nine degrees below zero. The forecasters promise that clear, cloudless weather will continue tomorrow, though there is a chance of light snowfall in places. Now we're presenting a program of popular music for our boys working in the Far North."

"We're not frightened of any ninth wave, or any permafrost we know!" a hearty Komsomol voice boomed out.

Siegfried turned the transistor off. All the intoxication and other delights of the evening left him instantly; his whole body grew stiff with fear. So they'd lied about the weather in Tyumen. That meant they'd taken him off the plane and carried him off to this reservation deliberately so as to . . .

Icy suspicion gripped his heart. Of course: the KGB wanted to deprive him of his profit! On December 17, when the international committee of experts signed the pipeline protocol, the Western European banks would hand over \$9 billion to the Russians, and Siegfried's commission would be \$225 million. But a generous promise of 2.5 percent was one thing; paying out $225 million was another. Siegfried had been in business a long time; he knew how reluctant people were to part with money. And Russians surely love money—especially foreign currency. They had needed him earlier, to extract such an enormous loan from the German and French banks—18 billion dollars! Even backed by government guarantees in France and Germany, it had been no easy matter getting a loan like that, dammit. Although he was ignorant of the precise figures and had no real facts, he had a strong hunch that somebody in the upper echelons of government in France and Germany had been on his side in the matter, somebody there had been "oiling the wheels," as the criminal slang has it, for the USSR. True, after that, the French had realized the situation and Mitterrand had thrown out nearly a hundred Soviet spy-diplomats last summer.

Still, getting the banks' agreement to provide a loan to the Soviets hadn't been the end of the matter; the money was paid in installments every two or three months as construction work progressed, so that every time payment was suspended as the Russians went about rocking the international boat, now in Afghanistan, now in Poland, an attempt on the life of the Pope, exiling Andrei Sakharov to Gorky, using convict workers on the pipeline, then the Korean airliner! Every time there was an international row, the banks got nervous and wanted to stop payment of the next loan installment.

INTO THE VALLEY OF DEBT

. . . result of some political prodding. And Russia's request for an extra DM 300m last December for financing the Urengoy Siberian gas pipeline sent the bankers scurrying to Bonn for consultations.

As bankers and governments become more aware that bankers' decisions to lend or not to lend, reschedule or not to reschedule are decisions of importance not only for banks' profits but also for their country's international relations . . .

The Economist
March 20, 1982

FRANCE—IT'S BACK IN CHARACTER

. . . in a series of disagreements. Among other irritants:

French cooperation in construction by Moscow of a trans-Siberian gas pipe line to Western Europe, a project the U.S. strongly opposes. Secretary of State Alexander Haig has said he is "appalled" that French banks, with loans guaranteed by the government, are helping finance the project. France dismissed U.S. objections . . .

U.S. News & World Report
April 5,1982

RUSSIAN GAS PIPELINE; BANKERS TIGHTEN THE TAPS

The natural-gas pipeline to deliver, eventually, about 40 billion cubic meters of gas a year from Siberia's remote Urengoi fields and Yamal peninsula to western Europe is catching Polish flak. West German banks are most at risk in Poland and experience there has made them leery about increasing lending to other communist countries, including Russia.

In consequence, when representatives of 20 banks met in Frankfurt this week to sign an agreement to reschedule Poland's debt, it very quickly became apparent in informal discussions that West German banks are most unhappy about Russia's recent request for an extra DM75m (about $30m) of unguaranteed loans for the trans-Siberian pipeline that is now under construction.

This sum will not make or break a project costing at least $15 billion. West German lenders have already extended DM2.5 billion in credits and are poised soon to announce agreement on a further DM300m the Russians asked for in December. Even so, the West German hesitation is significant because it reflects a general dampening of enthusiasm that may delay completion of the pipeline.

The DM2.5 billion loan was extended by a consortium of 16 West German banks and largely guaranteed by the state export credit insurance agency, Hermes. It was founded on a promise by the Russians to make a 15% down payment from their own resources. In December, the Russians said they could not keep their promise, and asked for another DM300m.

Members of the banking consortium were divided over what some of them saw as a dangerous breach of principle. Bankers say the credit is likely to go ahead once haggling over interest rates is over; but some banks, led by Bayerische Landesbank, may opt out.

These banks were particularly annoyed by Russia's request for the extra DM75m early this year. Even the big banks, Deutsche, Dresdner and Commerzbank, are not keen to lend a lot more money unguaranteed. There have been three main reasons for the shift from the go-go fervor of a year ago, when there was talk of DM10 billion in German financing alone.

First, the collapse in Comecon creditworthiness has chilled enthusiasts. The rescheduling of Poland's and Rumania's debts has made bankers fretful about the size of the Soviet Union's pipeline borrowing. Repayment of the loans (from gas sales) is still supposed to be assured, but delays in construction could mean expensive delays in repayment.

Second, America's opposition to the project found more effective expression in President Reagan's post Poland trade sanctions. The American export ban blockaded one of the pipeline's vital turbine parts, to have been manufactured in the United States. This slowed the pipeline more than any amount of political jawboning.

Three European firms—AEG Telefunken, Nuovo Pignone and John Brown Engineering—that had signed contracts last autumn to supply 125 turbines based on the American General Electric's rotary parts are hunting for ways round the ban—and so are the Russians. According to the Swedish consulting firm PetroStudies, the Russians have brought forward their pipelaying schedule; and have accelerated programs designed to give them the capacity to manufacture near-substitutes for the American-designed turbines. Reliance on Soviet manufacture, however, would set completion of the project back far beyond the 1984 target date.

Third, as oil prices have dropped and gas supplies increased, European consumers are no longer in quite such a hurry to sign long-term contracts for Soviet gas. Two other new gas pipelines are on the way: Algeria's to Italy via Tunisia (now completed) and Norway's from the North Sea (to be ready by the mid-1980's).

Only West Germany and France have signed firm supply agreements with the Russians. Italy's state-owned utility, Eni, put together an agreement in principle last year, but has yet to get government approval. Holland, Belgium, Switzerland and Austria are still talking. Russia was expected to receive between $8 billion and $10 billion a year from sales of 40 billion cubic meters a year. Firm contracts to date guarantee Russia less than half as much income as that.

The Economist
April 10, 1982

RISING HOPES
West German banks agreed to lend Russia $1.13 billion for the Siberian gas pipeline.

The Economist
July 17, 1982

In the history of the construction of the Siberia–Western Europe gas pipeline, there had been several such episodes, and every time Siegfried had dashed around in airplanes between Moscow, Paris, Urengoi, and Bonn, spending incredible amounts of money to retrieve the situation. Only the Russians believed he had pocketed the first half of the commission. Who had organized that trip for French bankers to Urengoi so they could see there were no convicts there? And who was still retaining agents at the Algerian and Norwegian construction sites to report on exactly when the competition went on stream and what firms they had contracts with? And who had gone without sleep these last four years getting the Russians their regular $3 to $5 million every three or four months? Then, of course, they were all over him and rolled out the red carpet; he got the best girl in Moscow as a mistress, parties at government dachas, free holidays at Black Sea resorts, and no customs inspection at airports—take icons out if you want! And that was nothing compared with his treatment in Urengoi, Salekhard, and Tyumen. There, he was a king, the bosom friend of party and Gee Bees, and of the chief geologists of the territory.

But now that was all over. The pipeline was built,

in three days the commission would sign the protocol bringing it into service and the Russians would get their $9 billion. That's why they were in such a hurry to get it over with, and he, Siegfried, had been a complete idiot giving them the chance to entice him into this Udmurt trap. Khanov was nothing, a minor official of the Udmurt KGB, but tomorrow the boys from Moscow would be rolling up. They would show Siegfried a photo album of his whoring exploits in the USSR—with Tanya in Moscow and on the Black Sea, those mulatto girls in Alma-Ata, and the Udmurt girls today. They would show him the album and say: either you sign over your $225 million voluntarily to the International Movement for Peace and Disarmament or tomorrow these photos will be sent to *Der Spiegel* or *Playboy*.

And if, God forbid, they knew about that business in Salekhard five years ago as well, they would just sling him into one of those arctic camps he'd asked to have moved well away from the eyes of Western European bankers. American citizenship would be no help at all. The KGB knows how to frame foreign nationals too. Incidentally, they had a camp for foreigners somewhere around here; was it Udmurtia, or Mordovia? He'd read about it in the papers. . . . Yes, indeed, they'd wrapped him around their little finger and no mistake. Six years they'd allowed him the freedom of the store—make hay with the Russian girls—while they put together their little album and planned their trap in Zataika.

Siegfried lay, petrified by the awareness of inescapable disaster. Even if he ran away from the dacha this instant, they would pick him up as soon as he got to Moscow; he wouldn't make it from the airport to the embassy. The bastards! The lot of them! Even Tanya, the KGB bitch—her and Dynkov's flu—all lies . . . Got to do something. Now. But what! Nip out to the bathhouse and check for hidden cameras?

The door opened partway, and the figure of one of the waitresses slipped into the room without knocking. She was wearing a transparent nightdress and carried a bottle of champagne and two glasses. Placing them on the bedside table, she scuttled into bed, although Siegfried was lying with his eyes closed, pretending to be asleep. She pressed up against him with her glowing body and kissed him hungrily on the lips. But now even her youthful, juicy flesh evoked in Siegfried nothing but disgust. No doubt Khanov had sent her, so as not to leave him on his own even at night. Siegfried moved away, mumbling, "Don't . . . I want to sleep."

The girl froze in astonishment. "You want me to go?"

"Yes, I'm tired."

She sighed. "Oh dear. And I won you for the whole night."

"What do you mean, won me?" Siegfried was now the astonished one.

"Well!" she said, relaxing onto the pillow. "Only old farts come here from Moscow—ministers. It's really boring with them. They keep us shut up here, like in a harem. So we have to throw ourselves at some old man who can't even get it up. And suddenly we get a young, husky fella, an American as well, knocking back booze better than a Russian. So us girls drew lots for all three nights. Is it because you don't like me? Should I send somebody else?"

"No, I'm just very tired. Let's postpone it till tomorrow."

"It's not my turn tomorrow," she said, rising from the bed. "Do you want the other one, the Russian? She's busy with Khanov anyway."

"No, I'm going to sleep."

"Should I come back near morning?"

"Thank you, no."

She looked at him with desolate eyes, gave a profound sigh of sadness, and went out. As she left, she contemptuously clicked off the light.

Siegfried lay, listening intently to the noises of the house. It took about twenty minutes for everything to quiet down in the waitresses' room below and in Khanov's on the first floor. Siegfried, however, lay another hour more to make sure everyone was asleep. He had worked out a plan of escape. He got up, got dressed, and quietly went downstairs, fearing that every step would creak. If they found him here, though, it was all right, he could say he was looking for something to drink.

But the house was absolutely silent. Siegfried reached the hall, slipped on his sheepskin coat, hat, and shoes, and wrapped his scarf around his throat. He just wanted a breath of fresh air, didn't he?

He didn't need an excuse anyway. The house slept.

Siegfried rummaged through the pockets of Khanov's coat, which was hanging close by, and took out the keys to the black Volga. From this moment on, there was no going back. He got a sharp knife from the kitchen and slipped two unopened bottles of vodka into his coat pockets before going outside.

The Volga was standing by the gate next to the pickup, in which the waitresses had arrived earlier, no doubt. Beyond the cars the gates were closed, not locked. Past the gates, he recalled, there was a slope down to the river, where the road ran into town.

Of course, he could run to the bathhouse and see if there were any cameras hidden somewhere under the ceiling, but was it worth wasting time? Even if there were no cameras, that didn't mean there hadn't been three hours before during that mindless orgy.

Siegfried approached the pickup slowly, as if out on a stroll; he walked all around it, slitting each tire with the kitchen knife. The truck quietly settled into the snow. He waited several seconds—would a light flash on in the house? Then he climbed onto the fence, reached out for the telegraph pole, and cut the wire. The end of the wire fell inside the fence, onto the snow. Siegfried climbed down and sliced it off close to the house. About thirty yards of telephone wire now lay in the snow. He coiled it up and placed it in the Volga. Like his parents, he always did everything thoroughly, thinking out every detail. If his flight was discovered, Khanov would have no pursuit car available and no telephone to raise the alarm in Izhevsk. At any rate, for some time.

Now for the opening of the gates. They creaked a little, but to Siegfried the noise seemed loud enough to arouse the whole planet. Still, no one woke in the house. Too much to drink. Siegfried grinned to himself.

Growing bolder, almost scorning concealment, he put the Volga's transmission into neutral and, holding onto the wheel with one hand, put his shoulder to the door and pushed the car through the gates. The car rolled easily down the slope and was soon moving by itself. Siegfried jumped in as it got going and taxied along as far as he could. Only when he was down by the river and shielded from the dacha by the snow-covered pines and cedars of the taiga did he switch on the ignition.

The Volga leapt forward and raced along the forest road in the darkness. The souped-up engine, specially built for Khanov in the Izhevsk tank factory, enabled Siegfried to squeeze out up to one hundred kilometers an hour, even on this track deep in snow.

At first the road was empty, no oncoming cars, no lights of villages or settlements. Along either side, the headlights picked out only the dark snowy shapes of trees. It was as if he was speeding alone through the unpeopled Siberian countryside.

Half an hour's driving, however, brought him out onto a main road only partially cleared and just as poorly lit. There were no road signs whatsoever. Russian roads are not the same as American highways. Siegfried had no idea in which direction Izhevsk lay. Fortunately, the headlights of some sort of truck appeared in the distance.

Siegfried stopped and jumped out of the car; he quickly raised the hood and burned his hands unscrewing the radiator cap. Hot steam belched out. He ran out into the middle of the road, waving his arms at the approaching vehicle.

The truck stopped, and the driver's face stuck out of the cab. "What's up?"

"Fucking radiator's leaking," Siegfried said in the true Russian manner, switching at once into truck drivers' obscenities.

"No, get stuffed, I'm not towing a Volga," the driver said at once. "I've got a trailer already—can't you see?"

Sure enough, there was some sort of container on the back of the truck. But Siegfried was not interested in towing the Volga anywhere.

"I can see. Just drop me off at Izhevsk, the airport. I'll pay, look." Siegfried pulled the two bottles of vodka out of his pockets. "There's cash in it for you as well. My wife's flying in, see. If I'm not there to meet her, she'll smell a fucking rat, say I was on a screwing expedition."

Male solidarity, combined with cash and two bottles of vodka, carried the day. An hour later the truck rolled up to Izhevsk Airport.

The terminal building was cold and empty. There were no passengers, of course, from yesterday's Moscow-Tyumen-Urengoi flight; they had left the day before. Nor were there any groups in transit, as happened in bad flying weather. This was one more confirmation for Siegfried that yesterday's "forced landing because of blizzard" was just a KGB ruse to lure him off to Zataika. "Boarding is proceeding for flights Izhevsk-Moscow and Izhevsk-Siktivkar," came the announcement over the intercom. "Passengers are requested to board the aircraft. I repeat . . ."

Siegfried restrained himself. His first impulse was to make a dash for the Moscow flight, but Moscow was now the most dangerous destination of all. It was nearly four hours flying time to Moscow; by then news of his escape would surely have reached them, and a detachment of Gee Bees would be waiting for him on the runway. No, anywhere but Moscow!

"How long is it to Siktivkar?" he asked the drowsy cashier.

"An hour and five minutes," she answered.

That was what he wanted. An hour from now, he'd be in Siktivkar. Once there, change planes right away and off somewhere North, preferably into the tundra or the taiga, where no one would think of looking for him. In a couple of days—when dozens of foreign journalists would be flying into Urengoi for the opening ceremony—he would drop in out of the blue. He would be inseparable from the reporters and would fly out of the USSR along with them. In front of Western newspapermen, of course, the KGB wouldn't touch him.

Now it remained for him to do one more thing—get a ticket for the airplane without showing his foreign passport and without saying his last name.

"How much is a round trip to Siktivkar?" he asked.

"Seventy-four rubles."

Siegfried pulled a hundred-ruble bill from his wallet, put it down in front of the cashier, and said, "Keep the change."

The fat cashier, wrapped in a heavy overcoat, raised her sleepy eyes at him in surprise. It was simple arithmetic—a twenty-six-ruble tip. Reason woke her up.

"Passport," she said, getting the form for the ticket out of the drawer.

"That's the point, honey!" said Siegfried, pushing the bill toward her. "That's the whole point! I'm flying in order to retrieve my passport! A drinking buddy of mine flew off to Siktivkar wearing my jacket, and in the pocket of the jacket are my passport and all my papers. And today, I need them right up to here!'' He held his hand up to his chin, showing that he needed his documents, on fear of death. ''I'm signing up for work here at the paper factory—that's why I'm going there and back. When I return, I'll show you my passport, I promise! Give me the ticket! I tell you—keep the change!'' He again moved the hundred rubles nearer to the cashier and beseechingly looked her in the eye.

She stared at him for a few seconds. Siegfried's eyes shone with absolute sincerity, and his whole appearance—sheepskin coat, expensive fur hat, clean, sober face—suggested that he was a respectable person, an engineer, and not some kind of criminal whom the police could be looking for.

The cashier silently hid the hundred-ruble note in the drawer of her table, then, holding pen above the empty ticket, asked, ''Last name?''

''Thanks!'' Siegfried said. ''Ivanov. A simple last name! Ivanov, Boris Ivanovich.''

28

Only when he was on board the plane, a little forty-seater Ilyushin, did Siegfried allow himself to take a breath. He reclined limply against the headrest and thought, horrified, What have I done! On the run from the KGB, and where? Inside the USSR!

While he'd been driving the car, hurtling desperately through the taiga in the dead of night, getting his ticket, and boarding the plane, everything had been wound up inside him by the sheer dynamics of physical action; his thoughts had been totally occupied by the need for self-control—not to give himself away, not say a word out of place, not to make a suspicious gesture. But now they'd taken off and nothing depended on him anymore; all he had to do was wait passively till they reached Siktivkar. So his fear returned, and all his acrophobia, he thought, was nothing compared with the terror he felt now.

He looked about him. The plane had traveled from the South, the Caucasus, and was packed with black-mustached Georgians in huge cloth caps. They were talking noisily among themselves in Georgian. There was also a strong, unpleasant smell of sweat, garlic, and *chacha;** everybody carried an extra bag or box of tomatoes, mandarins, or flowers under his seat. For

*Grape vodka.

the first time in all the years he had been coming to the USSR, Siegfried had descended from the high standard of living enjoyed by the privileged elite to the normal everyday level. The abundance of Georgian black marketeers on the plane and the fact that the stewardess had obviously been bribed to let them bring their heavy bags and boxes into the cabin reassured Siegfried. It meant that at least there were no KGB operatives on board. His Georgian neighbor took his shoes off, and the air at once grew thick with the smell of long-unwashed feet—so what the hell! Better freedom and the smell of sweat than the fresh air of the game trap at Zataika. And, anyway, thought Siegfried suddenly, in a couple of days I won't smell any better—my suitcase is back in Zataika, and you can't buy deodorants in Russia.

His neighbor meanwhile, now shoeless, had dragged out of a voluminous wickerwork bag a roast chicken wrapped in a greasy copy of *Evening Tbilisi*. To be more precise, it was a chicken *tabak,* smelling sharply of garlic and spices. Out of the same bag appeared a large bottle of red wine, a round of fresh cheese, some greens, ripe tomatoes.

Siegfried had a sudden piercing pang of hunger, so much so that his mouth was filled with saliva. The Georgian, as if reading his thoughts, or more likely out of Georgian etiquette, broke the two-pound chicken apart and offered half to Siegfried.

"Go on, go on!" he said in a Georgian accent. "I'm Soso from Tbilisi. You?"

"My name's Siegfried," said Siegfried indistinctly as he tackled the chicken.

"A Jew?"

Siegfried, sinking his teeth into juicy chicken flesh, mumbled something between confirmation and denial.

"What's your line of work?" asked Soso, pouring wine for both of them into plastic cups.

"I'm . . . a translator," Siegfried managed to say.

Soso grinned. "You're a translator and I'm a transporter!" He lifted his cup of wine. "OK! Your health, friend!"

They drank. "What language do you translate from, *genetsvali?**" the garrulous Soso asked.

"English, German . . ." said Siegfried.

"Oh, dear-dear-dear!" said Soso, distressed. "If you know languages like that, why didn't you go off to America when Brezhnev was letting the Jews out?"

Siegfried was beginning to regret having accepted the chicken and getting drawn into this conversation. He shrugged vaguely.

"You're sorry now, of course," said Soso confidently, dragging a packet of Marlboros out of his coat and proffering it to Siegfried. Siegfried declined; he didn't smoke. "I was a fool as well," continued Soso. "In Tbilisi you could marry a Jewish girl for ten thousand and get away. But I just sat thinking—go or not go. If I went to Israel, a totally different country; if I went to America, I'd have to know the language, right?"

"Right," Siegfried confirmed.

"Wrong!" Soso contradicted emphatically. "I should have gone! There's no living here. None at all, know what I mean? Here's me taking mandarins up north. Before, when Brezhnev was in charge, I made eight thousand on a trip like this. So in Georgia you give the police a sweetener to let you take the stuff out, so in Urengoi or Norilsk you do the same and they keep their hands off. Two, three thousand I lose. But I still had five thousand; I could live! Now? Now I'm risking my life when I fly. Even if I give out half my profit in bribes, there's no guarantee I won't land in jail! Andropov!" Soso heaved a sigh. "No, we missed our chance, missed it. Should have gone with-

---

*Dear (Georgian).

out thinking. I'd be in America now, driving a Cadillac."

Before too long Siegfried knew a good many details about the clandestine market in fruit, vegetables, and flowers in the USSR. The cost of these goods rose with the polar latitude, but there were differentials even beyond the Arctic Circle. "You can't take fruit into Murmansk now," said Soso. "The whole police force has been changed over because Andropov banished Brezhnev's son-in-law there as militia chief. Not one policeman takes bribes in Murmansk now; they're scared. There's no business in Archangel for us; there's no money around. Different matter in Urengoi or Surgut! The geologists are well heeled, and your ordinary working man rakes in up to a thousand rubles a month. Risky, of course. Shatunov, the KGB man in Salekhard, is a real brute." No, thought Siegfried, the undercover fruit trade in the USSR wasn't much different from arms or drugs traffic; the state had a trading monopoly and couldn't run it properly. It persecuted its competitors as if they were selling people pistols and grenades instead of flowers and mandarins.

"Have you heard the latest one about Andropov?" asked Soso. "As soon as everybody on the Central Committee had voted for him as general secretary, Andropov says: 'Voters, you may lower your hands and move away from the wall!' Later on, at a press conference, some foreign correspondent asks Andropov, 'Comrade Andropov, are you confident that the Soviet people will follow you?' 'If they don't follow me, they'll follow Brezhnev!' answers Andropov. Do you know what Andropov's New Year's TV message will be? If he lives till then, of course. 'Dear comrades, Happy 1937!' "

FASTEN YOUR SEATBELTS. The red sign lit up. The aircraft banked and swiftly came in to land in Siktivkar, capital of yet another ethnic minirepublic, the

158

Komi ASSR. And now a double terror gripped Siegfried's heart—acrophobia and fear of the KGB.

The aircraft skis scraped along the snow-covered landing strip, and the plane taxied briefly before coming to a stop. Siegfried looked fearfully through the window. If a black Volga appeared on the runway, it was for him of course.

But no one met him.

From the wall of the concrete airport building, a gigantic portrait of Lenin, now resembling the slant-eyed Komi rather than the moon-faced Udmurts, gazed serenely down on the Georgian black marketeers as they dragged their boxes of fruit, flowers, and other bounty from the Soviet subtropics into the terminal.

Siegfried gave his new friend Soso a hand in hauling his cases of fragrant mandarins and chrysanthemums. As soon as they had traversed the frozen nocturnal airfield and entered the terminal, they were assailed by a wave of stale air. The building held several hundred transit passengers—shift workers along with the Caucasian fruit merchants. Both had to get to Salekhard, the workmen to the boring sites and the pipeline, the traders to their market. Salekhard, however, had been closed to passenger flights for two days now on Shatunov's orders. In winter, bad flying weather and postponed flights are no rare thing in the North, so the workmen slept as usual side by side—on the floor and on the windowsills. The black marketeers stayed awake, worrying about their perishable goods. The arrival of another thirty Georgians raised a gale of laughter. The traders hailing from the "fraternal" republic of Armenia found this especially funny. Armenians and Georgians love one another like the Flemings love the Walloons.

"Get in the line for Murmansk," shouted a young Armenian to the newcomers.

"Why Murmansk?" said another. "Actually Georgians can fly to Salekhard. They've got nothing in their pants, anyway; they're in no danger.''

A roar of laughter drowned out the end of the sentence. The new arrivals looked everywhere in their embarrassment. At last an old man took pity on them and explained. "In Salekhard the tundra spirits are cutting Russians' cocks off. That's why they're not letting anybody in or out of Yamal, so the panic doesn't spread.''

"What tundra spirits?'' asked Soso.

"Nobody knows,'' said the old man and pointed into the air. "Spirits, know what I mean? They're— nothing! But they're going around cutting Russians' balls off!''

"Thank the Lord,'' said Soso.

"What do you mean—thank the Lord?'' The old man was puzzled.

"Thank Him for starting the operation,'' said Soso. "Pity He started in the North, though. Couldn't He have made a start with our Russians in Georgia?''

Now everybody laughed, Georgians and Armenians together. Of course, nobody believed a word of the "tundra spirits'' business, but with the great love the Caucasian peoples bear for their "Russian big brother,'' everybody listened to the fantastic rumors about Russians being punished in this "interesting manner'' with keen enjoyment.

Siegfried, however, was in no mood for jokes or stupid stories about tundra spirits. He left the Caucasian company and walked out onto the airfield, deeply depressed. When Khanov woke up he could easily find out which were the flights out of Izhevsk that night, and this meant Siegfried urgently had to disappear from Siktivkar. There was only one flight scheduled in the next three hours: Siktivkar-Izhevsk-Tbilisi—the same one Siegfried had used to get there.

The realization that he was in an even worse trap

than in Zataika clouded his brain as if he had been drinking heavily. He looked around him.

To the right, a few yards from the terminal building, stood a two-engined Anton with a red stripe along the fuselage. It was equipped with skis. Near it was a truck with MAIL written on it. A young man, in a fur flying suit, pilot or mechanic, was throwing bags and boxes out of the truck and through the open door of the aircraft. In there, hands were catching the packages and stowing them further inside.

Siegfried approached slowly. Now he could make out the addresses on the parcels: NOVY PORT,* AMDERMA, DIKSON. Novy Port—that was on Yamal, about 150 kilometers north of Salekhard.

The boy loading the plane wiped the sweat from his brow. "Haven't got a smoke, have you?" he asked Siegfried.

For the first time in his life, Siegfried regretted the fact that he didn't smoke.

"Hold it!" he said to the boy. "Hang on a minute!"

He raced back to the airport buildings. As he ran, he was pulling Soviet money out of his jacket pocket. Since there are no credit cards or checking accounts in the USSR, Siegfried always changed ten or fifteen hundred dollars into Soviet rubles when he visited Moscow and always carried a thick wad of bills in his pocket. Now he peeled off two hundred-ruble bills and rushed up to Soso, who was sitting on his boxes noisily playing backgammon with his associates.

"Soso, be a pal!" said Siegfried excitedly. "Sell me some mandarins, twenty pounds."

Soso looked at him in amazement. Siegfried lied fluently: "I've just met a friend. It's his wife's birthday. And those American cigarettes I saw you had—sell me a pack, ten rubles . . . !"

Within a minute he was picking his way through to

*New Port

the exit, with Soso's wicker bag stuffed with mandarins and a pack of Marlboros in his hand. As he emerged onto the airfield, he saw the little mail plane. Both engines were running and the propellers were turning! The young man was standing in the doorway, dragging a metal gangway inside. Siegfried ran up, preparing to throw the pack of Marlboros.

"Catch!"

"What do you mean?" The boy was surprised.

"No, I only want one," he explained. "I've given it up; that's why I've got none myself."

"Go on, take the whole pack! American!" Siegfried thrust them at him vigorously. American cigarettes are rare in the USSR.

"Well, shit!" The youth grinned sheepishly. "How can I give up smoking at this rate?" He lit up with evident enjoyment and stowed the cigarettes in a pocket of his flying suit. "Whereabouts are you flying?" he asked Siegfried.

"Novy Port," said Siegfried and opened his bag of mandarins as if by accident. On glimpsing this subtropical "baggage," the lad glanced furtively to check if there were any bosses or witnesses around. He then addressed Siegfried in rough haste. "Well, get in then. Look sharp! What are you fucking waiting for?"

One minute later they were taking off into the dark polar skies.

Siegfried was jubilant. It was six in the morning, and even if Khanov roused the entire KGB, who would think of looking for Siegfried Shertz in Novy Port in the Yamal tundra!

When the aircraft was on course, the young fliers, pilot and mechanic, munched their oranges with relish and confided to Siegfried, "You were in luck, buddy, with us. Too damn true you were. A mouse couldn't get into Yamal now. Everything's sealed off."

"Why's that?"

"The place is a shambles, the Nentsi are in revolt.

You don't believe it? Fuck it! A few days back, three convicts made a break for it out of camp and sliced up three geologists or something on the way. They cut their balls off and their ears. Fuck it, it was the airport chief himself told us. But that's not the funny part; the funny part is, the Nentsi decided it was the tundra spirits doing it, giving them the signal to rise up, and they've started massacring us Russians all over the tundra. In Salekhard, they've even caused two explosions. Stuff them, though, our paras are going in today. They'll fucking restore law and order!''

And it suddenly dawned on Siegfried: so that's why they'd held him back in Izhevsk, that was the reason for Zataika and its unlooked-for delights. A revolt on Yamal! But, hell, this ridiculous revolt could disrupt the pipeline ceremony. That made his trip to Urengoi even more urgent. He was simply a genius escaping from Zataika! If the European banks didn't pay the $9 billion to the Russians because of the uprising, Siegfried could say good-bye to his millions. No, fuck them! The KGB was not going to stop him now!

III

ICE DRIFT IN DECEMBER

29

GOVERNMENT TELEGRAM
URGENT, SECRET

TO:
SALEKHARD DISTRICT COMMITTEE CPSU

TODAY 12 DECEMBER PARATROOP DIVISION OCTOBER REVOLUTION UNDER THE COMMAND OF MAJOR GENERAL GRINKO IS ARRIVING TO PUT DOWN THE DISTURBANCES IN YOUR DISTRICT.

THE SECOND SECRETARY OF THE DISTRICT COMMITTEE, COMRADE ROGOV, IS TO TAKE OVER THE DUTIES OF THE FIRST SECRETARY AND MOBILIZE THE TOWN PARTY ORGANIZATION AND ALL RESOURCES OF THE LOCAL KGB AND POLICE MILITIA TO ASSIST THE MILITARY FORCES ON THEIR ARRIVAL. FORMER FIRST SECRETARY PYOTR TUSYADA IS TO BE EXPELLED FROM THE CPSU FOR ABSENTING HIMSELF FROM HIS POST WITHOUT LEAVE.

COMRADE BOGOMYATOV, FIRST SECRETARY OF TYUMEN PROVINCE PARTY COMMITTEE, IS APPOINTED AS PRESIDENT OF THE PARTY COMMISSION FOR THE ELIMINATION OF DISORDER IN THE DISTRICT.

A. YEREMIN
HEAD OF PERSONNEL ADMINISTRATION, CENTRAL
COMMITTEE CPSU
MOSCOW, KREMLIN, 12 DECEMBER 1983

30

At four o'clock in the afternoon, a cavalcade of official cars and Sno-Cats, escorted by the three personnel carriers from the military garrison, set off from the district committee building. The new first secretary, Vladimir Rogov; the chief of the Salekhard KGB Directorate, Major Shatunov; the local chief of police militia, Colonel Sini; and other top brass were on their way to the airport to meet the October Revolution Paratroop Division. Shatunov had promised to drop me off at the hotel on the way; a night spent investigating Ryazanov's murder meant I'd had no sleep at all; then there were the two explosions at Yamal Gas and Northern Pipe Laying—then the attack on the local KGB headquarters by mobs of workmen. After all I had been through, I was just tottering on my feet.

A full moon, red because of the frost, hung over Salekhard. Beneath it, in the black skies of the polar night, three helicopters and three Annushki of the local arctic air service circled over the town. But the escapees made no attempt to slip out of Salekhard, even during the two morning explosions. In fact, not a single Sno-Cat or Nenets sled had left or even attempted to leave that morning.

We drove through the streets of Salekhard, empty, as if frozen solid, past buildings defaced by anti-Russian inscriptions and drawings. Usually from four to seven in the evening was the most lively time of the day. The shops were open—hairdresser, café, post office—and there was the normal urban hustle and bustle on the main thoroughfare, Lenin Street, with its bright street lamps. Until three days ago, that's how it had been, especially since the Yamaltrade and Yamalstore trusts, as usual before public holidays—in this case, the pipeline opening—had supplied the stores with imported boots and shoes, ladies' underwear, Finnish suits for men, transistor radios, and tape recorders. The food stores had real butter and even chickens! Naturally, the Salekhard streets had filled up at once with sleds loaded down with weighty bags of goods obtained by waiting in line for hours. It took more than a snowstorm to remove the smiles of happiness from the faces of those people. We've come through, we've tamed the tundra, and now we've got something to celebrate with!

But today all that holiday bustle had gone from Salekhard. The town was under siege, something like Beirut during the Israeli occupation. Only armed police patrols, tracked vehicles, and hoards of Nenets children were in the streets. Since their Russian teachers and boarding school staff had not come to work, the children went tramping around the central streets, or riding in dog sleighs; some even attached themselves with metal hooks to Sno-Cats and slid laughing behind them along the icy roads. Nenets adolescents, sixteen or seventeen years old, strolled around the streets in festive *malitsas* and *kisi*,* jeering at the police patrols and Gee Bee Sno-Cats in their own language. Practically none of the Russians understood what they were saying, but their gestures were eloquent. As if by chance, as soon as a patrol or Sno-Cat got near, they would pull out a handsome bone-handled knife (an essential part of Nenets national trappings) from the

*Thigh-length boots made from deer fur.

sheaths on their belts; this done, they would pretend to test the edge with their thumb to see if it was sharp. Inscriptions like RUSSIANS—GET OUT OF THE TUNDRA! and THE TUNDRA SPIRITS ARE WITH US! were their work, as were the drawings of blood-dripping penises disfiguring the faces of Russian tundra tamers on the triumphal posters.

The motorcade halted by the North Hotel, a three-story building with facade freshly painted for the arrival of the European visitors and an enormous plywood placard bearing in scarlet letters: THE PARTY—MIND, CONSCIENCE, AND HONOR OF OUR EPOCH!

Shatunov got out of the car with me, and we went into the hotel. In the middle of the empty lobby, Major Orudjev was playing cards with a police patrol detail—an extremely young sprig of a lieutenant and two vigilantes. Two guard dogs from the camp were dozing by Orudjev's feet.

On seeing Shatunov, the police detail and Orudjev sprang to their feet in alarm. The young lieutenant rapped out in a loud voice, "Comrade Major! Permission to report! All quiet in the sector entrusted to me, nothing to report!"

Shatunov nodded sourly toward the front desk.

"Where's the hotel manager?"

"The hotel staff have not reported for work, Comrade Major," the lieutenant informed him, and added with a smile, "They've sat at home, barricaded in, Comrade Major. Scared of spirits."

"I see," said Shatunov. "And who do you think is going to look after the military commanders here? Pushkin? Look sharp, get hold of a Sno-Cat, and get around to the houses! Everybody is to be at their posts within half an hour! Clean linen in all bedrooms! The divisional staff are going to be based here, understand?"

"Very good, Comrade Major. Permission to carry on?"

"Carry on." Shatunov's eyes followed the policemen as they rushed out of the hotel. Then he turned to Orudjev, who all this time had been standing at attention by the counter. "Why haven't you gone? You should be back at the camp."

"There's no diesel fuel, Comrade Major," said Orudjev. "Can't go on without it. The KGB transport stores won't refill us and neither will the police; they haven't enough. They won't even give me any meat for the dogs. They haven't eaten for two days."

"They haven't earned any meat, your dogs, that's why!" said Shatunov. "All right, while they're picking up the hotel staff, you can sit here on guard. Later, I'll issue an order for the diesel fuel. And then out of my sight right away, understand?"

"Very good, Comrade Major."

Shatunov sighed, gazed around the hotel lobby, and went out without a word. His Volga at once shot off toward the airport to meet the paratroop division, and Orudjev and I were left alone in the hotel. I started to climb the stairs to the second floor. Even through my back, I could sense Orudjev's beseeching, doglike gaze. A single gesture on my part, a single turn of the head, and he would have flown up those stairs to my room. But I did not look back. All that had been between us only three days ago in Camp RS-549, stayed there—on the straw mattress in the room where prisoners could meet their close relatives. There it had been one Orudjev, here it was quite another. Let him thank his lucky stars for what had happened.

I went up to my room and turned the key twice in my lock just to be on the safe side. I hadn't strength enough to take a bath. I wrenched my boots off, discarded my sheepskin, pulled off my fur coveralls, and flopped into bed. The last thing I heard was the heavy drone of aircraft way out over the Ob.

31

OPERATIONAL REPORT

Special Military Communication

To: Minister of Defense USSR
    Member of Politburo Central Committee CPSU
    Marshal Dmitry Ustinov

From: Commanded Paratroop Division
      October Revolution General Grinko

In accordance with your orders, today, 12 December 1983, at 16:30 the Paratroop Division October Revolution, consisting of three parachute regiments, two independent armored batallions, and nine helicopter squadrons, disembarked at Salekhard Airport.

After an examination of the strategical situation I decided to surround the town with the military forces at my disposal and tighten the ring gradually, entering the town and searching every house, leaving patrols beyond the town limits, and using observer helicopters.

The division completed the operation by the time Comrade Bogomyatov, first secretary of the Tyumen

Province Party Committee, arrived from Tyumen with his entourage, i.e., 20 hours 40 local time.

As a result of the operation, the following have been arrested:

• 42 traffickers in fruit—all persons of Caucasian origin—present in Salekhard with intent to sell fruit and vegetables brought in from the Caucasus, at black-market prices.

• 39 youths aged 17–18—all persons of Nenets origin—for venturing disparaging remarks during the operation, and other anti-Russian activities.

• 132 prostitutes living in Salekhard without a permit.

• 7 persons of Tartar origin, resembling one of the wanted criminals, to wit T. Zaloyev (all seven subsequently released after careful police inquiries).

Despite meticulous care being taken during the operation, the criminal-murderers were not discovered in Salekhard.

Jointly with the province party leadership from Tyumen and with the assistance of the chiefs of the local KGB, police militia, and CID we are proceeding to widen the sphere of operations across the Yamal-Nenets District.

General V. Grinko

Salekhard, Divisional HQ, North Hotel
12 December 1983
21:30

32

I'd managed to get in exactly three hours of sleep before the hotel was filled with the crashing of army boots and voices issuing military commands. It was the staff of the paratroop division getting settled in.

I got out of bed and took from my rucksack a pair of calf-leather boots, my gray uniform skirt, officer's shirt and tie, and my tunic with its militia lieutenant's epaulets. There was nowhere to iron them, but if I dabbed a bit of water on the creases, my tunic and skirt would hug my figure—a long way from the worst in the world—and everything would be OK.

I got dressed, put my eye makeup on, had a good look at myself in the mirror, and went downstairs to the lobby. So recently empty and quiet, it now resounded with the rumble of male voices, the crackle of radios in constant communication with the helicopters circling above the town, the to and fro of messengers, and that peculiar army smell—a complex mixture of men's sweat, soldiers' pig-leather boots, shag tobacco, and the squeaky leather of officers' shoulder belts.

Far down the lobby, officers of the militia and KGB were questioning those who had been arrested—Georgian and Armenian fruit traffickers, prostitutes, Nenets youngsters, and Tartars who resembled or did not resemble Zaloyev's photo. Many of the young Nentsi were stubbornly refusing to talk to the investigators in Russian.

Aware of the interested eyes of the paratroop officers—my dress uniform hadn't been a waste of time!—I walked the length of the lobby to Major Zotov's table and saluted. "Investigator Kovina present and reporting for duty."

"Had your sleep?" he asked, and, without waiting for an answer, looked at the four arrested persons—three lads and a girl. They were standing in front of his table, narrowing their already slit eyes, pale, scowling.

"Who's been writing 'Russians—Get out of the tundra'?" asked Zotov in Russian.

There was an answering silence. I translated the question into Nenets; in the four years I'd been working on Yamal, I'd become fluent in that rather simple language. I was bound to, although to be honest I'd not once opened *Nenets Fairy Tales and Legends,* which Hudya Benokan had long ago given me as a present.

"You think they don't understand Russian?" Zotov smiled. "The inscriptions are in Russian, no mistakes." He addressed the boys again. "Why have you got knives?"

Silence. I translated the question again.

"Nentsi have always carried knives," the eldest answered me in Nenets. "A Nenets would be lost without a knife in the tundra, however."

Zotov understood the reply perfectly, but asked in Russian nevertheless.

"This is not the tundra, however. This is the town. Why do you need a knife in town?"

Silence.

"The Russians brought you out of the tundra and into boarding school, taught you to read and write, gave you electric light," said Zotov. "Why don't you like Russians? Me, for example?"

"The Russians gave us light and took away the tundra, however," said the youngest, about fourteen, grinning.

"They kidnapped me on the tundra and brought me in to boarding school, the Komsomol, and then the Komsomol secretary wanted to shag me in his study!" said the girl. She would be about sixteen, no more.

This pronouncement was no news to us. Every autumn, before the start of the new academic year, people from the District Education Department went out in helicopters to the Nentsi grazing their reindeer on the most northerly areas of the tundra, close to the Arctic Ocean. Nentsi don't want to part with youngsters older than eight or nine—they're the best hands with the reindeer and around the house. Any ten-year-old Nenets knows how to lasso a wild reindeer, or deliver a reindeer calf, or find a runaway animal on the tundra, and much else besides. So the Education Department people apply a simple method that has stood the test of time: they get the obstinate parents drunk on vodka, both father and mother. After that, they exchange the children for bottles of vodka—one bottle per child.

The youngsters are carried off to boarding schools in Salekhard, Nadym, and Urengoi. There the Komsomol leaders (sometimes non-Komsomol at that) allow themselves to have a little fun with the young Nenets girls. From the legal point of view, even a sixteen-year-old Nenets girl is theoretically below the age of consent, but on the other hand the Nentsi themselves give their daughters in marriage at thirteen, sometimes even eleven! Generally speaking, up till relatively recently, our men had no trouble sleeping with a Nenets girl. Any Siberian who's been around will tell you about the Nenets hospitality ritual: the head of the family would tuck up his own wife in the bed of any Russian visitor staying the night in his choom—a treat. He was even insulted if his "treat" was declined. As recently as fifteen or twenty years ago, women in Nenets settlements, if they saw a helicopter of Russian geologists, would run out to meet them with joyful cries of *"Lyucha** have come, now we'll have some fucking!''

But over recent years the situation has begun to change. It's either because a new generation of more or less literate Nentsi has grown up or because the demand for women has risen incredibly with the influx of hundreds of thousands of single men into the sub-Arctic and the Nenets girls have discovered their market value. Most likely it's a bit of both. Some young girls at the boarding schools have stopped being compliant in this sense. In fact, our town court in Urengoi has several times settled claims for alimony made by underage Nenets mothers against local geologists and engineers!

I glanced at Zotov, wondering how he would react to the sixteen-year-old's statement. Another time he might have tried to find out the name of the corrupt Komsomol secretary who had tried to seduce her in his study. Now he merely gave it up as a bad job.

''All right, let them go. Write her name down and we'll sort it out later.''

I wrote it down on my notepad: "Ayuni Ladukai, 16 years, 8th class, Boarding School No. 3, 9 Gagarin Street.''

*Russians (Nenets).

33

Everything was quiet by the time Bogomyatov arrived at the hotel. Ye gods, the faces of our party leaders have certainly started changing over the last few years! There's no comparison between Andropov, Aliev, and Gorbachev and those who were in the Politburo before. If you did a composite of a typical member of our old governments—put together Khrushchev, Brezhnev, Podgorny, Bulganin, and the rest, whose pictures have followed me since I appeared in the world—you'd get a well-fed, rosy-cheeked face with a double chin. The eyes would be devoid of any hint of intellect, romance, or even basic strength of will. I remember when I was about twelve or thirteen this used to annoy me a lot. For our country, building a new road into the bright future for the whole world, I wanted handsome young men as leaders, like Vyacheslav Tikhonov, the film star who played Prince Bolkonsky in *War and Peace*.

Bogomyatov, first secretary of the Tyumen Province Party Committee, didn't resemble either a prince or a film star. But he was clearly a man of a new mold, *ours*. I mean he's older than me, of course, about fifty, but he doesn't have the Khrushchev-Brezhnev falling-apart look in the face. He has the intelligent, forceful, even harsh face of a leader who knows what he's about. He wasn't wearing the standard short overcoat either;

instead, he had a becomingly fashionable, well-cut sheepskin. With swift steps he and his entourage—the chiefs of the Tyumen Province KGB and police militia—passed through the lobby and went up to the deluxe suite of General Grinko, commander of the paratroop division. There the secretary of the Yamal-Nenets District Committee, Rogov, Major Shatunov, and Colonel Sini were due to report to Bogomyatov on the current situation in Salekhard. Ordinary investigators like us, and that included Zotov, were not invited to this conference, of course.

I had no time to feel annoyance or hurt vanity, however, because into the hotel came Rasim Salakhov. The man was a legend, the geologist who had first discovered oil in western Siberia, twenty-two years before. Salakhov is a separate page in my biography, a special page I should say. Now they make films and write plays about him; now he's the manager of the Tyumen Oil and Gas Trust, Lenin Prize winner and Hero of Socialist Labor. Only eight years ago, though, he had just been the head of the geological expeditions. Our affair then didn't reach the bed stage only because I was an eighteen-year-old idiot, a virgin, all atremble over my innocence. I can still remember that taiga clearing above the Irtish River when the air was heavy with summer heat and the scent of taiga flowers. Salakhov, with typical Caucasian ardor, covered me with his body and I convulsively pressed my legs together, whispering in shame, "Anywhere but there! Anywhere but there, please!"

Of course, if I'd been brought up somewhere like Moscow or Paris, that stupid stopper wouldn't have been there—in any event, by the age of eighteen, it wouldn't have been there anymore. But it was my first year at Moscow University and I was still the provincial girl from Voronezh with the powerful volleyball player's legs. So Salakhov didn't go in "there," something I think I haven't forgiven him for yet. All the rest did happen between us; in fact, I was half-dead with desire myself and with my hands held his hot prick to me, touching all around my fuzzy maidenhead.

Having come on my belly, Salakhov calmed down, laughing at my "daftness" and, possibly to distract himself from another onset of desire, started telling me the story of the discovery of Tyumen oil and gas.

During those feverish white summer nights, in my confusion of thoughts and desires, I scarcely listened to him and remembered nothing apart from isolated episodes in his adventures over twenty years in the wild Siberian taiga and the Nenets tundra. Apparently as long ago as the 1930s, the celebrated academic geologist Gubkin had predicted the presence of oil in Siberia. On the basis of certain resemblances between the geological structure of the west Siberian platform and other oil-bearing regions of the world, he calculated that there ought to be oil in the taiga. But where should searches be made? That the academician did not know. But Siberia is vast, the Yamal-Nenets National District alone is larger than France. And Salekhard is not Paris; the taiga and tundra can't be compared with the Bois de Boulogne and its neat gravel paths.

Geological parties wandered through the impenetrable wilderness for thirty years, drowning in the summer bogs and freezing in the polar night. For thirty years the state threw money away on exploratory boreholes that yielded nothing apart from refutations of the celebrated academician's theory. Among these failed geologists was the twenty-three-year-old Rasim Salakhov from Baku. On his chestnut stallion Kasbek, he wandered through the taiga and the tundra, feeding the mosquitoes with his young blood, falling into swamps, fighting with his workmen—former criminals, of course, who else worked on taiga expeditions in those days? With true Caucasian stubbornness, he squeezed out enough money in Moscow to equip new expeditions.

In 1960, however, all this came to an end. The Ministry of Geology halted oil prospecting in Siberia as being completely hopeless. The last geologists abandoned the taiga. Autumn navigation barges ferried out drilling rigs and the rest of the bulky oil-prospecting equipment. There was only one drilling derrick they couldn't manage to get out—ice had gripped the tundra river Plotva. Salakhov kept the Moscow evacuation order a secret from his workpeople and sank a last borehole near Surgut—but nowhere near where the geologists had said it should be.

"You see," he told me in his Caucasian accent, "oil is lighter than water, and geologists had always found it in the anticlines of oil-bearing strata. But here there was no oil in the anticlines. For thirty years people drilled bores into those domes and no oil, no nothing! But at least a century ago the Nentsi had seen 'greasy patches' on the lakes. They reckoned it was the 'earth sweating.' But that was oil, oil! Well, so I decided to go against the rules and not drill into the domes, but at the very base of the anticline.

"Five months the drilling went on; imagine, five months! In winter, with no wages, no bread, we just ate venison. I don't know how many times the workers wanted to murder me—I had some canisters of liquor and I swapped it for reindeer meat from the Nentsi. Well, the workmen wanted the booze as well—the whole lot at once. In March 1961 the bore exploded in an oil gusher, the drilling rig collapsed, and such a torch of burning oil roared out over the tundra that six Nenets camps up and bolted while we jigged around the blaze and rubbed oil over each other. Now they want to make a film of it all; some writer flew out from Moscow to see me. They'll never do it like it really was! They'll never put on the screen that I was held by the KGB for six months while they tried to pin sabotage charges on me asking who gave me permission to set fire to the oil, national property!''

We sat there above the Irtish, Salakhov smiling bitterly as he remembered the past and I smoothing his curly hair, black but with a hint of gray, kissing his prickly mustache. In a few minutes we were rolling around again among the fire flowers and willow herb. When it came to sex, however, Salakhov was not so invincibly persevering as he had been searching for Siberian oil, and I left my first student practice a virgin. Two years later the film about Salakhov, *The Land of the Long Winter,* was released, and then there was a play, but neither film nor play, of course, contained the KGB episode. Either the writer had been scared to put it in, or the censor had cut it out.

Another two years after that, I got my law diploma and requested a posting to Tyumen Province not without romantic daydreaming. When I arrived in Tyumen, I discovered that Salakhov was now the chief geologist of western Siberia, head of the Tyumen Oil and Gas Trust, Lenin Prize laureate. How could I, just one out of thousands arriving in the taiga in those days, fight my way through to such giddy heights of authority? And what reason could I state to get an appointment? Report to him that I was no longer a virgin, but that I'd dreamed dozens of times in the students' hostel at Moscow University of being with him in that clearing above the Irtish, filled with fire flowers and willow herb?

I spent a week in Tyumen, striding around like a complete fool under the windows of Tyumen Oil and Gas all my nonworking hours. I was rewarded by a glimpse of Salakhov arriving at the trust in his personal Volga. He walked into the building three paces from me, hurrying as usual. Of course he didn't notice me, with all those passersby! And no doubt there had been plenty of probationers in those clearings with him after me, and not so stubborn either. After all, Salakhov was now a celebrity, hero of stage and screen. I applied that very day to the Tyumen Province police chief requesting a transfer to some newly built tundra settlement as far as possible from Tyumen.

And now the romantic hero of my girlish dreams was walking into the lobby of the North Hotel. Short sheepskin coat, tan trousers beneath a fur coverall, dog-fur boots, and the same stiffly curly hair, now completely gray and beautifully barbered, above dark Caucasian eyes. A number of people, evidently from Tyumen, were coming in after him, but I only had eyes for Salakhov. A sort of oppressively warm wave of tenderness and sadness swept over me from head to foot.

*"An torovo, hasava!"** was his loud and cheerful greeting to one and all. "Well now, are these tundra spirits giving you a hard time?"

Of course, only Salakhov could permit himself to joke in a situation like this! He was at once surrounded by the heads of the local geological authorities, who had wandered in here under various pretexts, but really for the protection of the paratroopers. He shook hands with them, joked, clapped someone on the shoulder, and then caught sight of me in a gap between the figures. For several oppressively long seconds he looked into my eyes, then abruptly moved someone aside and walked straight toward me. It seemed to me that in those moments his gaze caressed my hair, shoulders, eyes.

"Anya?" he said as he came up.

Close to him, I could see how he had grown older. Wrinkles and furrows had creased his brow and face. In his eyes lay the deep weariness of an aging man.

"What on earth are you doing here?" I asked quietly.

"It is Anya, isn't it?" he asked again, switching his

*Hello, friends (Nenets).

astonished gaze from my face to my militia lieutenant's uniform.

"Yes, I'm Anya. I'm an investigator now. But what are *you* doing here?"

He seemed to understand what lay behind my question.

"I?" he said cheerily for the whole lobby to hear. "I'm just getting a bit closer to the Nenets spirits. I mean, if they're castrating the people who discovered oil and gas here, they should have started with me! The point is, I want to take a walk by myself around Salekhard. Just to show there's no such thing as these ridiculous tundra spirits, and put an end to the panic. People have stopped work all over the Yamal. But you can keep me company if you like. I don't think a woman will frighten the spirits off. Will you?"

"What do you mean? Are you serious?"

"Of course I am!" he added softly. "None of my expeditions have been operating for three days. People are on the run from Urengoi, Tarko-Sale, Nadym. Imagine what that means! Are you coming?"

I shrugged. Perhaps he was right. Maybe if they wanted the panic to stop, the top people shouldn't really be hiding in here under the wing of the paras, they should be out on the streets. But only Salakhov could hit on the idea; tomorrow, the word would go around the whole territory that Salakhov *himself* had strolled through Salekhard freely and without any bodyguard— and no "spirits" had laid a finger on him. This would bring Russians and Nentsi to their senses.

As an atheist, I've got no time for mystical nonsense, and anyway, when you've got a good hundred of our gallant paratroop officers around you, the devil himself wouldn't scare you, even if his existence were scientifically proved. So Salakhov and I left the hotel as if we were on a lyrical stroll—accompanied by jokes from those present.

"Have you got your pistol with you?" asked Salakhov in the doorway.

"Yes."

"Leave it here."

"Why?"

"Leave it, I said."

I pulled my TT out of its holster and, in front of paras, investigators, geologists, and the youthful Nenets prisoners, I handed it over to Salakhov.

"Ah, the purity of the experiment above all!" said one of the geologists. "But we should check to see if Salakhov has got his male tool with him!"

Out on the street in front of the hotel, the engines of the paratroopers' personnel carriers were wreathed in gray exhaust fumes. Beyond them, though, the street was empty and dead. The frost nipped at our faces, and the snow crunched under our feet.

"Scared?"

"I should think not," I lied, because in fact the farther we got from the hotel, the more uncomfortable I felt inside. I believe I began to understand those people who had so easily panicked. You can be an atheist a hundred times over, but when you're face to face with a dead, frozen town in the dark of the polar night, every rustle, every dog coming around the corner can seem like a ghost, a murderer, a tundra spirit.

"OK," said Salakhov, taking my arm. "Tell me about yourself. How long have you been in Salekhard?"

"This is my second day. Actually, I work in Urengoi. Four years now."

"And never phoned once, never stopped in. You married?"

"No."

We let a patrolling armored car pass along the road; then I asked, "Are *you* married?"

"Yes, I've got three children already. Making up for lost time. You frozen?"

I was disappointed but not crushed by the news. "Not yet. . . . Look!"

An extraordinary display of northern lights had begun above the town and the tundra. It doesn't matter how many times you've seen it, there's no getting used to a sight like that. The dark sky suddenly seemed to fly up from the earth—up, up, and up! And at every corner of this huge and instantly luminous heaven appeared broad, shining, ghostly-icy, multicolored bands of flickering fire. They resembled shining ribbons fluttering across the sky, constantly changing altitude, tone, and color. And all this in total silence, soundless, as if it really were what the Nentsi say, the spirits of the dead flying through the sky.

The changing hues of lifeless light illuminated the squat, snowbound houses of Salekhard, its dark dead streets, and, directly in front of us, on the wall of some official building, a large red poster bearing the legend THE RICHES OF THE TUNDRA—FOR OUR BELOVED HOMELAND! The poster was of the standard type; beneath the slogan was a picture of a young workman with a clear and open Russian face. He stood against a tundra backdrop, with oil derricks scattered over the landscape. The workman's face had been disfigured in the usual obscene manner: a bleeding penis had been drawn onto his mouth. In rough, uneven lettering the inscription read: RUSSIANS— OUT OF THE TUNDRA!

Salakhov inspected the poster in silence.

From around the corner came a sudden rush of feet, voices—low as if stifled—and the sound of muffled blows. Salakhov and I wordlessly raced in that direction to see what was happening.

Under the northern lights, beneath the window of a workingmen's hostel, about ten Russian workers were beating up a Nenets. The latter was a short fellow, in all probability drunk—he didn't cry out and was putting up no resistance. Wrapped in his thick reindeer *malitsa,* he kept falling down like a sack under the blows, but they pulled him up again and hit him with savage enjoyment, using fists and feet. The shapes of approving spectators stood at the hostel windows.

As Salakhov and I ran up, the crowd took us for their own and stood aside for us to do our bit. But Salakhov didn't start hitting the Nenets, of course. He seized somebody by the collar and asked brusquely, "What's up?"

"Nothing! Thump him!" The workman tore Salakhov's hand from his coat collar and rushed toward the Nenets again. The rest meanwhile kept on hitting him. Someone held the Nenets up by the *malitsa* so he wouldn't fall over.

"Stop it!"

Amazed by my feminine voice (in winter clothes, a woman can easily be mistaken for a man here), they let the Nenets go for a moment, and he fell like a sack of potatoes.

"What's he done?" asked Salakhov.

"Ah, nothing! He's a Nenets, shit! We'll show them tundra spirits now!" And the speaker slammed his boot full force into the recumbent Nenets.

At the same second Salakhov slashed the workman with his fist, so that he fell onto the ice-covered pavement with his legs kicking in the air.

"What're you hitting your own for, bastard?" The rest rushed toward Salakhov, and I at once regretted leaving my pistol in the hotel.

"Stop! This is—Salakhov!" I shouted at them.

"We don't give a shit for Salakhov or whoever he is! We were beating up a Nenets, why the fuck's he interfering? We're going to squash the lot of them now, the shits. With tanks—our troops have arrived!"

The legendary name of Salakhov, however, familiar to every worker in the tundra, restrained their knotted fists.

"Are you really Salakhov, *the* Salakhov?" someone asked, calmer now.

"*The* Salakhov," he brought out, lifting the Nenets from the ground. His eyes were closed; the broad face with its prominent cheekbones was smashed, and a thin fountain of blood had spurted from his mouth. His head lolled forward on his chest like a doll's.

"You've killed him," said Salakhov, lowering the Nenets to the ground.

"Well, fuck him!" said the one Salakhov had knocked down. He was now on his feet. "One yellow bastard less, who cares!"

But he didn't manage to finish the phrase. A blow from Salakhov flush on the teeth made him choke off the last word and crash into the road next to the dead Nenets.

"What's up, chief, have you gone fucking crazy?" asked one of the workmen, astonished. He pointed at the man Salakhov had twice struck. "What's he done to you?"

"I'm a 'yellow bastard' too!" Salakhov shouted at them and, for the first time in my life, I saw a furious Caucasian. He walked toward them. "I'm an Azerbaijani! To you Russian pigs, I'm a yellow bastard, like that Nenets! Well, who's going to hit me, eh?"

"Come on, all right, all right, chief, cool down!" They were backing off and turning away from his fists. "Nobody means you. Nobody's touched you."

But if I hadn't intervened and hung onto Salakhov, he would have provoked them into another fight. It was no problem for me to restrain him. I had been taught in the police how to grab a man from behind so that he can't move.

"You cheap bastards! Strong if you've got tanks." Salakhov was struggling to be free and suddenly shouted at me, "Let me go, dammit, Russian idiot!"

I shuddered as if I'd been slapped, and let him go.

He turned and spoke to me face to face. "Should

have fucked you that time, no pity! All of you should be . . .'' He went off without finishing. Again, I regretted leaving my pistol in the hotel. But I would hardly have dared to shoot at him, Salakhov! Besides, at that moment, the echo of another explosion rolled out over Salekhard.

34

On the evening of 12 December, after operational
units of our division had entered Salekhard, local
workingmen in a drunken state began to seek out
and assault Nentsi. Six cases of fatal assault were
registered, and 23 of grievous bodily harm . . .

At 22 hours 17 minutes local time, a twelve-year-
old Nenets, a pupil of Boarding School No. 3, Vauli
Litkoi, set fire to a personnel carrier parked near
the North Hotel by dipping a smoldering bundle of
reindeer hide in the gas tank. The explosion dam-
aged the hotel building. Seven soldiers and two of-
ficers were wounded.

Immediately after this, assaults on Nentsi became
extremely widespread.

35

We ran up to the North Hotel before the powdered snow raised by the explosion had had time to settle. Fragments of the destroyed personnel carrier were still burning at various points on the roadway, along with the placard: THE PARTY—MIND, CONSCIENCE, AND HONOR OF OUR EPOCH, which had tumbled off the hotel facade. The pale faces of the party leaders peered out of the shattered hotel windows as soldiers hauled the wounded indoors.

In the lobby paratroopers, geologists, and police stood in a dense crowd by a sofa on which lay a mortally wounded Nenets boy, twelve years of age. I pushed through the crowd after Salakhov. The boy's shoulder and side had been mangled by splinters from the destroyed vehicle. His tattered old *malitsa* was drenched in blood. The paratroop medical officer stood up and waved the stretcher-bearers away: no one could help the boy now. The last signs of life were quickly fading from the broad face with its high cheekbones. Hudya, however, kneeling in front of the boy, cried, "Why? Why did you do this? Who put you up to it?"

The boy opened his narrow eyes and, or so it seemed to me, even smiled slightly.

"Vauli . . ." he replied softly.

"Vauli who?"

The boy was clearly gathering his breath to answer. We froze.

"Vauli Piettomin," he brought out. "He has come."

One of the paratroop officers next to me asked, "Who's this Vauli? One of the escapees?"

"He's their national hero," said Zotov. "Like Spartacus. Two hundred years ago he raised a rebellion against the Russian czar. He was caught, escaped from forced labor, fomented another rising, and was killed. But the Nentsi believe he will return."

"And the other two explosions—was that you?" Hudya asked the boy.

"Us . . . ," sighed the boy, and in that *us,* there was pride.

"But why? Why?" Hudya cried out again in despair.

"Because I . . . ," the boy got out in a feeble voice. "I am Vauli. But you . . ." Here, with his last reserves of energy, he was clearly intent on spitting in Hudya's face. His strength failed him though—the bloody spittle froze on his lips and his eyes closed. The doctor took his hand and felt the pulse.

"All over," he pronounced after a few seconds.

Hudya rose and surveyed us all with his narrow eyes, now almost white. He seemed about to shout something at us, or say something. But without uttering a sound, he walked with the slow, heavy, waddling gait of all Nentsi through the crowd, which made way for him, and out the hotel door into the street.

In the ensuing silence the words of the duty staff officer sounded crisp and clear. Clutching a number of radio messages in his hand, he went up to the paratroop commander, General Grinko, saluted and said, "Comrade General, permission to report. Aircraft have observed three drilling sites on fire in tundra regions Anaguri, Nugma, and Yunarta. None of the three have responded to radio calls."

Three sites on fire! At any other time, even one fire would have been enough to set off a general commotion, but now the news made no special impact on us. Only Shatunov sighed and said, "It's started. This is what I've been afraid of."

Lakes Anaguri, Nugma, and Yunarta lay at widely separated points on the Yamal peninsula, three hundred, even four hundred kilometers to the north of Salekhard, so there could be no thought of the escaping prisoners being responsible for the fires. They had only lit the fuse of Nenets hatred for us Russians, bottled up for centuries.

I saw Salakhov go pale and approach General Grinko. "Connect me to your airmen, the ones who can see the fires."

"Why?" asked the general.

"If it's only the derricks ablaze, that's not so bad. If there's been a gas blowout . . ."

"I think we'd better get out there in any case," said the general and turned to a youthful colonel. "Scramble three squadrons on operational alert!"

36

Anybody might envy the efficiency of the paras in action. Within minutes the military helicopters had taken off from Salekhard Airport and set course for Anaguri, Nugma, and Yunarta. At the same time, three enormous Mi-10 helicopters landed close to the hotel, right on the snow-covered wooden roadway; they picked up the investigation team and all possible top brass, including Shatunov, Salakhov, and Zotov. I wasn't in any of the teams investigating the fires. Zotov hid his eyes as he said to me, "Kiddy-wink, you've worn yourself out these last few days. Besides, it's urgent that we find out who's been spreading rumors among the Nentsi that their Piettomin's come back."

"You've got Hudya Benokan for that," I answered, furious. "It's his field, let him do the job. Especially as he's a Nenets."

"I don't trust him," said Zotov.

"You don't?"

"You saw how he was when that kid died? No, it's better if you deal with these Vauli rumors. Who's spreading them? Why? Go around the schools; you can speak the language. The children will talk better to a woman."

Of course, the assignment was an excuse for not taking me to the fires. It was obvious that they were more serious crimes than a boy setting fire to an army vehicle, so us men will deal with that, you stay in Salekhard and do a bit of snooping on the Nentsi.

Zotov apparently read all this in my eyes. "If there's anything interesting at the fires, I'll send for you, kiddy-wink, honestly!"

I snorted contemptuously and went back into the hotel and up to my room.

Once there I plunked myself down on the bed and began to bawl. Not because Zotov hadn't taken me with him to investigate the reason for the fires, but because of what had happened between Salakhov and me two hours ago. I couldn't have a good cry anyway, because frost was blowing in through the window, which had been smashed in the explosion. I got up and wiped away my tears as I walked over to shove a cushion in the window. Outside, the last Mi-10 was taking off, its engines roaring. Bastards, the lot of them, bastards—Zotov, Salakhov, Hudya, the whole blasted lot!

I opened my duffle bag and drew out my emergency store—a bottle of Stolichnaya vodka—poured out half a glass, and tossed it down.

Now I could do Zotov's bidding. The twelve-year-old Vauli Litkoi who set the personnel carrier alight had been a pupil at Boarding School No. 3.

I took out my notepad. Ayuni Ladukai, the sixteen-year-old girl who had told me and Zotov that some Komsomol secretary had tried to rape her, was at the same school. All right, it was a perfectly good pretext for paying this Ayuni a visit and taking a look around the school at the same time.

37

A fat little puppy dog, stumbling around on uncertain legs, came running joyfully toward me from along the corridor as soon as I opened the door of Boarding School No. 3. In the corridor, half-filled with battered school desks and children's boots, *malitsas*, and coats, a boy's voice, high and breaking, echoed and re-echoed:

> And like wolf packs on their quarry
> There came streaming like a river,
> Russian hordes upon our homeland,
> Pushing us away to northward,
> Far off to the Icy Ocean,
> Stripping us of all our pastures,
> All our rivers, all our fishing,
> Beasts and fowl and all our reindeer,
> Everywhere intent to ravish
> Wives and sisters and our daughters. *

"So-o-o! Some poem!" I thought as I closed the outer door. Carefully, so as not to step on the silly pup or knock against the stuff piled up in the corridor, I

*Here and on the following pages are genuine verses from "Yangal-Maa," a nineteenth-century Nenets ballad. It was only published once in Russia, in 1933.

moved along the corridor toward the classroom from which the boy's voice was coming.

> *Hear us, hear us, Lord Almighty—*
> *This the voice of all thy peoples,*
> *All thy peoples now in bondage,*
> *Worn out by the weary burden—*
> *By the battle never ending*
> *To sustain a bare existence.*

I glanced in at the partly opened door. It was a normal school classroom, but with all its desks apparently thrown out into the corridor. The blackboard remained though, and on it was chalked: RUSSIAN OCCUPIERS— OUT!

A short, slit-eyed boy of about thirteen was standing beneath the blackboard, holding a copy of the book Hudya had given to me—*Nenets Fairy Tales and Legends.* He was reading from memory, however, not looking at the book.

> *Well thou knowest Lord Almighty,*
> *How the strangers came among us*
> *Into our beloved homeland*
> *Came the Rus with fire of cannon,*
> *Came with ax and deadly poison*
> *In he came with priests of cunning*
> *Rus came thieving—took with iron,*
> *Priest—with cross and honeyed speeches.*

The most remarkable thing in that classroom, however, was not the boy-reciter or even the blasphemously defaced portrait of Lenin on the wall. It was the audience. They were sitting on the floor, densely packed together—about two hundred people; there were children eight to ten years old and young people of sixteen, seventeen, or eighteen. They wore reindeer *yagushka* unbuttoned in the heat and had long hair, broad cheekbones, slit eyes. Their figures were bent toward the reader in what seemed to be one concerted movement. Their eyes were riveted upon him.

> *Then the Russian war detachments*
> *Conquered us with swords of iron,*
> *Did away with all our elders*
> *Put in posts of power above us*
> *Many bloodsuckers and bandits*
> *Holding court, dispensing justice,*
> *Taking from us furs in tribute*
> *And dishonoring our women!*
> *These days all our wives in childbirth*
> *Bear us feeble, breeding weaklings,*
> *Like the seventh pup, the last one,*
> *Born in an old bitch's litter—*
> *Far too weak to rise in anger*
> *Strike for freedom.*

At this point, the indescribable took place. A savagely angry cry of ''No-o-o!'' rose suddenly from every throat. Part of the audience leapt up in fury; somebody rushed toward the declaiming boy, seized the book from his hand, tore out the page, and angrily ripped it into pieces, shouting, ''That's it! Enough! That was before. Now—that's it! Read on from here!'' He showed the boy another page.

The boy raised his hand for quiet, but the hall still seethed with angry exclamations. Then, like an experienced orator, the boy said quite quietly:

> ''Nut i shar''—*the bear's my witness!*
> *I would wish that every Nenets*
> *Shout out loud with voice triumphant:*
> *''Death to the insidious strangers! . . .*
> *''Nut i shar!''*

By the end of the first two lines, the hall had fallen silent, and after "Death to the insidious strangers" had been pronounced calmly and harshly, the audience spoke in one voice with the boy:

> "Nut 1 shar!" *The bear's my witness!*
> *Yamal will one day see its peoples*
> *Seize again their ancient freedom!*
> "Nut i shar!"

They leapt to their feet, eyes blazing, their broad faces alight. Among them I recognized Ayuni Ladukai. Of course, any heart-to-heart talk with her was now out of the question; she was swearing along with the rest:

> "Nut i shar!" *The bear's my witness!*
> *Times of terror! Keep your courage!*
> *Death will be here, fire and famine;*
> *From the old crone's scarlet death grin,*
> *Like a pack of wolves in panic,*
> *Leaving all, from tundra flying,*
> *People running for the mountains—*
> *Russian people from destruction!*
> "Nut i shar!"

About the loud chorus rose the high, breaking voice of the reciting boy:

> "Nut i shar!" *The bear's my witness!*
> *I can see the glow of fires,*
> *Smell the burning, night draws nearer,*
> *Smoke in clouds blots out the heavens*
> *As the hated Russian bandits*
> *Flee in terror from our forests!*

He seemed to have gone into a trance, a shaman's ecstasy. His whole body shaking; he shouted forth his prophecies:

RED SNOW

"Nut i shar!" The bear's my witness!
After this will come the dawning
Of an age that's new and other
Time of justice and of freedom
From the God-accursed Russians!

"A tambourine! Fetch him a tambourine!   someone shouted.

A youth sitting by the door jumped up and rushed into the corridor and . . . stumbled over me. I had no time either to jump to one side or to hide behind the door—I was discovered, and for a second everything went silent and still, as in a pause in the theater. But in the next instant they had recognized me and the roar of voices shook the school: "Russian! Spy! Bloodhound! Grab her!"

The older boys, around eighteen, flung themselves on me. Their narrow eyes made me realize that this was no place for joking or for words. I grabbed my pistol. "Stop! Or I'll fire!"

The boys halted.

I began to step slowly back toward the corridor.

But the corridor was obstructed by broken desks and other school equipment; it was hard to back off in a straight line. Suddenly from behind the backs of the senior boys rang out the voice of the boy-reciter, who was walking directly up to me.

Go on, shoot, yes, shoot, you bastard!
Nenets oil is not sufficient?
Nenets fish are not sufficient?
Let my blood then flow in rivers
Nut i shar! Then shoot, you bastard!

He was clearly in the same kind of trance that Nenets shamans at one time induced in themselves. But I couldn't shoot a boy. I turned away and ran toward the exit.

A leather lasso caught me just by the door; the noose lashed around my neck. Well, those Nenets youngsters know from childhood how to bring down a healthy bull reindeer at full gallop. I felt a sharp tug as if my throat had been cut, and I lost consciousness as I collapsed.

38

"I can see the glow of fires"—this prophecy of the little shaman from Boarding School No. 3 came true that night with frightening swiftness.

From Urgent Report of Party Commission for Elimination of Disorder in the Yamal-Nenets District to the Soviet Government and Politburo of the Central Committee of the CPSU

It was not possible to approach the drilling sites or execute a parachute drop: at all three sites gas flares are burning to a height of between 700 and 1,000 feet, with a diameter of between 150 and 300 feet. For a radius of 1,200 to 2,000 feet around the flares, the permafrost has melted, as have the swamps and lakes. An aerial survey of the burning sites showed that all equipment, including the derricks, has been destroyed and the site workers either killed in the fire or drowned in the melted permafrost and swamps.

Owing to the intensity of the flares, the investigation teams are not in a position to determine how the fires were started or by whom. However, the premeditated character of the fires is shown by their simultaneous incidence in widely separated parts of the Yamal tundra. At 4:15 in the morning, information was received concerning similar fires at drilling sites in the region of Lake Mirigi, the river Haide, and near Kamenni settlement.

Geological specialists have calculated that each minute the burning fountains are consuming thousands of cubic meters of gas, but the flares can only be extinguished by drilling inclined boreholes to conduct gas away from the vents that are on fire. Drilling shafts of this nature will take no less than three to four months.

Simultaneously with the fires, a mass flight of workmen from the tundra has been observed, which has resulted in a cessation of drilling operations, the freezing of the clay compound in boreholes, and twenty-two drilling sites being put out of action. Daily losses are being estimated in millions of rubles and rumors of the "white terror of the tundra" are threatening to paralyze the entire Russian population in the territory, provoke uprisings in the labor camps, and prevent the gas pipeline Siberia–Western Europe from becoming operational.

According to the heads of the local KGB and police militia, the arson is being carried out by the native inhabitants of the territory—the Nentsi, influenced by rumors of the return of Vauli Piettomin, who twice led the Nenets people in uprisings against the Russians in the last century. The possibility cannot be excluded, however, that the escape of the three prisoners from Camp RS-549, the brutal murders of pipe-laying and geosurvey chiefs, the explosions in Salekhard, and the firing of the drilling sites are all a planned operation by American intelligence aiming to disrupt the Siberia–Western Europe gas pipeline project.

Bearing the above in mind, the Party Commission suggests that the Paratroop Division October Revolution by itself is *patently insufficient* to restore order speedily throughout the district. The commis-

sion judges that to prevent a total revolt of the Ne-
nets population and the spread of such a revolt to
the Khanty-Mansi, Taimir, Evenki, and other
neighboring districts populated by northern na-
tional minorities and also to prevent uprisings in
labor camps and the threat of the destruction of the
gas pipeline and gas enterprises *it is essential for
additional military units to be transferred to the Ya-
mal-Nenets District immediately and to occupy all,
repeat all, inhabited points in the district with these
forces, to prohibit all movement across Yamal on
the part of the local population.*

>President of the Party Commission,
>First Secretary Tyumen Province
>Party Committee
>V. Bogomyatov

*Salekhard, 13 December 1983
5:00 local time*

39

I regained consciousness to a familiar combination of pain and pleasure. Next to me, literally by my ear, a tambourine was beating loudly and rhythmically, and, in time to the beat, a man was forcibly entering my body, producing both pain and sexual languor. I automatically wriggled my body to escape my assailant and only then realized what was taking place.

I was lying absolutely naked on some sort of table; my arms, legs, and head were roughly bound to this table with narrow leather thongs, my eyes were heavily bandaged, and I was gagged. I could not move or shout and couldn't see who was violating me. Only the weight on my body and the fact that the emission occurred very quickly told me it was a boy of about fifteen.

"Next!" said a girl's voice in Nenets.

I was horrified: surely they weren't all here, the whole school, girls as well?

The next boy came into me and, ignoring the tambourine rhythm, finished literally in a few seconds—probably aged 12.

"Next!"

Now something enormous, like an elephant's cock, was forcing its way into me, literally tearing my insides apart. My shriek must have penetrated through the gag. The pain, however, subsided as instantly as it had begun; my violator spurted the scalding liquid of his sperm into me even before he had fully entered.

"Next!"

And all of a sudden, through the incessant rapping of the tambourine, a quiet boy's voice, the familiar voice of the boy-reciter. "I don't want to," he said, in Nenets.

"What!" the girlish voice screeched in indignation.

"I won't do it, however."

"Ah, fuck you!" swore the girlish voice in pure Russian. "But Russian men can fuck *us*? I've already had two abortions! They sent Okka to the next world! But you, you cowardly son of a crow, scared to touch a Russian woman. Now then, where's your *khote*? Soon you'll be able to manage anything, however. I sure learned a lot from those Russians!"

I didn't see what happened next; I only heard general laughter and the steady beat of the tambourine. In half a minute, no more, the next boy's *khote* entered my body and spent itself at once.

"Next!"

I swore to myself that if I survived, I would kill that little girl. The others as well, but her first.

The beat of the tambourine was bursting my brain.

Yet another almost instant injection of sperm. I'd already lost count.

Actually, it was this inability of the boys to sustain sexual activity for long that saved me that evening from severe injury or, as they put it in forensic medical reports, "damage to internal organs." The youngsters simply spurted the load they had been accumulating in their scrotums, swollen by the erotic dreams boys have; the table under my buttocks was very wet already. No doubt the moisture had even dripped onto the floor. I suddenly heard a muffled blow and a squeal of protest from a puppy as it flew off out of the way. The same girl's voice gave instructions. "Get rid of the dog, however! Otherwise, it'll get used to licking up sperm!''

The tambourine banged.

The next *khote* entered my body.

Close by my ear, the girl's voice sounded. ''Well, Russian bitch? How do you like it, however? That's the way you've been fucking us for three hundred years now. Nice? Me as well they . . .''

She did not finish. There was a distant opening of doors, the tramp of running feet, and a voice—the voice of Hudya Benokan!

''Stop this!'' he bawled.

The tambourine became silent.

I couldn't see what was happening. The one thing I realized was that belated salvation had arrived; I could let myself go and sink into oblivion. It would have been even better, I thought, if I could have lost consciousness an hour ago, so that I wouldn't have to know that Hudya, who had been head over heels in love with me five years back, was seeing me naked and tied to a table, raped by a bunch of schoolboys.

But I did not lose consciousness. I waited for the boys to race off at the sound of Hudya's voice, but that didn't happen either. All I felt was my hands, head, and legs being freed from the thongs. Hudya, moving around the table, cut each set with one swift movement of his sharp knife. While he was at it, he shouted, ''Why? Why did you do this? You'll all go to jail, the lot of you!''

Sensing that my body was now clear of the straps, I turned over on one side, crossed my legs, and curled up tight. Hudya drew the gag out of my mouth and cut through the bandage around my eyes. I didn't cry out or weep—I was trembling violently and in dire need of a drink. But I was too weak even to ask for water. I didn't want to open my eyes either. I didn't want to see, to know, to live.

But all the same, I saw and heard.

RED SNOW

That sixteen-year-old Ayuni Ladukai, whom Zotov and I had interrogated in the hotel lobby, went up to Hudya and said in that voice which I would never mistake for any other in the world, "We were avenging Okka! You're not a man—you can't take revenge on the Russians yourself. Just the opposite, you serve them like a faithful hound, however! Tfu!"

I don't know who her spit was aimed at, me or Hudya. Probably both of us. But I clearly recall that Hudya made no reply to her. He bent down to retrieve my clothes scattered on the floor and glanced in my holster. It was empty.

"Give her pistol back!" he said harshly—so harshly, in fact, that one of the boys gave him my pistol without argument. Hudya replaced it in the holster, then, wrapping me in my sheepskin, lifted me and carried me out of the school into the street.

"And we're not scared of Russian courts!" someone yelled after us. "There're no prisons beyond the tundra, anyway!"

The thirty-degree frost burned my lungs and froze my knees, which were sticking out from under my coat. But it cleared my head, and I revived. I burst out crying and buried my head in Hudya's chest. Still holding me in his arms, he quickened his pace.

There was no one on the empty street—Salekhard seemed dead and frozen.

40

Hudya took me to his place—he lived three blocks from the school, on the second floor of a concrete building raised on piles. His tiny one-room flat was clean, with reindeer skins on the floor and books lining every wall. There was no furniture whatsoever, just the skins on the floor, as in a Nenets wigwam. Instead of a hearth, no doubt, a homemade Dutch stove stood in the middle of the room, with a metal pipe leading out through a window.

Hudya bore me into the bathroom, sat me down on a little stool, turned on the hot water in the shower, and left, closing the door behind him. I threw off my sheepskin and forced myself to get up and step into the shower. I didn't have the strength to stand, however; I sat down in the bathtub and listened and listened to the warming, reviving water flowing and flowing over my skin. I sat motionless, like a mummy, an idol. Just the tears poured unbidden from my eyes. The water washed them from my face.

After about ten minutes Hudya knocked on the door.

I made no reply, didn't even budge. I felt utterly indifferent; it was as if I were stupefied and totally deaf and blind.

He opened the bathroom door and saw me motionless under the shower in the overflowing bathtub, just sitting and silently crying. He started washing me with soap and a cloth, talking to me softly. "Never mind. Never mind, however. Forget about it. It never happened. Shall I tell you a fairy story? One of ours, Nenets. About how a little mouse talked with the whole world. Listen, then. A little mouse had a hole right on the bend of the river. In spring the sun came into the sky at last and began to warm the whole earth. The snow began to melt on the ground and the ice on the river. And ice floes floated down the river and ran into one another with such a crashing, it was like thunder or someone firing a rifle, however. The little mouse got frightened and came out of his hole and said, 'Hey, ice floes, float away! You'll break my house down!' At this, the ice floes spoke up. 'Hey, little mouse, what are you talking about? We're ice floes! If we're going down a river, nobody can stop us and nobody can tell us where to float! If there are mouseholes in our way, we'll break down mouseholes as well!' Now the little mouse said, 'Hey, ice floes, who do you think you are, however? Throw you on the bank and the sun melts you.''

I knew this Nenets fairy tale, they often broadcast it on the radio. The little mouse talks in turn with the ice floes, the sun, the clouds, the mountains, and so on, defending his hole. Now the tale had taken on a secondary meaning—about the crushing passage of the ice floes, which nothing could now stop. The thought kept coming and going, fading and losing itself in the rim of consciousness—most likely because Hudya's warm, slightly hoarse voice and rough, hairy hands so cautiously touching my back and shoulder blades made me feel cozy in a poignant sort of way, as in childhood. And I really surprised myself when I suddenly turned my head, caught his hand on my shoulder, and pressed my cheek against it. I used to press my father's hand against my shoulder like that when I was a child.

"What made you come into the boarding school?"
I asked.

"I was going around to all the boarding schools. Our children had been left without supervision; all the teachers had run away. I wanted to tell the children to stop blowing up cars and armored trucks."

"Where is your daughter?"

"She's in the tundra, staying with my parents."

Later, wrapped in a sheet, I lay on the floor in his room, on reindeer skins, covered by the hide of a polar bear. Hudya didn't have a bed. Like all Nentsi, he still preferred sleeping on the floor, despite his attempts in his student days to get used to a bed. I half-lay on the skins while Hudya fed me strong tea from a saucer and firewood crackled cozily in the stove.

Thinking it over now, I am struck by the complete illogicality of my behavior. By rights, once I'd recovered from my humiliating violation, I should have rushed back to the Paratroop Division HQ, got hold of a company of paras, and arrested the whole fucking school, all the Nenets boys in one go! And there I was lying and drinking tea from Hudya's hands. Why? Very simple. How could I, the "Urengoi Alsatian," go to Division HQ or the CID directorate and say, "I've just been raped by some Nenets boys"? How could I say that? Who could? In spite of the law and official public morality being on my side, I would still have been a laughingstock in the eyes of the whole CID and everybody else in Salekhard and Urengoi.

It's because of these hidden sneers, this silently contemptuous attitude of the public toward rape that thousands, even tens of thousands of women and young girls in the northern hostels, and throughout the country, don't go to the police or even the hospital following a rape. The Moscow prosecutor Malkov revealed an interesting statistic to us when we were on investigator practice: 70 percent of the women alleging rape in 1979 were prostitutes, settling accounts with clients or lovers in this fashion.

The normal woman finds it easier to endure the fact of rape than to display herself as the victim to public— what? Scrutiny? No, virtually always, secret mockery. In the heat of wild drunks in the men's and women's hostels where the young tamers of the North reside, not a night goes by without rape, most often in groups—but even from the victim of a group rape you'll never get honest evidence.

Now I had joined the ranks of women shielding rapists from justice. But I honestly gave no thought to it that night in Hudya's flat. I gave no thought to anything. I just drank hot tea from Hudya's hands and almost naturally felt myself to be a little, put-upon girl, not a CID investigator.

Hudya sat in front of me on the floor, tucking his legs beneath him Nenets fashion; he poured the tea into the saucer and brought it to my lips. I drank, my eyes half-closed, and with the hot strong tea, my heart recovered and the pain in my lower belly eased. Hudya's quiet voice was unhurried; like all Nentsi, he softened the *d* till it almost sounded like *t*, giving his words an added charm, as if it wasn't an adult, but a child telling you an interesting story, soothing away the pain, the Salekhard explosions and rapes.

"When I was just a little lad, however," Hudya was saying, "my grandfather, Eptoma, often used to tell us about a certain country. If you could cross the ice floes and keep heading north and pass through a wall of circling winds, you would get to a place where people love one another and know neither enmity nor spite. Those people have only one leg each, and nobody can move independently. But they love each other and walk around embracing, loving. The more they love, the tighter they embrace and the better they can walk and even run, faster than the wind.

But when they stop loving, they immediately stop embracing and they die. When they love, they can achieve miracles. So my granddad used to say. And I always used to dream of heading north. I wanted to get through the wall of circling winds and find that land, where there is no enmity, no spite, only love. Are you asleep?''

"No, Hudya. Talk some more." I stretched my hand out for his hand and stroked it. "Please."

Hudya got up and put some dry birch logs on the stove. The fire raced swiftly over their bark. Hudya shut the light off; now only the orange glints from the stove lit up the dark walls and windows. Hudya, without undressing, lay down beside me on the skins.

"Good—listen," he said, putting his hands behind his head and settling in half an arm's length away from me. "Only this is not a fairy tale, it happened to me when I was a kid. These last few days, I keep remembering the story."

"Is it frightening, Hudya?" I snuggled up to him, just as I had done long ago in childhood, when I used to get up on the couch and arrange myself at my father's strong shoulder. My father was a military man; he'd worked his way up to lieutenant colonel and now lives quietly on his pension in Voronezh.

"No, it's not frightening. It's lyrical." Hudya, it seemed to me, smiled in the darkness. "One summer we had brought the reindeer up to the very north of Yamal, to the shore of the Arctic Ocean. There were good grazing grounds there. Not like now, however. I was a boy, ten years old. We had a large herd of animals, two thousand reindeer we had. The dogs knew their job, though, so I could leave the herd and go walking on the tundra. I used to go off to the shore of the ocean. There, you could find something interesting every day. After a storm all kinds of things get thrown up on the beach. I've found American whiskey bottles, colored buoys with yachts' names on them, and even

rubber sneakers, ripped, of course. The chief thing I
was searching for, however, was planks with nails in.
Nails and screws, that's what we're short of here, real
riches. You asleep?''

"No, Hudya, go on."

I thought I had never felt so warm, uncomplicated,
and comfortable—not with a man, I mean. I lay on
Hudya's shoulder, feeling his unshaven cheek on my
temple, glints from the fire drifting across us. I knew
that Hudya was trying to take my mind off what I had
been through, to help me to fall asleep with his sto-
ries. But no matter how comfortable I got, I could not
sleep. Apart from a great weariness, pain, and weak-
ness, there was some nervous thing beating in my pulse
and temples, which would not let me sleep. So I just
listened.

"So one day after another ocean storm," said Hud-
ya, "I found two sea gulls on the beach. Ocean gulls.
There are a lot of birds on the North Yamal, the
shores are full of auks and geese, but we don't get
many gulls. These two were lying quite still on the
shore; one of them was already dead. The second,
the male, was still alive, but so weak he didn't stir
as I came up to him. Just looked at me with his round
eye, and I well remember there was already a kind
of quiet death film in that eye, however. I'd found
dead sea gulls before and hadn't paid them too much
attention—so one had died, the other would lie for a
while, then fly off.

"But I came the next day and found the two sea
gulls in the same place. The live one was sitting mo-
tionless next to the dead one. When I got near, he tried
to rise, but he didn't have the strength to stand up,
even though he used his beak to balance on. I ran off
and came back with a small fish. I wanted to feed her,
that is, him, you haven't got a word in Russian for a
man-gull. We have, though. Anyway, he wouldn't eat.
I pushed the fish into his beak, but he just took it and

threw it to one side. He didn't want to eat. If he'd had the strength, he would probably have pecked me, but he didn't have enough even to get up on his legs. Still, he refused to eat. And then I understood what was going on. He wanted to die next to his mate. He had decided to die next to her, and even I with my tasty bit of fish couldn't make him change his mind.

"I realized what had happened to these sea gulls. Out over the ocean they had run into a storm. She had succumbed and hadn't made the shore, just fallen onto the water unable to fly. He had likely flown around and around above her calling to her. Have you ever heard gulls crying in a storm? They're crying to those who've given in and fallen on the water and can't fly, however. But they don't abandon their loved ones. The one I found on the shore, he perhaps flew all night above the waves, over the body of his beloved, watching the waves tossing her, covering her in foam, and carrying her closer and closer to the shore. And he flew to that shore, reaching it with his last strength, and saw that the waves had tossed her onto the land.

"At first, breathless, he lay near her and waited for her to get up. But then day came, the ocean retreated from the shore, and the storm died down; he realized his beloved would never rise again. It was then he decided to die near her. If he'd been old, he'd probably have died the first day. But I came to see him for a whole week, every day, and brought him fish and water. On hot days I bathed him in ocean water and kept trying to feed him. But he kept throwing the food away and wouldn't drink the water. On the sixth night a storm rose. When I ran to the shore after the storm, I couldn't find either him or his mate. The storm had carried them back whence they had flown. And he, he had achieved his death next to her, just as he wanted, however. And I realized that the country my Granddad Eptoma had spoken of actually does exist. Those two sea gulls were from there. That's why they died together. You asleep?"

"Yes, Hudya. I'm quite, quite asleep." I whispered and asked him, "Hudya, do you love me?"

Hudya was silent.

I had never asked any man that question before. Especially in bed. If only because once you're *in* bed, a man will tell you anything you like, to get everything that comes into his head that night. The more varied his desires, the more lies he'll tell.

Today I couldn't have satisfied the simplest of male desires—all my insides were twisted and ached like one big wound, calming down now, but still open. But I don't think Hudya had that on his mind just then.

"Yes, I love you," he said after a pause—pronounced calmly, the way they announce an undisputed fact in court. "I've loved you for four years, even longer, however. That's why I didn't go with you to the concert that time. I didn't want to give in to that love. But I named my daughter, Anna, after you. And now sleep, however, please."

"However!" I raised myself on my elbow and kissed Hudya's stubbly cheek. And then—on the lips. His lips were dry and tightly shut. They did not respond to my kiss. Hudya lay like a stone; not one muscle trembled on his face.

I lay back. No, I was not after sex—how could I be after all that had happened just a couple of hours ago? But surely he could have just moved his lips a little in response? It wasn't my fault I'd been raped. I wasn't a leper, was I? Even for a Nenets. This was the second time this Hudya had said no to me. The second time! A mixture of wounded feminine vanity and exasperation made me clench my jaws to keep from bursting into tears.

And then I felt his hand on my cheek—dry, rough,

hairy. I turned my head sharply away. No, I didn't want his sympathy, no patronizing caresses!

"Anya," he said calmly. We were in darkness now; the wood had burned through in the stove. "You don't understand. I can't say more than I have said. But what I have said is the truth, however. I had no right to love you in Moscow and I don't have that right now. And now sleep, please."

At that a furious wave of anger lifted me, no, jerked me upright on the skins. A simple idea had occurred to me, and harsh, angry words flew from my tongue of their own accord, faster than I could think.

"You're lying! It's all lies!" I shouted. "About love and your sea gulls—lies! You're just scared I'll arrest those sniveling school rapists, and you're buying me off with your fairy tales and lying! But really you're a coward, a coward! You fell in love with me in Moscow, yes, but not to conquer me, oh no! You ran off into the woods. Let other people sleep with me! Let Moscow fuckers seduce me! Let officers in the zone fuck me! Let someone rape me! But not you, you 'pure romantic'—on one leg!"

I didn't know what I was saying myself, but it was buried under my officer's uniform—the simple dream of any woman about *one* man, caring, loving and beloved, the dream I had concealed from myself and dissipated, like some prostitute in bed, with the likes of Orudjev, proudly thinking it was not them seducing and using me, but I them. That dream suddenly burst out in spiteful insults at this man who could probably have become that one and only if he had just wanted to try. For it was only with him of all the men I had had that I felt at ease, as if he were my own father. That feeling, that instant of perception means more to a woman than sporting with twenty stallions like Orudjev. That was why I was shouting now at Hudya, as I got dressed, shivering, in the dark.

"You prevented yourself from falling in love with

me in Moscow not because it kept you from studying! No! You think I don't remember how you looked at us when that Nenets kid was dying at the hotel? You hate us Russians; you're a racist, yes you are! You're a racist and a murderer! You murdered your love because I'm Russian! Then you go and call your daughter Anna in honor of that love. You're a masochist, that's what you are!'' In the dark I slipped on the soft skins, swore, and groped for the lightswitch. I turned on the light.

Hudya was lying on the floor, unmoving.

I had already put on my tunic when he spoke. ''You're not leaving here. The door's locked, however. The key's in my pocket. You're not going anywhere.'' The words were spoken simply and convincingly, as if he was stating an obvious fact. I stood stock-still. Surely he didn't intend to keep me here by force? Hudya restrain me!

He looked at his watch. ''Yes, you're not leaving here for two hours, minimum. Because the boarding school lads are on their way out of town. I don't want them to be caught.'' He got up from the pile of skins with the look of a man who had decided exactly what he was going to do. Most probably, he simply intended to tie me up. Good God, that meant I was right. In the heat of my anger, I had guessed the truth!

Hudya hadn't even got to his feet when a powerful blow landed on his cheekbone. I punched him, me! I hit him the way they do in the police, the way they *teach* you in the police. I've got trained hands, believe me.

Hudya made no attempt to dodge the blows, though I put all the force of my resentment into them. The swine, swine and bastard! He'd carried me from the school, told me fairy tales of love, given me tea, told me he'd loved me for over four years—all that just to let those boy rapists slip out of town unnoticed. Of course! Who's going to stop youngsters when they're looking for escaped convicts?

I hit him, and Hudya stood there like a bull, legs firmly apart, holding his squat, sturdy frame craned slightly forward. My next blow hit him along the eyebrow, and blood flowed from the cut. I felt a sharp pain in my wrist and realized I'd dislocated it. The bone of his eye sockets must have been hellishly hard. God!

"Cretin! Give me the key, I'm getting out," I said, doubled up with pain.

"I've told you once: you're not leaving. Go to the bathroom and wash your hands. They're all covered with blood."

Blood was seeping in a thin rivulet from his cut brow into his eye, but he seemed unaware of it. He looked at me calmly, his eyes perhaps just a little whiter.

"You look as if you've dislocated your wrist. I can put it back."

"Oh yes, right away." I sneered. "What are you talking about?" But I was pacing around the room in circles because of the pain in my hand. At last I tried to set the joint myself, but my wrist responded with such a fierce stab of pain that I exclaimed softly.

Hudya strode over, took my hand, and gave a short pull. I cried out again, but the joint had gone back in. Hudya was squeezing my wrist softly with his strong, dry hands, talking as he did so. "You can believe me or not, it's up to you, of course. I told you the truth. About the sea gulls I found that time, and about us. I loved you and still do, however."

"Who's Okka?" I asked, suddenly remembering Ayuni Ladukai's words to Hudya in the school: "We were avenging Okka!"

Hudya went on squeezing my wrist, saying nothing. Then he went into the bathroom and returned with a bandage. The blood from his brow had reached his chin, but he paid no attention to it and began binding up my hand.

"So, who's Okka?" I asked again. With my free hand I wiped the blood from his face almost automatically.

"That I can't tell you," he said. "Go to bed. I can't let you out on the street alone at night. There're villains out there." A brief smile touched his lips, for the first time in the whole evening, I believe.

"Oh, I won't give your youngsters away!" I said contemptuously. "That's all I need, for the CID to know I was raped."

"I thought as much. But in any case I told them to get out of town. That's it." He neatly tied the bandage with a bow and tucked the ends underneath. "That bandage will remind you of me for a couple of days. You won't be able to break the door down with one hand, and the key's in my pocket. So let's sleep."

With these words he lay down again on the skins, stretched out full length, and closed his eyes.

I stood in the middle of the room, feeling helpless and ludicrous. It was true I couldn't break the door down with one hand, nor had I any need to hurry to the North Hotel, where there were tons of army and police bigwigs. I really did look as if I'd been raped now!

I sighed, put out the light, and began to undress. Although the room was in total darkness I said to Hudya, "Turn away."

In the dark I heard him turn on his side.

I got my clothes off and guessed my way to where I had been lying before. And, of course, stumbled over Hudya's body; I trod on his back and toppled over. His arm caught me and cushioned my fall, but I hit my shoulder badly just the same. I was really unlucky that goddamn night. That stupid fall ended my endurance. I sat down on the floor holding my injured shoulder with my dislocated hand and began to whimper like a puppy—mournful, tearful, and forlorn.

Hudya put his arm around me and laid me down next to him. I lay on his arm and he pressed me to him, all of me from head to foot, my breast to his, and my tears flowed across his unshaven cheeks and the lips with which he gently kissed me.

"Sleep. Please, sleep," he kept saying softly.

I don't even remember when or how I dozed off.

41

The characteristic click of a Yale lock woke me up; I guessed this was Hudya closing the outer door. What a great idiot I was, when all was said and done! If he had a Yale lock on his door, that meant I could have just walked out during the night. Hudya didn't have any key in his pocket; he was just playing with me, like a child!

But I felt no anger toward Hudya anymore. Quite the opposite. I had slept half a night on his shoulder, and a quiet sense of peace and happiness had come to dwell in me, despite all the humiliation I had undergone in the school. I was even grateful to Hudya for deceiving me and not letting me go during the night. Now he'd quietly departed, and I didn't need to talk to anyone. He had given me the time to come to my senses so I could lie here on these skins and cherish inside me that rare feeling of having discovered *my* man, like a mother cherishes the baby at her breast.

I lay like that for about twenty minutes. All the turmoil of these last days, all the murders, explosions, and the rest, glided away from me into nothingness. No, I hadn't fallen in love with Hudya that night, but I felt like I suppose composers feel when the first notes of a new melody rise up in their mind.

After about twenty minutes I got up and turned the light on. My watch showed 10:40 A.M.; beyond the window was the polar night, darkness and some sort of vague rumbling. I put water for tea on the electric stove and switched on the local radio receiver. The set exploded into a hearty youthful melody:

We're not frightened of any ninth wave,
Or any permafrost we know!
For we're the brave lads, for we're the bold lads
Who work on latitude seven-oh!

I switched it off, revolted; these pseudohearty songs seemed repulsive to me now! I wandered around Hudya's little apartment and examined the bookshelves. Everything connected with his personal life had become interesting to me now. I even kept repeating his name over and over to get used to it.

There were lots of law books on the shelves, and books by virtually all the big names in criminology. There was also a whole shelf of books on Nenets history, Nenets fairy tales, legends, even anthropological research on the Nentsi. The experienced eye of the "Urengoi Alsatian," however, the specialist in sniffing out anti-Soviet literature, recognized at once among the spines of Soviet books such anti-Soviet editions as George Orwell's *1984,* Vladimir Bukovsky's *And the Wind Returns . . . ,* Abdurakhman Avtorkhanov's *The Technology of Power,* Menachem Begin's *White Nights.*

Now fancy that! I thought. I had seen anti-Soviet works, Solzhenitsyn and Orwell, for example, in the houses of high party and administrative officials many times, despite the fact that even possessing such writings could be punished by prison sentences of up to three years. But party leaders and KGB men of high rank even keep *The Gulag Archipelago* on their shelves, just to show their friends how much they are trusted by the party!

My Hudya Benokan, however, was not a party bigwig or even a KGB operative. He was a militia investigator, like me, and a Nenets to boot. Of course, I wouldn't inform on him, but I would have to have a talk with him about it—anybody might drop in for a cup of tea or a glass of vodka and then inform the KGB, and that would be it, his whole career over. I drank my tea and got dressed. Damn, Hudya didn't even have a mirror; I couldn't see what I looked like. A night like that and not even able to take a look at myself in the mirror! From beyond the window came the intensifying roar of aircraft. Hell, it was as if I'd dropped clean out of the stream of events that night and didn't have a clue about what was going on in Salekhard.

I pulled on my sheepskin, but before leaving I went to the bookshelves again and took out all the anti-Soviet stuff. Hudya had no furniture, as I've mentioned before. So I just shoved the books under the reindeer hides lying on the floor. In a few minutes I would see Hudya at Operations HQ and tell him to be a bit more careful with his ''literature.''

I buttoned up my coat and went out into the tiny hallway.

Only as I came up to the outer door did I see a note pinned next to the Yale lock. Written in a hurried but firm hand was:

Good-bye. And, please, go back to Russia.

Hudya

IV

HÄNDE HOCH!

42

On winter nights Moscow is deserted. Even in the city center, life dies down around one o'clock, when the subway stations close. Only the duty traffic police stand around at the downtown crossroads and stare intently at the rare passerby hurrying for a taxi, or stamping his freezing feet at a trolleybus stop. At one-thirty the doormen-cum-bouncers toss out the last drunken clients from the restaurants, get them taxis for a three-ruble tip, and, for another ten, smuggle them a pint of vodka for the journey. Toward two the city is sunk in sleep. Only the snowstorm scours around the deserted, frozen streets like a hungry beggar—fluttering the ripped newspapers in the garbage cans, probing under doorways, or bowling a tin can along the roadway.

It was on such a night, at 2:30 A.M., that three government limousines left the city and raced at high speed along a deserted Marshal Grechko Prospect, then turned sharply onto Rublyov Highway, which was kept meticulously clear of snow, narrow as it was. Here there were police posts every two or three kilometers in the shadow of snow-laden pine trees. As the black limousines proceeded, the duty militiamen would pop out of these posts, fully alert. They wore fur jackets, and none of them was below the rank of major. At the approach of the government vehicles, they came to attention and saluted. The limousines, without reducing speed, swept on, shrouding the sentries in slipstream and powdery snow.

Ten minutes later the cars reached a long, high brick wall, snow speckled and crowned with three tiers of barbed wire. This wall stretched on for many miles, with its watchtowers and high steel gates, an entry and exit barrier, and closed-circuit television concealed in the trees; it surrounded the group of government villas closest to Moscow. The security system here is very reminiscent of the camps, the only difference being that here, instead of prisoners, the inhabitants are the leaders of the country. Though which side of the wall is the camp compound depends on your point of view.

However that might be, around three in the morning, government limousines bearing the license numbers MOS-006, MOS-009, and MOS-012 rolled past the raised barrier, negotiated hastily opened gates, and found themselves in the Christmas peace of a pinewood park, with snowy paths sprinkled with yellow sand leading off into the interior. The cars turned confidently onto one of the paths and, moving much more slowly now, approached the last control point in front of the two-story dacha of Konstantin Ustinovich Chernenko. Here, the occupants of the limousines—Marshal Ustinov, General Fedorchuk (the interior affairs minister), and the president of the KGB, General Chebrikov—got out and walked the last twenty yards to the porch. A tall Christmas tree, half decorated with colored lights, stood in front of the dacha; next to it was an unfinished snowman with a child's sled, a box of Christmas tree decorations, and a toy machine gun of obvious foreign manufacture. Two of Chernenko's bodyguards stamped their feet on the porch. One of them opened the door for the nocturnal visitors.

Chernenko was sitting in the drawing room on a low stool by the fireplace, where crackling birch logs burned fiercely. He was smoking slowly and with enjoyment. This was the only cigarette he allowed himself per day, unbeknownst to his doctors, and he listened with repulsion to the hoarse bubbling sounds his chest made in response to every draw. He took pains to direct the smoke up the chimney. On seeing his visitors enter, he furtively threw the cigarette into the fire and covered it with birch embers. Then he grew ashamed of the gesture and made a wry face. "There you are. Shit, I smoke as if I was stealing something. Sit down. Kolya, tea for everybody and a bite to eat."

Kolya, a six-foot bodyguard, went out into the kitchen while the guests sat in armchairs by the hearth.

"Well, what do you make of it? What the fuck is with these Nentsi? Khe-kha . . ." Chernenko began a fit of coughing and rubbed his chest with a pudgy hand.

"We could put another few divisions in there," said Ustinov, when the paroxysm was over.

"Divisions. You're pretty free with your divisions. And what if the Americans pick up troop movements by satellite? They'll prick up their ears immediately. What the fuck do they want troops on the pipeline for, they'll ask."

"In the first place, it's the polar night up there now," said Ustinov. "Second, the forecasters guarantee total cloud cover in the area for the next three days. With clouds like that, especially at night, no satellite, even an American one, is going to see a fucking thing." He took a glass of tea from the tray Kolya had brought, but his gesture was irritated, and the tea spilled onto the hand-woven Persian carpet. Everyone pretended not to notice this. Everyone, that is, except Ustinov himself. The marshal stared demonstratively at the damp stain on the carpet and even rubbed at it casually with his black leather boot. Chernenko's indecisiveness exasperated him. An hour ago, when Bogomyatov's telegram about the scale of the situation in

Salekhard had arrived, the marshal had told Chernenko on the phone that he was sending another four divisions in. Chernenko, however, had forbidden this and asked him to come to the dacha. Any fool could see that delay in putting down this Nenets rising was dangerous, and not only because the contagion of rebellion might spread, as Bogomyatov had said, to other national districts or disrupt the opening of the gas pipeline.

That was bad enough. But even more important was something else: hesitation and the half-measures currently being employed in Salekhard by the local authorities and the October Revolution Division were giving an advantage to Gorbachev and the whole "young" echelon backing him up: Marshal Ogarkov, Aliev, Dolgikh, and that Siberian party upstart Bogomyatov himself. This was all they needed, to catch "the old men," him and Chernenko, unable to cope even with Arctic Nentsi.

"N-yes." Chernenko chewed his lips. "Forecasters . . . Cloud cover . . ." He glanced at General Chebrikov. "Well, what have you got to say? Will they get wind of it in the West if we open fire in Salekhard?"

"I guarantee—no!" Chebrikov said hurriedly. "We shall take measures. If we send our special Security Division in along with the army . . ."

"I would like the police militia to take part," General Fedorchuk broke in. "In Voronezh there's the Advanced Police Academy, one thousand three hundred men. Hand-picked officers as highly trained as paratroopers. After all, there will be lots of visitors, we have to guarantee security."

Ustinov smiled mockingly at the zeal of Chebrikov and Fedorchuk. The police and KGB had failed to notice the start of this rebellion; now they wanted to get in on things. "That should have been guaranteed before now," he said.

"Y-yes." Chernenko smiled again. "With things as

they are, we'll have to get the Politburo together and discuss the operation, then report to Comrade Andropov. But that's two days, maybe three. And Bogomyatov says we can't wait, eh?'' Chernenko looked demandingly at the servile Chebrikov. "Or is he trying to provoke us into overreacting, the son of a bitch?''

At long last he'd come out with what had been tormenting him since Bogomyatov's telegram had arrived. After all, it wasn't out of the question that this Bogomyatov was deliberately exaggerating the danger of the Nenets revolt; he'd even slipped in plots by ''American intelligence.'' He was either overinsuring himself, the son of a bitch, or deliberately pushing Chernenko to take extreme measures. And if it should turn out that there was nothing at all going on there, a few drunken hooligans, and he, Chernenko, had sent in thousands of soldiers, a KGB division, a police academy, all without the knowledge of Andropov and without the Politburo's permission . . . Gorbachev would make a laughingstock of him, not to mention Andropov! Can't stand the heat, they'd say, Comrade Chernenko, scared stiff when the chips were down. And the whole implication would be that Comrade Chernenko couldn't be considered for the post of head of state after Andropov died—he'd lost his guts in his old age. And what if American intelligence started stirring it up, not in the Far North with a bunch of lousy Nentsi, but nearer Moscow? What then? Would Comrade Chernenko start a nuclear war?

On the other hand, suppose the action in Salekhard really was American intelligence at work? You couldn't put anything past Reagan. Off his rocker since we crapped all over his sanctions and built the pipeline without American know-how. Suppose he sent a couple of spies into Siberia to touch off a Nenets uprising, and under cover of the uproar blow up the pipeline? The Americans had been telling the world for long enough that the Soviet Union was about to split apart because of internecine hostilities. And now, at the moment of decision, Chernenko's dragging his feet, displaying lack of character, hesitation. The young ones will be in for the kill all right, and Ustinov for one will change sides like a shot—saying, "I was the one who advised decisive measures," and so on, and so forth.

"Bogomyatov's not provoking anything," said Ustinov edgily, although Chernenko had made a point of addressing Chebrikov. "I was talking to General Grinko, the commander of the October Revolution Division, and he considers the situation extremely serious. The rising's only just starting, and the district's extensive, bigger than Poland. You can't get by on one division."

"Major Shatunov has also reported to me," said Chebrikov. "A mob of drunken workmen attacked our KGB directorate in Salekhard, smashed the windows, and broke the doors in."

"They did right," Chernenko grinned, looking him straight in the eye. "What's the point of us having a damn directorate in Salekhard if we get no early warning about the mood of the population? Kick the bunch of them out on their asses, understood?"

"Very good, Konstantin Ustinovich," said Chebrikov hurriedly, realizing that if the Nenets rebellion lasted another week, it would be his turn to follow Shatunov.

"So then . . ." Chernenko rose heavily. "So, we all agree decisive measures are called for, yes or no?"

So that's why you called us out here in the middle of the night. Marshal Ustinov smiled grimly to himself. Of course! It won't be Chernenko who makes the decision to squash the Nenets rising with the might of army, KGB, and police, it'll be a joint decision: minister of the interior, president of the KGB, and the defense minister. Crafty! And there was no evading a direct reply—those watery little eyes were staring hard, awaiting the answer.

"Yes," said Ustinov.

"Absolutely," Chebrikov at once chimed in. Fedorchuk simply nodded.

"Well, now . . ." Chernenko's puffy lips smiled in relief. "As Comrade Lenin said on the night of the storming of the Winter Palace in 1917, 'Yesterday was too early, tomorrow will be too late.' All right then: Ustinov will send in the nearest troops to Salekhard he's got; Fedorchuk his police academy, and Chebrikov his KGB division. What's more, he'll fly out there himself, this minute. And tomorrow it's all going to be over, got it?" He stared hard at Chebrikov, who had leapt to his feet and was standing at attention. "And the vital thing is—not the slightest leakage of information to the West, clear? Did you manage to nab that American, Shertz?"

"Of course, Konstantin Ustinovich. He's in Udmurtia, in a nature reserve." Chebrikov looked at his watch. "Right now, he's either asleep drunk or he's banging one of the girlies there, a cook."

"How some folk live! Yerch," Chernenko brought out enviously. "And here there aren't any girlies, and I haven't even got time to make a snowman for my grandson. Incidentally, Fedorchuk, your grandson gave mine a bloody nose here yesterday over some toy. That's all right, boys will be boys, fight a little. What's not all right is him going around to all the dachas boasting about it. 'I'm the one who punched Chernenko himself on the nose!' "

Everybody laughed except Fedorchuk.

"The scamp!" said Fedorchuk, flushing. "I'll show him! Can we go now?"

When the door had closed behind Ustinov, Chebrikov, and Fedorchuk, Chernenko stamped around the fireplace, raking among the burning logs with the steel tongs, as if hoping to find his half-smoked cigarette.

The butt had long since burned up, and Chernenko turned to his bodyguard.

"Kolya, can you give me another one?"

"Not on any account, Konstantin Ustinovich" was the reply, stern as if to a child. "We agreed."

"But I didn't finish this one."

The bodyguard shook his head.

"Well, fuck it!" Chernenko grinned. "Well, all right then, fetch me my boots. Let's go and finish the snowman."

A minute later, an outside observer (if such were possible in a Soviet government villa complex) would have seen an odd picture: in the dead of night, at twenty below zero, Politburo member, secretary of the CPSU, and soon to be the head of the Communist Party of the Soviet Union, Konstantin Ustinovich Chernenko, wearing felt boots and a Siberian fur coat, constructing, with the help of his two bodyguards, a snowman for the grandson who had recently been hit on the nose by the grandson of General Fedorchuk. He knew very well that from the minute Ustinov and the others got into their cars, their radio-telephones would be in action and terse coded instructions would be delivered to all corners of the sleeping land. These instructions would set in motion the vast and mighty machine of Soviet power. Red alert sirens would go off in paratroop formations, the Voronezh Advanced Police Academy, and the Dzerzhinsky KGB Special Division. Night-shrouded airports would resound to the roar of plane and helicopter engines; thousands of soldiers were already being issued ammunition. All in the cause of preserving Soviet authority in the Far North, protecting the Siberia–Western Europe gas pipeline, and foiling the intrigues of American intelligence. But no, Chernenko was no longer thinking of that.

"Anyway, you," he was saying to his bodyguard, who was adjusting the snowman's head, "you were the one who promised to teach my grandson self-defense. Why the fuck didn't you?''

''I did teach him, Konstantin Ustinovich, honestly,'' said the bodyguard. ''He just panicked.''

''Just panicked!'' mocked Chernenko, nettled. Surely his own irresolute nature hadn't been transmitted to his grandson? ''You teach him to keep his head.''

43

The frost had already penetrated his sheepskin and trousers, and the chill was heart stopping. Siegfried jumped in place and slapped his arms, all to no avail. If they didn't open this damn trading post in another ten or fifteen minutes, he felt, his legs, face, and ears would drop off. He did not suspect that at that very moment, in a still-dark Moscow, Chernenko himself was envious of him, for Chebrikov did not yet know of Siegfried's flight from a warm bed in an Udmurt nature reserve.

Next to Siegfried, a Nenets hunter rolling a plug of chewing tobacco behind his lip spat on the ground, or rather on the snow, crisscrossed by sled tracks. The spit froze in flight and struck the snow as a lump of ice, rebounding like a stone. Minus fifty Celsius, calculated Siegfried. At one time—in those great days when he had been an honored guest of the Tyumen territory bosses, Bogomyatov, Salakhov, Shatunov, Ryazanov, and the other party, Gee Bee, and administrative chiefs of Siberia—it had been the height of sophistication to walk out of a warm hotel, casual, Siberian-style, and calculate the temperature with one spit. If it landed on the ground without freezing, that meant it was less than forty below; if it froze in flight and didn't bounce off the frozen tundra, it was minus forty-five; but if it froze before it hit the ground and bounced like a piece of ice, then it was all of minus fifty Celsius. After that, Siegfried would get into the waiting managerial Volga and admire the beauties of the Siberian winter and the polar tundra from the safety of a warm car.

Now, however, there was no cozy hotel or managerial Volga. In fact, Siegfried had hardly jumped out of the mail plane onto the snow of the Novy Port Airport, when his self-confidence declined sharply. It was one thing to be without lines of communication or contacts (but with credit cards in your pocket) somewhere in Alaska, Taiwan, or even Honolulu. In five minutes Hertz would hire you any car you liked, from a cheap Toyota to a Mercedes. And if you had a pilot's license, you could rent an aircraft or a helicopter. While you were filling out a few forms you would get coffee and, in between times, book a room in a hotel. Siegfried took all this standard Western comfort and convenience so much for granted that even though he knew of the total absence of such service in the USSR, he couldn't imagine what it was really like to do without a hotel, a car, a telephone, hot coffee, and a warm toilet.

The toilet in Novy Port was a decrepit plank box raised above the permafrost on little wooden stilts. Leading to this edifice was a well-trodden path through the snowdrifts bordered with ornamental yellow initials. In the few minutes anybody needs to adjust his clothes, everything that had to be exposed in that box was likely to be frostbitten. It was this first meeting with unexhibited, untouristy Russia, with everyday Soviet reality, that utterly shook Siegfried's faith that, with one youthful bound, he could board a passing Sno-Cat and hurtle down from Novy Port to Urengoi or Salekhard.

But there was no turning back now. Anyway, if a Nenets uprising was threatening the pipeline, then to hell with these Russians and their playing at secrecy!

The pipeline wasn't just the Gee Bees' private property. There was $225 million of Siegfried's in there. So he had to get to Urengoi urgently, to see with his own eyes what was going on.

However, there weren't any passing Sno-Cats going to Urengoi or anywhere else. Novy Port is the most northerly river port on the Ob—above the Arctic Circle. It is out of service during the winter and wrapped in the pale, frosty phosphorescence of the polar night. However, the icebound jetties, the frosted cranes, and the barges and tankers sunk in the yards-thick ice of the Ob didn't mean the port was in total hibernation. No indeed, the settlement lived in winter too—there was the airport, the technical workshops, a club, a trading post. Most important, it was from the warehouses here that daily convoys of trucks set out by the "winter roads" across the frozen swamps with food, clothing, and technical equipment for geologists, oilmen, and gas pipeline workers out in the depths of the tundra. No doubt at any ordinary time it would have been easy for a couple of bottles of vodka to go with a truck driver to any of the tundra settlements. But today the winter roads were deserted.

Armed guards were strolling around near the port warehouse, wearing long-skirted fur overcoats, fur hats with earflaps, and felt boots. They were stamping their feet, hugging their Kalashnikov automatic rifles to their chests, and glancing suspiciously across the road at the score or so reindeer sleds. The owners of these sleds, Nenets hunters and fishermen dressed in bright *malitsas*, were grouped around the closed door of the trading post, patiently waiting for it to open. And Siegfried stood with them. Unshaven and short of sleep, his sheepskin coat stained and baggy after the long journey from Zataika to Novy Port, he no longer looked like a prosperous foreign businessman. It was a lot easier to set him down as a hard drinker, anxious for the store to open so he could get drunk again. There're enough of that sort in the North, and such a type the Nentsi and the armed warehouse guards no doubt took him to be.

Siegfried had no need of liquor, though. He wanted food, and Novy Port had no restaurant or diner. Even the tiny buffet at the airport was closed, like everything else today. Only this store remained, and it should have opened an hour ago. Siegfried waited impatiently and marveled at the unshakable calm of the Nentsi. If everything the helicopter pilots had told him about the Nenets uprising was true, these Nentsi should have disarmed the guards—surely a trifling matter for polar hunters like them—and rifled the store rather than wait for it to open. Seizing supply dumps was the first act of any uprising, thought Siegfried.

But the Nentsi seized nothing. They talked quietly among themselves, smoked their pipes, and chewed tobacco. Close by, the harnessed reindeer snorted and twitched. Their breath rose in clouds of steam above their branching antlers as they cocked their sloe eyes in all directions, jaws phlegmatically chewing on wads of dried lichen. As usual in the vicinity of Russian food stores, stray dogs wandered, rummaging in the snow. The post's chimney was giving out smoke, and the fact that the stove was going inside gave Siegfried, the Nentsi, and the dogs hope that sooner or later the store would open up.

Compelled by lack of anything else to do, Siegfried glanced over at the Nentsi. They were the usual old Eskimos, looking like Japanese. Squat, powerful frames, calm, wide-cheeked faces, framed in fur hoods, frosted by their breath. Their *malitsas* gave off a penetrating smell of dog.

"Your Russian cheeks is white, however," said one of them in Russian to Siegfried. He bent down, scooped up a lump of snow, and held it out. "You should rub it with snow, however." As all Nentsi, he pronounced the letter *d* like *t,* which softened his speech and made it sound childlike.

"Thank you." Siegfried took the snow and said, "I'm not Russian, I'm an American."

The Nentsi stared silently at him with their narrow eyes.

"I'm from America. A translator," said Siegfried, rubbing his cheeks with the snow. These savage Nentsi were hardly likely to run off and report him to the KGB.

"Oh, America!" exclaimed one of them. "America—good, however. America lives good law: it sells vodka to anybody. No different there, white man or Nenets, sells vodka to everybody, *savo*!"*

"And you like vodka?" asked Siegfried, interested.

"My likes vodka very much, very much!" The Nenets even screwed up his eyes, so much did he like vodka.

Just then, a stout Russian woman emerged from a wing of the shop and headed for the door, crisscrossed from head to toe in gray fluffy shawls. At her appearance the stray dogs at once scampered up to the porch and the Nentsi clustered closer. She opened the sizable barn lock and thrust the dogs away with her foot.

"Get lost!" She then turned to the Nentsi. "Don't push now! No pushing!"

Opening the frosted door, she entered the store in proprietorial fashion. Nentsi and dogs followed; Siegfried went in last.

It was warm inside, and Siegfried drew a blissful breath. The Nentsi meanwhile were crowding around the counter, inspecting the shelves, which held nothing except pyramids of tins labeled TOURIST BREAKFAST and cans of eggplants and peppers.

A subdued grumbling began.

*Good (Nenets).

The woman disengaged herself from her coverings and approached the counter.

"Well? What do you want?"

One Nenets indicated the shelves.

"Nenets can't eat that, however. Give bread, give tea, give flour. Powder also give."

"At once! I'll run and get it!" The woman sneered. "They burn our oil sites and we give them bread! Take what there is, while it's still there."

"Nenets can't eat this," said the Nenets again. "Such law not, not sell flour to Nenets. Only for vodka is such law. Not for flour. You will give me as much flour as I give you money, macaroni you will give also." Saying this, he pulled a bundle of rags from the leather bag at his belt. Undoing it, he placed money on the counter. "Take money, give butter, give flour, tea."

"Come on. Don't fuck around," said the woman. "You'll get no flour and no butter! Do you want the tins?"

The Nentsi started jabbering among themselves.

"Well?" said the woman impatiently. "I'll be shutting up the store in a minute."

"Such law not—close store," the Nenets began again.

"Don't 'the law' me! That's it, shit! Out of here!" She waved her arm in the direction of the door and picked up the lock from the counter.

The Nenets sighed, took four sable pelts from his bag, and placed them on the counter. She thrust them away decisively.

"No! You should have come before with this. I've got instructions now: for you—just that." She indicated the pyramids of cans. "Take them while you've still got the chance." Her regretful gaze followed the pelts, which the Nenets was tucking back in his bag. She took the money from the counter, swiftly counted it, and announced, "There's enough for three cases. Which'll you have? One of each?"

The Nenets nodded wordlessly.

In twenty minutes or so, the Nentsi had cleared the shelves. They hauled sackfuls of dusty Tourist Breakfast out of the store, as well as the prehistoric canned eggplants and peppers. The woman was flushed with her exertions, the counters on her abacus were going like a machine gun, and Siegfried suddenly realized that this old woman was not only unloading old stock on the Nentsi, but robbing them as well; uneducated as they were, how could they check her lightning arithmetic!

Now only toiletries remained on the emptied shelves—dusty cakes of Fragrance soap, Pomorin toothpaste, and Red Moscow perfume.

"Scent also give," said one of the last clients.

"I won't; you'll drink it," replied the woman, tired now.

"My won't drink," said the Nenets. "My old woman give present, however." It was only now that Siegfried perceived that the figure in the *malitsa* standing next to this Nenets was indeed female.

The storekeeper, if only to rid herself of this last Nenets, handed him a bottle of perfume. In one second the Nenets had unscrewed the plastic top and given the bottle to his wife. Before Siegfried's astonished eyes, she drank half of it, gurgled, and returned the rest to her husband, who finished it off.

"Drunkards!" sneered the storekeeper. "And you want freedom as well. If you did get freedom, you'd drink yourselves to death! Tfui!"

"It's you, *lyucha*,* made the Nenets a drunkard, however," said the Nenets peaceably. "When the *lyu-*

*Russian (Nenets).

244

cha didn't come to the tundra, the Nenets was a hunter, never see vodka."

"All right, all right, on your way! No meetings here," she interrupted roughly. "This isn't the town council, making speeches!"

"Never mind . . . ," the Nenets went on, "soon Vauli will come here as well."

The Nenets couple left the store, towing the last case of canned goods with them. The storekeeper seated herself on a stool, wiped the sweat from her brow, and unhurriedly retrieved a round of sausage from under the counter. She broke a piece off and trimmed it, throwing the skin to the dogs.

"Well? And what do you want?" she asked Siegfried.

"I'd like some sausage as well . . . and a bottle of vodka. Two would be better."

"There's no vodka and no sausage," she stated, gnawing at the hunk of sausage, only now staring at Siegfried with her prominent, brazen blue eyes.

He calmly withstood her gaze. He well knew that from Moscow to Kamchatka there wasn't a storekeeper in the USSR who didn't have at least two or three bottles of vodka tucked away.

"I'll pay triple," said Siegfried and placed a brand-new hundred on the counter.

They continued to look each other in the eye for several instants, during which time the woman's eyes took on a lively light, intrigued not by the hundred but by Siegfried himself. Then she rose from the stool with a sigh and went into the back room, swinging her powerful hips coquettishly.

"Four bottles," Siegfried called after her.

44

A few minutes later Siegfried walked out of the store carrying a heavy bag. Out in the street the Nentsi were busy around their sleds, tying on their sacks and cases of provisions.

Siegfried went over to the Nenets who had advised him to rub his cheek with snow and put his bag on the sled.

"I am Siegfried. What's your name?"

"Ani-Opoi," said the Nenets.

"And where are you going?"

"Over there." The Nenets waved a hand toward the tundra.

It was fifty below, unsuitable for subtle diplomacy. Siegfried spoke directly.

"If you take me to Urengoi, we'll drink a lot of vodka."

"I can drink a lot of vodka," said the Nenets. "I can't go to Urengoi, however."

"Why can't you?"

"Today I have to catch fish, however, to feed children. Ani-Opoi not kill Russian boss, Ani-Opoi not set fire to Russian gas site. But Russian store give nothing to Ani-Opoi, however."

The situation was desperate. This Nenets was Siegfried's last chance to get out of Novy Port and reach Urengoi.

"All right," said Siegfried. "Today we'll catch fish, tomorrow you take me to Urengoi. In Urengoi we'll buy flour, we'll buy tea, we'll buy butter, and we'll drink a lot of vodka."

It would be an adventure, riding with Soviet Eskimos some three hundred miles on a reindeer sled across the Arctic tundra. Later on he could give an excellent interview to *The New York Times* or even *Playboy*.

"I want to drink a lot of vodka, I want very much," the Nenets said, almost dreamily. He was probably about sixty, short, with an expressive, wrinkled face with high cheekbones. "Can't go to Urengoi all the same. Very long distance, however. Three changes of reindeer. Ani-Opoi poor, Ani-Opoi no money change reindeer three times."

Siegfried felt he was freezing again in this damn cold.

"How much does it cost to change reindeer?"

"Dear, very dear," replied Ani-Opoi, finishing the distribution of goods on the sled.

"Well, how much?" Siegfried persisted.

"Maybe three hundred rubles," said Ani-Opoi thoughtfully. "Maybe one hundred and twenty!"

Siegfried realized that figures were relative for this Nenets. He asked, "Would they change reindeer for vodka?"

"Oh yes," Ani-Opoi answered joyfully. "Of course they will, however!"

"How much vodka?"

"One bottle!" the Nenets said quickly. "Don't give more! If there's more, we'll drink it ourselves, however. We'll drink as we go!" He screwed his face up in anticipation of delights to come. He then surveyed Siegfried from head to toe and added despondently, "You won't get there alive, however."

"Why?"

"Your parka's thin. Can't go tundra with such parkas. With such parkas you go to *Khalmer*."*

And although Siegfried didn't know what *Khalmer* meant, he got the gist from the way the Nenets was looking at his clothing.

"Never mind," said the Nenets. "Now you be running behind *agish*,† very warm will be. When we come choom I will give you warm clothes, our clothes." He sat down on the empty space in front of the sled, then pulled a long stick out of the snow, brought it down on the crupper of the lead reindeer, and shouted: "Hokh! Ho! *Otte tsort!*‡ Hokh!"

The four reindeer sped off. Stunned by such a simple turn in the business, there was nothing left for Siegfried to do but run after the sled, holding his bag tightly.

They had barely turned off the street onto the tundra, which opened immediately after the houses adjoining the store—Novy Port consisted really of one street along the banks of the Ob—when Ani-Opoi also leapt down and ran beside Siegfried.

"Hokh! Ho!" he shouted to the reindeer.

Siegfried thought of taking the Nenets's place on board, but the whole sled was bumping so heavily on the rough patches and icy hummocks that he would hardly have kept his seat. So he had to run, sinking into the brittle crust. Snow got packed into his boots, he was steaming and soaked in sweat and he unfastened his sheepskin as he ran.

"*Savo!*"§ shouted a broadly smiling Ani-Opoi to him as they ran. "*Savo*, tundra warm!" and struck his reindeer with the switch. "Ho! Hokh!"

*Cemetery (Nenets).
†Sled.
‡Shit!
§Good (Nenets).

45

The spike, a special seventy-pound gouge with a weighted end, echoed and boomed on the ice of the river, chopping out large, jagged fragments.

Ani-Opoi stood chest deep in the excavated hole, lifting the spike with both hands and driving it down powerfully, gouging and gouging into the river's icy armor. His face was pitted and cut by flying splinters of ice; blood was trickling down his cheek and forehead, but he went on furiously smashing the ice. The last dark layer was quite close now, and Ani-Opoi didn't want to give the spike to anyone else, although another dozen Nentsi were standing around the rim. But it was he, Ani-Opoi, who had brought the whole clan here, and it was he who had promised them that at this point there would finally be fish.

A few days before, while tracking a marten—a rare animal nowadays, driven out of the tundra like all the rest by the Russian tractors and the smell of gas—Ani-Opoi had stumbled upon the Techida River, right at its source. He had been taken at once by its clean, untrodden snow. That white snow, with no trace of soot, not one speck of dust, had typified the whole tundra thirty years before. Only dog and reindeer sleds had disturbed that whiteness then, while arctic foxes, martens, and squirrels wove upon it a *tynzei** of spoor. But no beast, bird, or reindeer sled had spoiled the tundra, and even the hooves of reindeer had not sullied it the way the iron tracks of Russian machines, stinking of gasoline, had disfigured the landscape. The smoke of these machines settled on the tundra as soot. Wildlife fled, and men fell ill from the airborne dust.

The Techida, however, lay far from Russian roads, hidden away among frozen bogs, and the snow on her banks was clean and white. Ani-Opoi stopped tracking the marten, kicked away his broad, fur-covered skis, and set to work digging up the snow on the bank and on the river's icy plating, sniffing it and even tasting it. No, the Techida didn't smell of oil! So that meant there must be fish. When Ani-Opoi was a little boy, there wasn't a Nenets in the tundra who didn't have as much fish as his heart desired—not ordinary fish either but sturgeon with caviar, Siberian salmon, pink and white. Dogs were fed dried salmon; they wouldn't touch pike or catfish. The Nenets used dried pike to light campfires with. And there was a special abundance of fish in winter, when the pressure of the ice in the Ob forced them into the smaller streams, where they could be netted or even scooped up by hand.

But when Russians began pouring petrol, oil, and other filth into the tundra's rivers, the fish began floating belly up. And now there wasn't enough fish for the people, never mind the dogs.

But there ought to be fish in the Techida, so said Ani-Opoi to his children and all his clan—the Haryuchi, named for the proud crane. Would a strong, cranelike man give up the gouge to anyone else when any moment water would spurt up, dark living water, bearing oily, precious caviar-rich fish? When this non-Russian guest who was standing with all the rest of the Haryuchi above the hole, watching Ani-Opoi at his

*A woven leather belt (Nenets).

work, had asked him for transport to Urengoi, Ani-Opoi had thought immediately that he would take a caviar fish along to Urengoi and get plenty of provisions in exchange for it—Russians were avid for caviar fish.

The spike suddenly broke through the ice and almost slid into the water, so carried away was Ani-Opoi by his thoughts. But Ani-Opoi kept hold of the spike, pulled it out of the water, and flung it to one side, then at once sank to his knees, feverishly tearing off his fur mittens and, scooping up the dark water, brought it to his lips.

The clan watched him tensely. If Ani-Opoi said the river water was living, they would at once cut another hole about ten yards from the first and lower nets between the two on a long pole. Some hours later, if Num, the God of the tundra, was merciful to the Nentsi, they would, as in years gone by, haul from the water an enormous sturgeon with a bellyful of caviar. The sturgeon would smash its tail furiously on the ice, but Ani-Opoi, as was the right of the first provider, would still it with a blow on the head from the spike, and then slash the belly with his sharp knife. From the opening would pour a dense mass of caviar to fill the waiting bucket. Everyone would pull a spoon from the top of his boot, and the caviar would be eaten up quicker than a fox can run from one riverbank to another. Then, thus fortified, they would haul the nets out of the river with sturgeon, salmon, and beluga, drive new holes, and again lower nets, while Ani-Opoi rested on the bank, shouting, "Eh? Ani-Opoi knows where to find living water!"

But Ani-Opoi was in no hurry to gladden his relatives. He drank all the water from his palm, cupped up more, and swirled it around in his mouth. His ice-pitted face was covered in blood, but he was indifferent to that.

"Well?" Someone's patience broke. "Tell us! Is it living water?"

Ani-Opoi made no reply. He peeled back his *malitsa* and, on all fours over the hole, lowered his bare arm up to the elbow in the dark waters of the river. Down there, he broke off a piece of dark ice and drew it out. Oblivious to the water literally freezing on his arm, he began examining the ice fragment from all sides, even sniffing it.

At last he straightened up, threw the ice away, and scrambled out of the pit. He shouldered the spike in silence and headed off upriver without a word.

The Nentsi followed him, and so did Siegfried. Siegfried was already decked out Nenets fashion—fur socks, *ichigi;* fur boots, *kisi;* suede trousers and shirt, *yagushka;* and, on top of it all, a *malitsa* and a *sokui,* a sort of heavy suede smock, which Nentsi wear only on long journeys. Siegfried was warm in this getup. His feet no longer froze in his fur boots with the straw insoles, and the arctic fox edging of his hood protected his forehead and cheeks from the tundra wind.

Ani-Opoi went about three hundred paces upstream, halted, and crashed the spike onto the ice, starting another hole. He did not like the water he had tasted at the first hole. It was dead, but not because the river was polluted with oil that might have seeped in with the spring meltwater. It was dead from a cause Ani-Opoi did not want to, could not believe. This was why he had begun desperately to gouge out a second hole.

After watching another hour of exhausting labor, many of the Haryuchi had returned on their dog and reindeer sleds back to the encampment. Ani-Opoi took the spike from Siegfried, who had been awkwardly pecking at the ice, quickly excavated a hole down to the water, and scooped up a handful. Blood dripped into it from his lacerated face, and he poured the water onto the snow and tried again. He held the water in his mouth for some time, swirling it this way and that with tongue and palate before spitting it out and reclining against the cavity wall.

"Well, then? Tell us!" said someone.

Ani-Opoi raised his face. There was such profound, unaffected grief on that wrinkled face with its dried crust of blood that Siegfried experienced for the first time a genuine compassion for these people. Six years before, when Bogomyatov, Salakhov, Ryazanov, and Shatunov had ferried Siegfried by helicopter around the Yamal and shown him the Nenets herders, hunters, and fishermen, he had seen them as simply quaintly exotic in their reindeer-skin garments. It was as if he was being taken around Disneyland and shown models dressed up in Eskimo clothing.

Later, five years ago, the fat bon vivant Ryazanov, chief geologist of the Yamal Oil and Gas Exploration Trust, had "treated" Siegfried to a twelve-year-old Nenets girl from a Salekhard boarding school. This little thing had easily convinced Siegfried that she was no model; she was alive, a savage of wondrous flesh, a bronzed body, a warm little bosom, provocative gray eyes, and a scalding hot slit under a tiny black pubic triangle. Siegfried, try as he might, was unable to recall the name of that gray-eyed twelve-year-old, though after the first night in Ryazanov's cottage she had come to Siegfried every night in the North Hotel. That had been one of the sweetest weeks in his experience as a man. So sweet indeed that at the farewell party in Ryazanov's cottage, he had behaved like a proprietor, a lovelorn boy; to every suggestion that he share the girl for group sex he had said no, and they had had to make do with another Nenets girl.

Convinced as he was, however, in the most direct manner possible, that the Nentsi were people of flesh and blood, Siegfried had never regarded them as people in the full sense of that word, in the way we regard ourselves and people like us. Consequently, when, about eighteen months later in a routine flight to Salekhard, he had learned from Ryazanov of the tragic death of his "sweet Nenochka"—she'd died immediately after Siegfried's departure of an asthma attack, according to Ryazanov—Siegfried didn't so much pity the girl—hell, what was her name?—as feel saddened that there would be no more sweet nights on this trip. In any case, Ryazanov with the aid of his contacts easily made good the loss with another Nenets maiden, no whit the worse between the sheets. Siegfried had decided that these ten- to twelve-year-old Nenets girls had a primitive, or more precisely savage lack of inhibition as far as sex went, and an almost prehistoric temperament, so it followed that these people were a kind of arctic Neanderthal with sensual, early-maturing girls. Siegfried had even been proud of his strikingly original anthropological analysis.

Now, however, after half a day with Ani-Opoi, observing his exhausting toil and even assisting in it, Siegfried regarded these "polar savages" in a somewhat different light. They lived in the snow of the tundra in chooms, alongside their dogs, with no light, no electricity, and they obtained their food by hard labor. And the result of this labor now was nothing, only grief and despair on the face of Ani-Opoi.

"Water dead," said Ani-Opoi. "All dead. Even no grass under water, however. Even no air in water, however. They killed water."

He didn't know how to explain to his non-Russian guest that when the weeds die in a river, that special taste which distinguishes river water from melted snow disappears. It meant not just the destruction of a river but the death of everything around—birds would no longer come to rest on the water, animals would desert the water holes and perish because the Russians had poisoned the other rivers too, and the reindeer pastures along the riverbanks would also die out. And without fish, without birds, without reindeer, without animals, death would come also for all the cranelike race of the Haryuchi.

Ani-Opoi could not explain all this to his non-Russian guest; he had neither words nor desire enough to do so. This guest, however, seemed to have understood everything without words. He got a bottle of vodka out of his bag, tore off the aluminum top with his teeth, and held out the bottle to Ani-Opoi.

46

But perhaps Ani-Opoi and the whole Haryuchi clan need not wait till the Russians had poisoned all the rivers in the tundra, destroyed all the reindeer pastures with their tractors, and driven out all the wildlife down to the last lemming. Perhaps Ani-Opoi should abandon his wigwam and go where three days ago his eldest son, Sanko, and five other boys from the Haryuchi and neighboring clans had gone—to help the spirits drive the Russians from the tundra. But no, the young folk wouldn't take oldsters like him. They'd laugh. You've drunk a lot of Russian vodka, they'd say, how can you fight against Russians now?

Ani-Opoi stood in the path of a reindeer herd being driven toward him by husky dogs and his camp neighbors. A long *tynzei* plaited from leather thongs lay coiled in his hand; his eyes sought out a female yearling. Of course, he could have killed some draft bull reindeer from those that were old or lame, but the meat of draft and working animals is stringy and tasteless; one couldn't entertain a guest on meat like that, especially this guest—from America!

Ani-Opoi had wanted to ride to Urengoi at this American's expense and exchange his fish for a huge quantity of foodstuffs and drink a good deal of vodka— that's how Ani-Opoi had laid his wicked plan! For that, the tundra spirits had punished him at once, had not given him fish in the Tcchida. But Siegfried didn't know how Ani-Opoi had wanted to trick him and had given Ani-Opoi vodka to drink. Now it was an urgent matter to recover the goodwill of the spirits; they must be placated by the sacrifice of a female deer yearling, and all his encampment neighbors, and Siegfried, must share in eating this animal.

Ech, how lovely Siegfried's vodka was! Of course, he'd take him to Urengoi, the very next day. He'd take with him a bagful of squirrel furs, four fox pelts, and seven martens out of the stocks he kept in his choom against hard times. And he would bring a month's supply of necessities to his son and his friends so they would fight well against the Russians. Butter he would bring, salt he would bring, sugar, and maybe tobacco and gunpowder. How else could an old man help his children, when the three-sided arrow was flying across the encampments with its signal for revolt—and all must go to the battle, both valiant warrior and common man?

The thud of reindeer hooves rolled ever nearer. The gray mass of the herd bore down on Ani-Opoi, pulverizing the tundra snow. Beneath the blows of those hooves, the frozen tundra rang like a shaman's tambourine. The branching antlers rolled above the herd like the waves of the Ice Ocean. Like a little boat, they disclosed, then obscured a beautiful yearling with a graceful breast and head held high. Ah, if all the Nentsi could have gathered into such a herd to fall upon the Russians and with one blow hurl them out of the tundra!

But only the legendary hero Vauli Piettomin had known how to drive Russians out of the tundra with one blow. And that had been long ago, long, long ago, when the Russians had no airplanes or tanks. And now, said his son Sanko, the Russians had to be defeated another way—they had to be so frightened they would flee the tundra of their own accord, like animals running from a forest fire. "How can you frighten them?" Ani-Opoi had asked. "The spirits have taught us how." Sanko had grinned and reminded his father of the old Nenets fairy tale that Ani-Opoi had heard from his own grandfather as Sanko had from him. "From their living enemies, they cut off the ears and *khote* and made them eat their own *khote*. Thus the fathers avenged their blood, thus do the sons likewise."

The herd was almost upon Ani-Opoi, about twenty meters away. Ani-Opoi must cease thinking. He must coil himself like a spring, as if he himself, and not his leather *tynzei*, were to swoop on this beautiful deer with the large black eyes and tender ears. Now!

"Ho!" Ani-Opoi hurled his *tynzei*.

The lasso flashed in the air like a snake and lashed around the yearling's neck.

As if cut down, the yearling collapsed into the snow and turned head over heels, dragging Ani-Opoi after her with her whole body weight. But Ani-Opoi's arm was strong, and his legs were strong; even after a glass of vodka, he could lasso a reindeer and stay on his feet! Sanko should not call him an old man.

The herd raced past; only the lassoed yearling remained, and got to her feet. Two Nentsi, assisting Ani-Opoi, rushed toward her, threw another loop of the *tynzei* around her neck, and stood at either side of her head. Each held one end of the *tynzei*. One quick and powerful tug on these ends and the yearling, instantly suffocated, with neck outstretched and hind legs buckling, subsided heavily onto the snow.

Only now did Ani-Opoi take the hunting knife from its carved walrus-ivory sheath. Those Russians slaughtered their domestic animals with knives or, as Ani-Opoi had heard, even axes! Tormenting animals and spilling valuable blood needlessly. No, not a single Nenets would kill a reindeer with a knife—that would be a sin in the sight of the tundra and the spirits.

Swiftly and neatly Ani-Opoi made an incision in the

reindeer's hide from fore to back leg, and continued it to the end of the body. No drop of blood issued from this cut; Ani-Opoi cut only the hide, not the meat. He inserted his knife in the incision and began to prize the skin away from the carcass. His left hand tugged at the skin while his right fist pressed down on the meat where the hide was being detached from the muscles. Under his deft hands, the skin came off easily, like a dress.

Siegfried watched this virtuoso performance with a mixture of squeamishness and curiosity. In a few minutes the whole skin of the reindeer lay on the snow, fur side down—without a single piece of subcutaneous tissue adhering, no blood either, just clean, smooth hide. On the hide, as if on bedding, lay the naked carcass of the deer.

The Nentsi seated themselves around this original table.

"Come here, however! We're going to *aurdat!*"* shouted Ani-Opoi to Siegfried, as he carefully opened the animal's abdominal cavity and rib cage with his knife. A second cut near the backbone, and the entire flank of the carcass came off along with the ribs. In another minute Ani-Opoi had tipped out the innards onto the snow. Once more, no drop of blood was spilled.

One of the Nentsi dragged the guts off and gave them to the dogs. Meanwhile, Ani-Opoi sank to his knees in front of the carcass and plunged his arm in somewhere under the yearling's throat. He gave a strong tug, and from the animal's torn windpipe came a fountain of scarlet blood. It quickly filled the abdominal cavity, where the heart and lungs floated in it. Steam rose from this scarlet "soup"—the blood was still warm, no, hot.

Women and children came running from the en-

*Eat raw meat (Nenets).

campment and formed a noisy circle around the felled reindeer. Each one had a knife and kept looking at this enormous dish with anticipatory relish; Ani-Opoi, however, raised an admonitory hand.

The hubbub ceased. Ani-Opoi pulled out the liver, neatly sliced off a long thin piece, and proffered it to Siegfried.

*"Savo syunze!"** he said. Seeing that Siegfried was regarding the morsel with evident distaste, he dipped the liver in the warm blood and again held it out. "Eat, eat! However! Your dick will stand good."

The Nentsi broke out laughing—men, women, and children. Siegfried, under the eyes of all present, took the piece of liver and nibbled it. It was warm and seemed to him tasteless. As soon as he had taken the dainty from the hands of Ani-Opoi, everyone else eagerly set about eating the warm and raw reindeer flesh, dipping it in the blood. "Tya, tya, ah tasty," the children kept repeating. "Siegfried, take salt. Salt for meat. So tasty, however!"

The Nentsi were amazingly neat about their eating. Each person would take a piece of blood-dipped flesh in one hand and seize an end in his teeth, but without biting through. In the other hand, everybody carried a knife as sharp as a razor. Using this, they gave a quick cutting stroke upward and sliced off the meat, almost grazing their chins and lips. Siegfried felt that they would injure their noses, so close did the knives pass in front of their faces.

Of course, Siegfried had often heard of Eskimos drinking reindeer blood and eating raw reindeer flesh; it protected them from scurvy. Still, it was one thing to hear about it, quite another to be the guest of honor at such a banquet. From a detached point of view, it no doubt looked picturesque, Siegfried reflected—a group of Nenets families in motley reindeer *malitsas*

*From all my heart (Nenets).

sitting on the snow around a freshly slaughtered rein-
deer, wolfing down raw meat with scarlet drops of
blood raining onto the snow like strawberries. All
around stood the dogs, impatient for their turn; close
by a couple of dozen conical choom of reindeer skin;
near every wigwam harness gear, several draft ani-
mals, and a three-year-old child who had harnessed a
grown pup to a washing trough, riding and laughing
over the snow. A real patriarchal idyll! On the other
hand, how could these patriarchal-savage Nentsi raise
a rebellion against the Soviet empire?

Later, in Ani-Opoi's choom, reindeer meat boiled on
the hearth in a blackened cast-iron pot, especially for
Siegfried, who was unused to eating raw meat. The
hearth divided the choom into two parts: in the front
area, nearer the entrance, lay an old, dark, foot-worn
reindeer hide; the dogs slept here during snowstorms.
In the rear, beyond the hearth, lay mats of soft grass
and clean reindeer skins—beds for Ani-Opoi and five
of his children, four daughters from five to eleven and
his two-year-old son. Now all his children, apart from
the eldest left at home, eleven-year-old Melkune, were
lying there, tucked up in skins and peeping at Sieg-
fried out of the semidarkness with curious little eyes.

Melkune was waiting on the adults: from the left-
hand corner of the tent, where all the crockery was
kept, along with stores of dried fish, tea, salt, and
sugar, she fetched a large glass cup, wiped it energet-
ically inside and out with cloth strips, and filled it with
strong, brick-colored tea. She then handed the cup to
Siegfried. The rest of the Nentsi, including Ani-Opoi,
drank tea from plain aluminum mugs. Siegfried, as a
guest, got the glass one.

The smoke went out through an aperture in the
choom roof; the fire gave out heat and the Nentsi,
copper-faced in the firelight, sat cross-legged close to
the hearth. They had taken off their *malitsas* and were

half naked in their suede pants and vests. They smoked pipes, placing their chewing tobacco behind their lips. They drank tea, not with sugar but with dried fish, which lay in front of them in a wooden basin. They had studiously avoided talking about recent events in the tundra, but Siegfried egged them on.

"I've heard somebody has been setting fire to the drilling rigs," he said.

The old men said nothing, glancing questioningly at Ani-Opoi or averting their eyes altogether and spitting out tobacco juice. Ani-Opoi replied diplomatically, "Nenets knows nothing. Nenets wanders over tundra, grazes deer. Tundra spirits set fire on Russian sites."

"Why?"

"Don't know why." Ani-Opoi turned his eyes away. "Russian peoples came, lots of bad did to tundra. They killed rivers, frightened animals, made little holes in the ground—woke up the spirits altogether, however. While these little holes were not in the ground, the spirits couldn't get out. Now Russian peoples wanted to drive the spirits out of the tundra through a tube. They opened little holes in the ground and started driving the spirits into the tube, like into a trap. So the Nentsi would have no friends left. But the spirits broke out and punished the Russians." Here, Ani-Opoi noisily sipped tea from his mug.

Not a bad interpretation of the Siberia–Western Europe gas pipeline. Siegfried smiled to himself. Aloud, he spoke otherwise. "When the Russians reach the gas under the ground, the tundra will be warm and light. The Russian people will build you warm houses, power stations."

"Then the Nenets will be dying altogether, however," sighed one old man, and he began rocking his body as one doomed.

"But why?"

"The tundra will be altogether dirty. While Russian peoples didn't come here, the tundra was clean, Nenets was never ill. But Russian peoples came and brought many of their spirits to the tundra, however.''

"But surely they built hospitals, schools, boarding schools—I've seen them myself in Salekhard and Urengoi!''

"Hospitals—tfu!'' said another old man in sudden indignation. "They don't cure you at all! My belly hurt, very bad—they took me on reindeer to hospital, to Novy Port. Doctor says give him a sable, he will give medicine. I say, you give me medicine, I will go choom, I will bring you sable. No, he says, first give sable, however. So he not give medicine, till I went choom, ill stomach, get sable for doctor.''

"Now it's all like it was before the revolution, long long ago,'' said a third old man. "Even got worse, however. Russian peoples don't give us Nentsi passport. Without passport, police not one town allow to live. To Moscow not allow to live, Leningrad, even Salekhard not allow. Tundra live! But how tundra to live? In shop you give sable—shop give you nothing. Flour don't give, tea don't give, butter don't give. Only paper money for sable give. Nothing nowhere for paper money. Mine daughter went trip. Moscow, says to me: Moscow even for Russian peoples no meat, however! My old head don't understand: if Russian peoples for selves nothing, why Russian came to tundra? Nenets can't feed all Russian: few Nenets, very many Russian peoples, however.''

The dogs came running into the tent to get out of the wind that rises on the tundra toward nightfall. With their tongues lolling, they settled down on the tattered skin, glancing now at the heat of the fire, now at the Nentsi and Siegfried. Droplets of melting snow glinted on their bushy coats.

"Russian peoples bad peoples, bad head,'' the oldster went on to explain. "Dog, see? My dogs—right dogs: herd the deer, attack wolves, very likes children, however. Russian peoples not so—others lands war, build a camp for themselves in the tundra, prison! And other Russian peoples they put in camps—own people put in camps, prison! And spoil dogs, teach fight men, however." The old man shook his head disconsolately; he had never considered such savagery—teaching a dog to attack a man and put other men, his equals, in jail, like martens in a cage!

"You talk a lot, Labuta," Ani-Opoi chided him, clearly not relishing the direction of the conversation.

"My name means that—talk a lot," replied the old man. "And what means your name?" he asked Siegfried.

Siegfried shrugged. "Nothing . . . just a name."

"It can't be nothing. Every name means something, however. Teta, for instance." Ani-Opoi became more animated, obviously delighted at this chance to change the subject. He pointed at the old man whose doctor had demanded a sable in return for treatment. "Teta means has lots of reindeer."

"Now not so many," said Teta. "Now *lyucha* has spoiled the tundra, no moss for the deer, many deer die, however."

"So your name is wrong now," said Ani-Opoi and indicated Labuta. "But his name is right. Talks a lot, it means."

"And what does your name mean?" Siegfried asked Ani-Opoi, placing the next piece of boiled venison in his mouth and sipping his tea.

"My name means 'one more,' " said Ani-Opoi. "My father called his children so: firstborn Opoi. One, that means. The second was born, Side. Two, that means. Third was born, Nyagar. Three. So seven children were born. So when I was born, he began again—Ani-Opoi. Another one, it means."

The Nentsi laughed indulgently, as if all of them were qualified mathematicians. Siegfried looked at them with something approaching astonishment at the open childlike laughter.

"And where is your wife?" he asked Ani-Opoi.

"My old woman gone to the *Khalmer*," said Ani-Opoi, at once saddened. He explained to the uncomprehending Siegfried. "My old woman was bearing a son. The Russian doctor took five sables, but he still cut her belly open and then sent her to the *Khalmer*. Didn't give sable back, however."

All the Nentsi grew sad at once; their faces were filled with sympathy for Ani-Opoi.

"Two years, I live alone," he went on. "Eight children to feed—very hard, however. Therefore, five children here, one son is hunter in tundra and two older daughter gave to boarding school. Didn't want to give, there Russian men will spoil, fuck them. But eight children Ani-Opoi cannot feed. Tundra became very bad—no animal, no bird, no fish also, however."

The old Nentsi men took to sighing noisily.

"What do they call your eldest daughters?" asked Siegfried with inner misgivings.

"Tadane and Padane."

Siegfried took a relieved breath; that hadn't been her name. He asked, "Why did you make so many children?"

"What else to do?" His eyes glinted slyly. "No television, no light also, however."

Once again all the Nentsi burst out laughing—a gay, frank mirth.

All of a sudden the dogs leapt out of the choom barking loudly. Ani-Opoi and the other Nentsi rose to their feet and, pulling on their *malitsas* as they went, followed the dogs.

Siegfried remained alone with the five children. Melkune was busy in the corner. Out of pieces of fur and cloth, she had neatly fashioned a tiny figure in *malitsa* and *kisi*.

"What is it?" asked Siegfried.

"It's a doll. A toy for youngest sister, however," Melkune responded, eyes lowered.

Damn, thought Siegfried, dirty, unwashed, living with dogs and reindeer, these people are also—people. Of course, that didn't mean that the pipeline should be canceled for their sake and $225 million lost, not that it was in his power to stop the project. But sacrifice $150,000 to $200,000 on some tundra Disneyland for these kids, that he would do right away. Especially because something had to be written off for tax purposes.

Unexpectedly, one of the children's heads poking up from the skins asked, "Siegfried, are you going to sleep with us?"

He shrugged his shoulder. "Probably."

"Will you sleep with Melkune?"

"Why Melkune? I'll sleep on my own."

"Alone—sleep bad. Cold, however. You sleep with Melkune, be warm. Take Melkune for wife, good wife will be. You want to take Melkune for wife?"

"What's your name?" Siegfried smiled.

"Me you can't take for wife yet. You want to wait three years for me; I am only eight years old. My name is Okka."

Siegfried felt it like a whiplash: Okka, that was her name! That had been the name of that twelve-year-old five years ago. The name again drove Siegfried into recalling that week of sweetness with that fervent, wild, debauched, and innocent Nenets girl.

He got up, pulled his *malitsa* on awkwardly, and went outside. About ten paces to one side near the still unloaded sleds on which Ani-Opoi and the other Nentsi had come from Novy Port, something was being discussed. At Siegfried's approach everyone fell silent. Siegfried saw the figures of six young Nentsi whom he did not know. They had hunting rifles, and their reindeer were breathing heavily.

"Why did your come out of the choom?" Ani-Opoi asked Siegfried. "Your better sit in choom, drink tea."

"I came out for some fresh air," said Siegfried.

The Nentsi began speaking among themselves in their own language. It seemed to Siegfried that the young ones were speaking out, displeased with the old men; Ani-Opoi appeared to be defending himself. Then the boys harnessed fresh draft animals to the sleds and shouting "Ho! Hokh!" drove off into the tundra night. The dogs accompanied them to the outskirts of the encampment, then returned to the old men, who stood and watched in silence.

"Who are they?" Siegfried asked Ani-Opoi.

"My son Sanko hunter," said Ani-Opoi, unyoking the weary reindeer from the sleds the visitors had left behind. "Gone to find squirrel, long way tundra. Your go choom, however. Sleep, however. Tomorrow we go Urengoi, *savo?*" He looked embarrassed and lowered his eyes.

"*Savo,*" said Siegfried.

47

From *Operational Report to Government*
From *President of KGB General Chebrikov*

Secret, urgent

I bring to your attention several points from operational reports received from various regions of the Yamal-Nenets District.

Point 1

In extending the search area for the criminals who burned the drilling rig at Lake Mirigi, Lieutenant Zvyagin, commanding a helicopter squadron, noticed from the air the tracks of reindeer sleds leading away from the lake in a northwesterly direction along the bed of the river Techida. Following these tracks, Lieutenant Zvyagin's squadron of three helicopters observed and detained in the tundra six reindeer sleds along with six Nentsi. During questioning the detained persons stated that they were on a hunting expedition in the tundra. According to them, they heard the explosion and saw the fire rising over the tundra near Lake Mirigi. Deciding that this was the "tundra spirits" blowing up the drilling sites, they left their hunting area and were proceeding home. A search of the sleds revealed hunting rifles, eighteen squirrels, and three martens, an extremely small amount for such experienced hunters as the local Nentsi. The hunters explained, however, that as a result of the laying of the pipeline, the catch of fur-bearing animals in the tundra has sharply diminished, and the traps and nooses they had set near the lake perished, in their words, from the fire.

Although the presence of the Nenets hunters close to the scene of the incident raised Lieutenant Zvyagin's suspicions, their statements and the absence of direct evidence of their involvement in the arson compelled him to release the detainees.

Point 2

Similar tracks of dogsleds were observed by helicopter crews in the area of Site No. 727, near the settlement of Kamenni. The investigating team, led by experienced detectives who came with me from Moscow, followed these tracks to a Nenets state fur farm, Dawn over the North. In the words of Nentsi questioned here, a group of hunters from the farm had actually been near Site No. 727, following a wolf pack. The Nentsi affirm that the development of gas fields has caused "all beast gone from tundra," and the wolves, for lack of other food, were attacking not only reindeer but also Nenets encampments. Here the Nentsi showed a child bitten by wolves and three pelts of wolves they had killed. A search of the encampment yielded no evidence of the involvement of Nentsi in the burning of Site No. 727. Another detail, however, merits attention. In connection with the forthcoming visit to the district by members of the Soviet government and foreign journalists, the farm Dawn over the North was selected as a showpiece, and a month ago all the workers were moved from their chooms into snow-shielded houses. The team of investigators has discovered that the Nentsi have dismantled the interior walls of these houses and erected their wigwams inside. They are now living in their chooms and burning the wooden house partitions and the furniture in their hearths. In reply to questions about the reasons for such behavior, the Nentsi stated that they did not wish "to live Russian-style." Similar information concerning Nentsi moving back from the houses to their chooms has begun to come in from other parts of the district.

Point 3

In the areas of site fires—Lake Anaguri, Nugma, Yunarta and river Haide—no tracks have been discovered, but pipe layers on the Anaguri-Urengoi section saw several dog and reindeer sleds on the tundra some hours before the fires occurred.

Point 4

In the Nenets settlement Red North, the former first secretary of the Yamal-Nenets District Party Committee, Pyotr Tusyada, has been discovered and arrested. During questioning, Tusyada stated that he had deserted his post because he considered that the exploitation of the tundra gas fields would bring disaster on the Nenets people and he did not wish to be involved in this "crime." Explaining the burning of the gas rigs, Tusyada stated that the oil and gas of Yamal belonged to the Nenets people and the people had the right to burn the gas as they saw fit. By this Tusyada indirectly confirmed that the Nentsi are responsible for the arson attacks.

All these points—the mass exodus of Nentsi from houses to chooms, their open declarations of the harm done by the pipeline, the traces of their presence in the vicinity of the site fires, as well as all the preceding incidents in Salekhard and the rumors of the return of Vauli Piettomin—the leader of anti-

Russian rebellions in the eighteenth century—testify in my view to an ORGANIZED CONSPIRACY AMONG THE NENETS PEOPLE *against Soviet power in general and the construction of the pipeline in particular. It is perfectly obvious that the Nentsi have selected the tactic of "invisible terror" in subverting Soviet authority, i.e., using the polar night and their excellent local knowledge, they attack the drilling sites, kill the workmen, and cover the traces of their crimes by setting the place alight. On returning to their encampment, the criminals melt into the general mass of Nentsi, while the crimes they have perpetrated create panic among the Russian population of the territory.*

IN VIEW OF THE NECESSITY FOR AN IMMEDIATE END TO THE DISORDERS, NOW TAKING ON THE CHARACTER OF A NATIONAL ANTI-SOVIET UPRISING, THE JOINT COMMAND OF THE ARMY, KGB, AND POLICE IN SALEKHARD, TOGETHER WITH THE PARTY LEADERSHIP OF TYUMEN PROVINCE, HAVE MADE THE DECISION TO CARRY OUT A SERIES OF PUNITIVE OPERATIONS IN VARIOUS PARTS OF THE YAMAL TUNDRA.

48

Siegfried sat on the sled behind Ani-Opoi, trying to ape his pose exactly. The compact figure of the Nenets in his dark *sokui* clung tightly to the sled; no hill disturbed his balance. His right leg was tucked under him and the left stretched out, pushing with his toe against the edge of the sled runners. In his left hand was an eight-meter stick with which Ani-Opoi not so much beat as frightened the reindeer, shouting, "Ho! Hokh!" His right hand held the rein of the lead animal, and with it he guided the team.

How Ani-Opoi found his way through the icy silence of this totally monotonous tundra shrouded in polar darkness, with its lightly phosphorescent spurs of blue-white hills, Siegfried did not know and didn't attempt to understand. There are situations when you can neither control events nor even guess at their logic and direction. You can only relax and go with the current, as the Russian poet has it, "whither the destiny of events draws us on."

It was only some twenty-four hours ago that Siegfried had fled from Zataika, his soft warm bed, the hospitable Khanov, but it seemed to him now that it had been long ago, almost in another life. The monotony of the tundra, its pure, frosty air, the rhythmic thudding of reindeer hooves, and the warm fur clothing he wore, all prompted Siegfried to doze off. Hell, he hadn't slept for three days now.

You couldn't call his night's stay in Ani-Opoi's choom sleep, could you? Siegfried had lain fully clothed on reindeer skins, covered with furs. But even through the skins, his body, unused to such a bed, sensed the icy strength of the yards-thick layer of permafrost. Apart from that, Ani-Opoi snored all night; the dogs fidgeted and whined in their sleep by the choom flap; and, in the middle of the night, the two-year-old kid suddenly left the pile of sleeping children and made his way on unsteady legs to the flap, raised it, and stood there barefoot in the snow, piddling straight onto the tundra. Gusts of wind carried spray and snow into the choom as the child got back under the furry hides, but the entrance flap remained open and slapped in the wind like a sail, wafting a whole snowdrift into the choom before Siegfried, cursing, crawled out from beneath his covers and closed it. It seemed that all Ani-Opoi's family slept on as if nothing had happened, but on the way back to his place, Siegfried suddenly encountered the fixed, expectant gaze of Melkune. He would not have laid a finger on her for all the money in the world—in the choom next to her sisters, her snoring father, and the whining dogs, certainly not!

But now he was in the sled, alternately dozing off and being jerked awake by the next ice mound; not without a certain feeling of self-satisfaction, Siegfried thought of the mature gaze of the eleven-year-old Nenochka. Who knew, perhaps in a year or two he would be in this part of the tundra again on business. Melkune in a bath of shampoo . . . she was a minor, of course. "Oh come on!" he said to himself, what was wrong with making love to a twelve-year-old girl if she begged for it? It meant she was ready for it; they matured early in these parts. That other one, Okka, hadn't been a virgin at twelve; she had been uninhibited and insatiable.

The roar of engines brought him out of his sweet reverie. Both Siegfried and Ani-Opoi looked up.

Three helicopters were flying from south to north, intersecting Ani-Opoi's route. Their noses and tails were brightly lit, and searchlights probed at full power. These made the helicopters look like huge birds of prey with white legs thrust ahead, prepared to seize their victims in their powerful talons.

Me! thought Siegfried, terror-stricken. It's me they're looking for, the Gee Bees! They'll land in a minute, pick me up, have a good laugh at my Nenets fancy dress, and then . . .

But the helicopters passed on to the north, the rumble of their engines dying away behind a distant hilltop.

Ani-Opoi brought his reindeer to a halt and anxiously raised himself to his full height on the sled, even craning in the direction the helicopters had gone. He listened intently. Then he sprang off the sled, threw back the hood of his *malitsa,* lay down on the frozen ground, and placed his ear to the ice. The reindeer pulled over to a bare patch of rock amid the snow cover, where some frozen lichen stalks could be seen.

"What's the matter?" asked Siegfried, but Ani-Opoi only waved his arms as if to say, quiet, let me listen to the tundra.

He sprang up from the earth sharply, as if he had been struck. His face was utterly transformed—it was cruel; the eyes, dark and narrow enough before, were now slits. He jumped onto the sled, struck the lead animal sharply, and roughly wheeled the whole team in the direction taken by the helicopters. Siegfried, hanging onto the sled with both hands, could barely maintain his grip.

"What's happened?" he yelled again.

But Ani-Opoi paid him no attention whatsoever. He

was standing bolt upright, bawling at his reindeer, and driving them with all his strength. The reindeer had probably never seen their master in such a state. With quivering ears and tails almost vertical from fear, they literally floated across the tundra, snorting and turning their thick muzzles toward their master.

To stay on the sled, Siegfried simply lay down, tucking beneath him his bag of vodka bottles and the bag of squirrel and sable pelts Ani-Opoi had been taking to Urengoi.

After some twenty minutes of this frenzied progress, when Siegfried felt his arms and legs could no longer keep him on board and Ani-Opoi, indifferent to the foam-flecked muzzles of his beasts, continued to beat them mercilessly with his stick, crying "Hor! Hor!" the roar of helicopter engines became audible once more. They were now flying from north to south toward Ani-Opoi's sled and a great deal lower than before.

Suddenly, one of the helicopters detached itself from the trio, dropped still lower before switching on its searchlights, and, with a roar, hurtled straight for the sled.

The reindeer, blinded and deafened, veered to one side, snorting with fear. Ani-Opoi controlled them by a miracle, but the aircraft came lower and lower, as if intending to ram the sled.

Recoiling, the reindeer trampled backward onto the sled as the powerful blast of the helicopter rotors flung the maddened animals, men, and sled in all directions.

Siegfried leapt crazily to his feet, waving his arms and shouting, "Stop it! What are you doing? There are people here!"

The helicopter banked to one side and then came straight for him, Ani-Opoi, and the overturned sled. "Stop!" yelled Siegfried. "I'm Shertz! I surrender! You've no right! I'm an American!"

The downdraft from the rotors once more toppled

him, but as he fell he managed to catch a glimpse in the aircraft's cabin of the young, laughing face of a pilot in army uniform.

The helicopter then soared and flew off to catch up with its buddies.

Ani-Opoi got up from the snow, looking around him. The sled was overturned and badly damaged; the reindeer, with broken reins, were racing headlong across the tundra.

Ani-Opoi dragged off his heavy *sokui,* threw it onto the snow, and, without a word to Siegfried, ran off in the direction the helicopters had just come from. Siegfried, totally at a loss, ran in pursuit, shouting, "What's up? Where are we going?"

He was soaked inside his heavy *sokui* and tried to take it off, but at that moment they came up onto the crest of a hill, and what they saw below made them both freeze.

A bloody jumble of human bodies, dead reindeer, and cans of Tourist Breakfast and marinated peppers machine-gunned from the air lay on the white snow of the tundra.

Ani-Opoi fell to his knees and crawled toward the shambles. His eyes had already found the body of his son, slashed by bullets. Sanko's *malitsa,* like those of the other five Nenets boys, was peppered with bullet holes, as if the helicopters had circled over the dead bodies and fired off all their ammunition. The same machine-gun bursts had mutilated the reindeer, who looked as if they had tangled with a drunken butcher.

Around these fragments of human and reindeer flesh, from which steam was still rising, punctured cans of Tourist Breakfast lay like a garnish. There was not one can left intact, as if the gunners had competed to see who could hit the most.

49

From *Instructions to Paratroop Division October Revolution*

Carrying out the government's operational orders, the Third Helicopter Regiment of our division successfully conducted an operation in defense of socialist property and the Soviet system in various parts of the Yamal-Nenets District.

As a result of the exemplary conduct of the operational mission, I order: that the commander of the helicopter regiment, Major Strigunov, and squadron commanders Lieutenants Zvyagin, Akhmerov, Ignatyuk, and Shevchenko be promoted to next officer rank; machine gunners taking part in the mission are to receive official thanks and ten days' leave.

Divisional Commander
Major General Grinko
Salekhard, 14 December 1983

50

Siegfried did not think that he would survive to reach any sort of habitation in the tundra. But whenever he fell onto the snow, Ani-Opoi lifted him roughly by the collar of his *malitsa* and hauled him along the ice until he recovered himself. Ani-Opoi did not stop once, even to throw a piece of ice or snow into his mouth to relieve his thirst.

After two hours of this run across the brittle snow crust, they saw the rows of snow-powdered open-air wired cages of the Nenets Bright Way fur farm. Light blue arctic foxes, chocolate-colored mink, and silvery dark foxes were kept there. Behind the cages were chooms and the living quarters of the farm, reindeer sleds, children in *malitsas*.

Siegfried pitched forward onto the snow.

Ani-Opoi went on alone to meet the huskies running toward him.

An hour later Siegfried recovered consciousness to the clatter of a tambourine, bright light beating into his eyes. Not knowing whether he was dreaming, he opened his sticky lashes and at once screwed up his eyes—it really was electricity, fluorescent lighting. Siegfried shaded his eyes with his palm and gazed around him.

He was lying in a large elongated room entirely without furniture apart from a long table and the portraits of Lenin, Andropov, and Marx on the walls. The main distinction of the room lay in the fact that the whole place was filled with heaps of sable, fox, and mink pelts. Siegfried himself lay on several piles of sables, hence the extraordinary feeling of gentle, soft warmth.

Siegfried stirred and at once heard a man's voice— low and cigarette-hoarse. "Aha! So we're coming around?"

Siegfried turned his eyes toward the voice. To one side, by the small dark window stood a tall, husky man of about eighty—one of those thoroughbred old men; years and stooping never seemed to age them. He had a thin, elongated face, a powerful nose, and a grizzled comb of a mustache. His large tobacco-stained teeth were clamped on an empty cigarette holder. He was dressed in a voluminous gray sweater. Over the sweater was a sleeveless fur jacket. He also had on trousers and high *kisi*. From beneath grizzled, bushy eyebrows, he gazed keenly and cheerily at Siegfried with his light blue eyes.

"Come on, up you get, up you get!" he said. "Or you'll miss the whole show!" He nodded toward the window, beyond which the tambourine was getting louder and some sort of lights were flashing. "You don't see this kind of thing too often. Get up!"

Siegfried looked around. On the floor there was literally no room to put his feet because of the pelts. The old man said, "It's all right, walk straight over the furs, don't be afraid! Let me introduce myself: Geizenrikh, Lev Nikolayevich, fur expert. I'm buying furs for the international fur auction in Leningrad, in January. And your name, if you'd care?"

Everything was unusual about this old man—the Russian aristocratic "if you'd care," the surname clearly un-Russian (and un-Nenets), his direct social manners, not to mention the fabulous riches of this interior.

"Siegfried Shertz," he said, stepping uneasily over the furs. "But where am I?"

"Wh-a-at?" the old man interrupted, raising his eyebrows in astonishment. "You're Siegfried Shertz?" He switched at once into German. "*The* Siegfried Shertz, the middleman between the USSR and the Western banks? I hope you speak German?"

"Yes," said Siegfried, astonished in his turn that an old man living in the depths of the tundra should know German.

"I've heard a lot about you, my friend," Geizenrikh went on, "but how did you turn up here with the Nentsi?"

"It's a long story," said Siegfried evasively. He had only now perceived the strong Russian accent in the old man's German, and his sentence structure was the high-flown style of Schiller's time.

"Well, tell me later!" said the old man complaisantly and pointed to the window. "Go and look, go and look! Even I rarely see it now and I've been in the Arctic sixty years. You're in the director's office of the Bright Way fur farm. Way, it's true, I don't see, but there's plenty of bright light, look!"

Beyond the double glazing of the window, it certainly was light, from an enormous bonfire, which the Nentsi had laid out on the wide snowy square in front of the farm director's hut. Near the fire on six sleds lay the bodies of the dead Nenets hunters, which had been brought in from the tundra. The bodies were wrapped in coarse cloth; by the right hand of each lay his smashed hunting rifle, by the left his portable cooking pot, knife, box of matches, packet of shag tobacco—all a hunter needed in this life and the next. Near these sleds, prepared for their last journey, stood a crowd of Nentsi with torches. By the bonfire, on a reindeer hide, was sitting a man in a strange costume: a handsome suede shirt with red cloth epaulets, edged with the same red piping and tufts of red fur. The man's entire face was covered with a piece of scarlet cloth; on his chest hung a kind of silver plate. He held a large tambourine.

Geizenrikh smiled. "Shaman. Soon he will *kamlat*, that is, commune with the spirits. Just now, he's warming up the tambourine to stretch the skin, make it resilient."

In fact, the shaman was moving the tambourine toward the fire and holding it there for a while; then, taking it in his left hand and a wooden stick in his right, he began striking the tambourine quietly and rhythmically, listening intently like a musician tuning his instrument.

"Of course, he's not a real shaman," said Geizenrikh. "It's Vaska Nogo, a veterinarian; he's about forty. But his granddad and great-granddad were real shamans; it's their costume he's got. Didn't drink it away, at least," he concluded, almost astonished.

"Are you a German?" Siegfried inquired finally.

"My ancestors came to Russia from Bavaria in the seventeenth century," Geizenrikh replied casually and turned back at once to the window.

There, the shaman had apparently decided that the tambourine was ready. The blows on it became powerful, delivered with all his strength, and as they increased in frequency, the shaman rose from his skin, part dancing, part performing some kind of ritual twitching movements. The Nentsi clustered closer around, their cheekbones lit by the glow of fire and torches. The shaman struck his tambourine and leapt, now approaching the sleds bearing the dead men, now retreating from them, shouting out in time to the beat, "Go-o-o-oi! Go-o-oi! Go-oi! Goi!"

"He's calling up the spirits," Geizenrikh told Siegfried. "By the way, his great-granddad really did it, I saw it myself." Since Siegfried looked at him with surprise and curiosity, Geizenrikh willingly amplified. "I've been spending a few months a year here since

1923. I'm a furrier by profession or, if you like, a fur expert. Well, Vaska, come on! Let's see what you can do!'' he said through the window, nimbly scrambling onto the sill and opening a fanlight to hear the shaman better.

The frosty wind and the smoke from the bonfire stole into the room. Beyond the window, the shaman suddenly stood stock-still and, throwing back his head, began shouting something in Nenets.

''Shall I translate?'' asked Geizenrikh.

''Yes, please.''

''He's asking the spirits of the dead, 'Who killed you, men?'' Geizenrikh began a simultaneous translation of the shaman's exclamations. He was now questioning the spirits of the fallen and immediately shouting out their answers:

''Airmen killed us, Russian airmen.''

''Why did Russian airmen kill you?''

''Because we burned the drilling rigs.''

''Why did you burn Russian drilling rigs?''

''Because the drilling rigs are killing the tundra and all our people on the tundra.''

''Is our hero, Vauli Piettomin, far from you?''

''No, Vauli is not far from us, he is here!''

''What do you say to us, Vauli Piettomin?''

''The Russians are killing you from their airplanes and helicopters,''

like hunting down wolves.
My spirit walks the tundra and seeks a bodily form,
to avenge the death of Nenets men.
I have loosed the triple-edged arrow across the tundra
with the signal for revolt.
and all must go to do battle,
both valiant warrior and common man.
But are there still men among the Nentsi
whose hands will not tremble

*and whose eyes will not blink as they shoot at the
Russians?
Are there?*

The shaman accompanied each question with a blow
on the tambourine and, running toward the Nentsi,
shouted in their faces, "Are there still men among the
Nentsi? Vauli himself is asking you. Vauli himself!
Who will go to wreak revenge on the Russians?"

"I will," said Ani-Opoi in a low voice as he stepped
forward from the ranks of bereaved relatives. "I will
set fire to one drill rig. For my son, however."

"I also." Someone else strode forward.

"And I also, however."

Eight men moved out from the crowd and stood eye-
ing one another. Then the shaman leapt high before
crashing to his knees and yelling, "Earth!" He banged
on the tambourine. "Bear them well on thy back, do
not overturn them."—bang—"King—Fire! By thee we
live, we are warmed by thee!"—bang. "Drive the
Russians from our land!"—bang. "To our tundra
without Russians make haste and come!"—bang. "We
beseech thee, O Sun, light of the earth—we wish to
live! To see our dear ones well! To graze our reindeer!
To catch our fish in the rivers! To hunt down our wild
animals in the tundra!" The shaman quickened the
tempo of his invocations, struck his tambourine faster
and more resoundingly; his dance became ever more
vigorous and his shouts louder. "Let the Russian peo-
ple run away. Let them fly away in their airplanes! Let
them depart with the night! With evil spirits let them
depart! With their diseases let them depart! With their
tractors let them depart! With their socialist commit-
ments let them fly away! The tundra cannot live under
socialism! There is nothing in the tundra as it is!"

Here Geizenrikh burst out laughing and stopped
translating, not that there was anything more to trans-
late. After a few more invocations, the shaman col-

lapsed onto his reindeer hide and fell silent. The Nentsi touched the animals harnessed to the sleds bearing the bodies, and the long funeral procession, accompanied by children and dogs, melted away into the polar night, the glint of its torches still visible in the distance. The last to go was the weary shaman. He had already taken the cloth from his face, but his shoulder now bore a Kalashnikov automatic rifle.

"Oho!" Geizenrikh grew serious at once and screwed up his face. "I'm afraid there isn't going to be an official opening of your gas pipeline on December seventeenth."

51

"Fur is—romance, my dear fellow," said Geizenrikh euphorically some time later, offering Siegfried strong tea with real Moscow *sushki*.* He took a pelt from one of the piles and jerked it around in the air as if shaking it out; then he turned it toward the bright fluorescent lamp. "See the play of colors? The height of fur? The density? But that's only a third-rate one. For the home market. Export begins with first-class furs, but there is something above first class—the extra-one and extra-two, not the farm-bred fur, not those beasties you saw in the cages—but the wild animals, from the tundra." Here, Geizenrikh walked over to some bundles of luxurious furs and picked up a blue fox pelt, lovingly ran his palm along the fur, and proffered it to Siegfried. "Have a feel. Know how much a pelt like that would fetch at auction? Fifteen hundred dollars. Now cast your eyes around this room, my friend. There are up to a thousand pelts. In other words, you and I are sitting on a million fur dollars, that's all. And that's the income of just two fur farms, a hundredth part, perhaps, of what will be on show at our January fur auction. That's why even Stalin, when he put an end to all private trading in Russia, didn't stop the Leningrad fur auctions! Currency, pure hard cur-

*Small dry bread rings.

rency! Every year the furriers of the whole world come to Leningrad for furs. And leave several million dollars behind after just a few days! Where else can you see that in the USSR? A real auction with bids in hard currency? Soviet rubles are never even mentioned. Good money only. But I was talking about romance, wasn't I? Romance, not money.''

The old man had clearly been starved for an audience, one that understood his native German too! Siegfried, warmed by the tea and feeling he was back in civilization, quickly took on his former image of self-confident businessman, calmly and smilingly indulgent toward his companion. Just as a ship emerging from a storm into a quiet harbor turns from a waterlogged eggshell into a proud and majestic vessel, Siegfried felt he had sailed through the icy sea of the tundra, if not as far as the mainland of civilization, at least to one of its islands.

"Romance lies in the furs themselves!" Geizenrikh went on. "Fur is love, yes, yes, don't laugh! I've had six wives, my dear fellow, all of them Bolshoi ballerinas! That's what fur is, my dear! Of course, your pipeline will kill off the tundra, and there'll be no more sables, foxes, or ermines here. And that's stupid. You can find gas in the Sahara or somewhere. Anyway, using oil, coal, and gas is characteristic of barbarous civilizations. In about twenty years, thirty at best, man will be extracting energy from the sea. All right, say a hundred years! But you won't get an ermine or an arctic fox from seawater or a nuclear reactor.

"Anyway, do you know what the tundra is? The tundra is the only health resort on earth, where the air as recently as twenty years ago was totally free of harmful bacteria! People terminally ill with asthma were cured here in a week. But instead of building health resorts here, they built labor camps!" Geizenrikh grinned. "Truly, the USSR is a land of paradoxes. Stalin killed millions of his own citizens; there isn't a family in Russia that hasn't had at least one relative driven off into the camps by him. I, if I might mention it, did time here from thirty-eight to forty-six, as a German-Japanese spy." He smiled bitterly. "But it was easier for me than for the others. I was used to the tundra. But the others . . . Every year here, even now, when the swamps melt human bones and skeletons float in the quagmires. And the Russian people still yearn for Stalin, 'the boss,' as they say. His picture's all over the country again, in any bus you get on. Even Zinovyev, the dissident, calls him 'a great man'!"

Siegfried noticed that a sort of fiery glint had kindled in Geizenrikh's eyes. Clearly it was the first time the old man had come across someone to whom he could tell everything without holding back, pour out his soul, as the Russians say.

"Still, no nation in the world knows how to draw lessons from history," Geizenrikh pursued. "A single individual yes, an individual learns from his mistakes. A child doesn't put his hand in the fire twice. But peoples are amazingly forgetful, that's the paradox of humanity. You want examples? Permit me. Israel exports flowers to Germany. No, just think. Israel exports flowers to Germany and Germany sends army uniforms to Israel. And you say—lessons of history!"

And although Siegfried had said nothing of the kind, the old man proceeded. "It's because nations have no memory that I don't believe Soviet power in Russia will ever be overturned, or any sort of democratic reformation will come about in this country. The Russians don't know what democracy is; they're afraid of it, they need 'a boss.' That's why the authority that's driven the population of the whole country to semistarvation is today the most powerful in the world. No dissident can stir the people to general revolt, no Solzhenitsyn, Sakharov, Bukovsky can do it, for all their quixotic heroism. Even during the hunger strike in Novocherkassk, there was no rising in the towns and villages nearby! The Russians just don't have any experience at fighting for democracy. If they ever did rise up, it was for a 'good' czar!

"The Nentsi though . . . Of course, they're a savage people, uncivilized and backward. But that's to their advantage, too. They haven't got a historical slave complex. Until they were enslaved by the Russians, they lived here as a primitive commune. They didn't have czars, kings, or even princelings. Their judges were the elders, who owned nothing, neither land nor people. I've studied this territory in Miller, Milton, and Georgi*—I know what I'm talking about! Nowadays just travel around the USSR and look: in every national republic, from the Baltic to Georgia, Russians are regarded as occupiers. The Russians know this, so they're always on their guard. The government stations troops in every republic, in case of an uprising.

"But here, in the tundra—well, who could have foreseen that Nenets savages would rebel? Nobody even regarded them as people. Probably the English thought the same about the Jews in Palestine in the 1940s. Having just destroyed Hitler in Africa, how could the British army and its generals regard ringleted Jews as serious opponents? Now remember the tactics the Jews used to gain the victory in Palestine, how they drove out the British. After all, in Israel, just like here in the tundra, there are no forests, no jungles for guerrilla warfare! Just like here, the whole country and its population wide open like the palm of your hand. Nevertheless, in the course of a few months, the Jews had thrown the British out of Palestine. How? What with? Terror! By simply using terror, they brought the British to a point where their army sat

*Milton and Miller were famous seventeenth-century ethnographers; Georgi shared their profession in the eighteenth century. All three were celebrated for their journeys through Siberia.

shamefully in its barracks, too scared to poke its nose outside. After that, they fled the country altogether.''

He's just a maniac, thought Siegfried suddenly. He's a madman, dreaming mad dreams about overturning Soviet power in the tundra.

''I don't know who organized the Nentsi for this uprising,'' Geizenrikh continued, ''or if they have a single organizer at all. But things are developing in the tundra now almost like in Israel before the British fled: first personal terror directed against prominent people, then scattered acts of sabotage, followed finally by sabotage across the whole territory—firing the drilling rigs. You follow my train of thought?''

''Yes . . . but I . . . I didn't think it was as serious as all that. So far as I've heard, it all started with murders committed by escaped prisoners. What have the Nentsi got to do with it?''

''You think that, do you?'' The old man smiled grimly. He walked across the furs to a corner of the room and removed a pile of sables from a cupboard from which he took a little book with a well-worn cover. *Nenets Fairy Tales and Legends* was written on the cover. The middle of the book held a paper bookmark. Geizenrikh perched his pince-nez on his nose and opened the book at the marker. ''There's an excellent legend here about seven Nenets hero-brothers and their seven sisters. One day, returning from a hunt, the brothers discover that enemies have destroyed their chooms, driven off their deer, and violated their sisters. The brothers leap onto riding reindeer, overtake their enemies, and . . .'' Here, Geizenrikh raised a finger and read from the book. '' 'However many there were of the enemy, all were slain. While alive, their ears and *khote* were cut off and they were forced to eat their own *khote*. Thus the fathers avenged their blood and disgrace, thus do the sons likewise!' You know what a *khote* is? It's what you've got between your legs, my dear. Now you tell me, what would be the point of escaped Russian prisoners carrying out the precepts of Nenets legends, especially so closely and accurately, cutting off ears and sex organs of such lovers of Nenets girlies as Ryazanov, Hotko, and Voropayev?''

"What? What was that?" Siegfried had been listening rather patronizingly to the old man up to now, as to one out of his mind, but now his whole body shot forward. "Did you say—Ryazanov? Which Ryazanov?"

"Pyotr Ryazanov, chief geologist of Yamal Oil and Gas Exploration," said Geizenrikh and looked at Siegfried with interest. "Did you know him?"

Did Siegfried know Ryazanov? Yes indeed, he knew all three—Ryazanov, Hotko, and Voropayev. They were the ones who had been in Ryazanov's cottage five years before at that very farewell party for Siegfried when he had refused to let his Nenets Lolita, Okka, be passed around the circle. Then they had consoled themselves with another young Nenets girl, doing hell knows what to her . . . and it had been those three the tundra spirits had killed!

"Do you . . . are you telling me they killed them and cut off their . . . because they . . . ?" Siegfried brought out.

"I don't know the precise order of events." The old man smiled. "Whether they killed them and then cut or cut first and then killed. The legend in any case definitely says: 'while *alive,* their ears and *khote* were cut off.' " Geizenrikh again stared hard at Siegfried. "So you knew Ryazanov?"

"N-yes," said Siegfried, embarrassed. "Not too well . . ."

But his knees came together from fear. This instinctive gesture of self-protection did not escape Geizenrikh's keen eyes. He laid the book aside and said with a soothing smile, "All that is my purely literary conjecture. You've got nothing to worry about in any case, you're just a visitor.''

I do have something to worry about, thought Siegfried as the sordid picture of group debauchery that drunken night swam up before his eyes. But, God, he hadn't had any hand in what Ryazanov, Hotko, and Voropayev had done with that Nenochka. He'd only made love to his Okka. And, anyway, it was all rubbish about "tundra spirits," Nenets legends and this old tundra hand with the piercing eyes, bookish German, anti-Soviet speeches, and portentous literary deductions. He'd had six wives himself, shouldn't wonder if he'd had his good times in Nenets chooms with the likes of Melkune, and Okka, but he's not running.

That cursed sense of fear had taken root in Siegfried's mind, however—a cold foreboding of disaster and catastrophe, as in a plane when a new fit of acrophobia strikes. All three of them had been in Ryazanov's cottage that night and now the "tundra spirits" had executed the three; logic suggested that it was the turn of the fourth, his turn. More than anything at this moment, more than his $225 million and the opening of the pipeline in the company of Western journalists, Siegfried wanted to be lost in the snows back at Zataika with KGB Colonel Khanov, who was so solicitous, so reliable.

But outside the window was the polar night of the Yamal, and the Nentsi coming back from the *Khalmer*.

"Have you got a line through to Urengoi or Salekhard?'' he asked Geizenrikh.

"No telephone, of course. There's the radio.'' He indicated with his eyes a tall pile of fox furs by the window.

Siegfried went over and removed the furs from a bulky object. It was a low stool with an antediluvian radio of the type known in Russia as Harvesters. He picked up the receiver and began turning the handle of the dynamo, listening intently to the crackling sounds in his ear. He would call up the Urengoi or Salekhard KGB directorate, say who he was, and surrender himself into their trusty arms. This would end once and for all his delirious flight into the tundra and the mystic threat of retribution for some passing peccadillo with a twelve-year-old Nenochka five years before.

But before the distant female voice of the radio operator sounded in his ear, he caught the boom of helicopter engines outside the window. He glanced outside as Geizenrikh came over.

In the dark sky of the polar night he could see the signal lights of heavy Mi-10 paratroop helicopters. They were swiftly descending toward the Nenets encampment of the Bright Way fur farm. Siegfried's ears were overwhelmed by the heavy booming sound, while outside reindeer broke their tethers from fear, chooms swayed in the blast of the rotor above them, and, in the cages and enclosures, mink and arctic foxes raced back and forth, deafened and terrified. It seemed inevitable that at any moment automatic weapons and machine guns would open fire.

But no—the figures of army paratroops began leaping soundlessly out of the aircraft. Using the butts of their rifles, they drove the Nentsi onto the square in front of the farm administration building.

One of the helicopters landed right by the porch of the building, where Siegfried and Geizenrikh waited. Loud, hurrying footfalls echoed along the corridor, and one of the paratroopers kicked open the door of the fur-sorting room.

Struck by the unexpected sight—the bright fluorescent light and the abundance of furs on the floor—the young paratrooper in his khaki jacket stopped short in the doorway.

"Hände hoch," said Geizenrikh quietly to Siegfried, to make him put his hands up.

At these words in German, familiar to every Russian

292

through films about the Second World War, the young para's eyes flashed triumphantly. Keeping his rifle trained on Geizenrikh and Siegfried, he turned toward the corridor and shouted, ''Boys! Hoorah! They've put us down in Germany!''

V

FIRE IN THE TUNDRA

52

It was only as I was going out of Hudya's flat into the street that I realized what the heavy drone of aircraft rolling over Salekhard actually signified. The noise had been muffled inside by the double glazing.

During the time I had been drinking tea and inspecting his bookshelves and suffering my initial astonishment at Hudya's reading anti-Soviet books and then at his strange note on the door—"Good-bye and, please, go back to Russia"—the droning had reached such intensity that hundreds of people were spilling out of their houses and waving arms and caps at the sky.

Dozens of transport aircraft were roaring overhead. The powerful noise of their engines rolled like a wave over the town from the west, northwest, and southeast. The semicircle of their landing lights shone out as they blinked in the high blackness.

Behind the airplanes came the enormous freight and paratroop helicopters. Over Salekhard itself the air brigades split up. The planes went on to land at the airport, while the helicopters came down close by the river jetty near the Wave Restaurant, on the thick ice of the frozen Ob.

These were the reinforcements sent by party and government orders into Salekhard to assist the October Revolution Paratroop Division; from Moscow, the Special Dzerzhinsky Division of the USSR KGB; from

Voronezh, 1,300 students of the Advanced Police Academy; from Murmansk, two divisions of marines; and from Khabarovsk, a paratroop brigade and special troops for guarding targets of particular importance to state security. Units of these forces had already fanned out across the tundra, dropping paras at oil and gas drilling sites, pipeline sections, shift settlements, and Nenets encampments. But even those operational units that had now arrived in Salekhard produced a stunning effect on the inhabitants by their numbers and military strength.

I imagine the Czechs experienced a similar shock in their time, when our paratroopers rained down on Prague during the airlift. The only difference was that the Czechs were unlikely to have been so pleased to see them as was the entire Russian population of Salekhard.

Hell, it feels good to be a citizen of a country that's got military strength like ours! Never mind the rationing, or that there's no meat or butter in the shops. At least we can sleep securely knowing we need have no fear of any Chinese, American, West German, or Israeli aggressor. My heart warmed to see the huge pot-bellied Antons disgorging tanks, armored cars, and tracked amphibians straight onto the frozen Ob. With revving engines, they formed into columns ready to storm through tundra, taiga, or desert, wherever the Homeland should require.

If I were a sickly "intellectual" or a college kid, what had happened to me yesterday might have knocked me off balance for at least a year, if not for the rest of my life. There are women who go crazy or become lesbians after the shock of being raped. I can't say I'm made of iron, but I'm not made of wet rags either. After all, I've been in the police force for four years, and this kind of work strengthens your nerves and character—believe me. And now, looking at the might of our armed forces and joining in the general sense of excitement in the streets, I almost completely forgot about what had happened to me only the night before. A sense of jubilation rose inside of me, and I felt a flood of renewed strength.

53

A euphoric atmosphere, literally festive in fact, prevailed in the North Hotel too. Here, right in the lobby, were the joint operational staffs of the army, KGB, and the police. Radio operators dictated the reports they had received to staff officers:

"Police militia landing at Dawn over the North!"

"Marines have taken Road to Communism!"

"KGB forces have blocked off Ilyich's Legacy!"

Nobody realized the double meanings of these phrases; the staff officers quickly inserted colored flags into a huge map of the Yamal-Nenets District, denoting the areas now securely sealed off by the troops sent in.

"Yes, our military machine works like a dream—no problems! These Nentsi—tfu! We'll snap them in half, wimps!" These loud words were spoken in the hotel dining room by a husky twenty-three-year-old Ukrainian tank commander, helping himself to a large plateful of macaroni navy style. The restaurant had been converted into a staff canteen and was now crammed with officers from all branches of the services. "If we don't cope with that lot, I'll telegraph my brother—he's in the special units preparing for a drop into Sweden," the Ukrainian went on. He addressed the cook through the serving window. "Chef, are you a local man?"

"Yes, I am. Why?"

"Listen, is it true what they say about the Nenets women having their cunts on sideways?"

This ludicrous idea—that Nentsis' vaginas are placed differently from everyone else's—dates back to prehistoric times. The hoax gets passed on, in some totally mysterious fashion, from one generation of men to the next coming into the North. There hasn't been a man yet who hasn't fallen for that one as soon as he arrives.

I ordered millet porridge and bilberry jelly—you can't eat macaroni navy style first thing in the morning! There were no free tables, but three groups of officers immediately offered a seat at their tables. I accepted the one where the cloth was cleanest. Of course, I was now the center of attention. After a brief, lightly flirtatious introduction ceremony, one of them decided to gain everybody's attention, including mine.

"Listen boys, have you heard the one about how Vanya Bugayev, one of the Khabarovsk paras, caught two German saboteurs? No? Well! It's the biggest laugh of the day. All HQ knows! Listen. Two Germans, one of them was a Russo-German, something to do with the fur trade, and the other wasn't a German at all, he was an American of German descent, but that's not it—anyway, two foreigners were at this Nenets farm, Bright Way, before our boys arrived. There they were sitting quietly having tea and *sushki* when suddenly the Khabarovsk paras drop out of the sky onto the tundra. Among them, Ensign Vanya Bugayev. I should say, Anechka"—this was just for my benefit—"that they collected all these paras, Bugayev included, on operational alert in the middle of the night, and shoved them into Mi-10s while they were so woozy they were wrapping their foot rags around their boots—they hadn't a fucking clue where they were going to fight! Anyway, Vanya Bugayev jumps out of his helicopter onto the tundra, bursts into the farm admin building half-asleep, and these two foreigners, as soon as they saw a soldier, came out with *'Hände hoch!'*—sheer habit. Of course, they said it to each other, but Vanya Bugayev goes crazy as soon as he hears *'Hände hoch'* and bawls at the top of his voice: 'Hitler—kaput! Hitler—kaput! Hoorah!' "

After everybody finished laughing, the storyteller added with a smile, "Do you think Bugayev got a stripe torn off for that? Not a chance! He only got official thanks from the KGB, that's all! It turns out that this American German or German-American, who the hell knows—anyway, one of these Germans is some sort of VIP. He's called Siegfried Shertz. The Udmurt Gee Bees let him slip and he got into the tundra. Decided to take a stroll around the Soviet Union, son of a bitch! But Vanya Bugayev grabs him by the collar. 'Hitler—kaput,' he shouts. . . . Anechka, where are you off to?''

"Business." I smiled. "Thanks for the company."

I didn't have time to sit around in a restaurant listening to combat stories. I had to find Hudya. He wasn't in the restaurant or the lobby; nor was he in the staff rooms on the first and second floors. However, when I opened a door on the second floor, I came across my boss, old Zotov, and the head of the Salekhard KGB, Major Shatunov. I was flabbergasted: amid all these events, in the very center of HQ bustle and tense operational activity, these two looked like they were on vacation. They were sitting in their underwear in the middle of a double hotel room, unshaven and playing cards. There was an empty brandy bottle on the table and the remains of a snack. They'd been eating—God, it couldn't be worse—a can of herring in tomato sauce.

"Good morning," I said. "You haven't seen Hudya Benokan?"

"Eh? Are you still here?" said Zotov vaguely. "I thought you were back in Urengoi."

"Yesterday you ordered me yourself to look into the rumors about Vauli Piettomin here."

"Ah, yes, so I did," he recalled. "But you look different somehow. Anything happen?"

"What do I look like?" I went through into the bathroom to take a panicky look at myself in the mirror. My face, it has to be said, wasn't as fresh as it might have been, but nothing drastic. And yet Zotov, old man meticulous, had spotted right away that something had happened to me. I quickly got busy with my makeup and heard drifting in: "King of diamonds! Nine! . . . Queen of trumps! . . ." Hell, why weren't they working, when all this was going on around them? Having powdered over the dark rings under my eyes, I came out of the bathroom.

"There's women for you!" said Shatunov. "A spit and a dab and they're as fresh as a daisy, good enough to eat!"

Even the style of the sentence was extraordinary coming from Shatunov. Yesterday, he had been a smart, brusque, taciturn KGB major, but now, as if making a show of it, he was playing cards with Zotov—in his underclothes, not shaved, brandy on the table. His talk was no longer businesslike, it was normal everyday chat. So I asked him frankly, matching his tone, "What're you up to here?"

Zotov, about to play his next card, held his hand above the table and looked at me in surprise. "You don't know?"

"What should I know?"

Instead of playing his card, Zotov lowered his arm and turned to face me, sneering. "And just where did you spend the night?"

I forced myself to grin. "W-well, that's my business."

"I see! There's been an exodus of officers," Zotov mumbled, returning to the game, adding, as if it were a minor detail, "We've been fired."

"Wha-at?!" My astonished question was so loud both of them looked at me.

"It's all right, now," Zotov said. "When guns speak, you know, the muses are silent." He turned to Shatunov. "Your turn, Major.

I roughly covered the cards with my hand.

"Will you explain properly what's happened?"

"Your officers are pretty decisive characters." Shatunov smiled at Zotov. "It's all very simple. The head of the KGB himself, General Chebrikov, flew in from Moscow and immediately relieved me and your chief of all duties. And after the army restores order here, we'll be court-martialed."

"What for?"

"For not catching the escapees. For not discovering that a Nenets rebellion was brewing and stopping it. In a word, for the whole shambles. Somebody's got to be the scapegoat! Chebrikov and Bogomyatov have decided on us, Major Orudjev, Pyotr Tusyada, and Colonel Sini—the longer the list, the more solid the case."

"Don't you worry, kiddy-wink," added Zotov. "You're not on the list. So you can fly off to Urengoi; they'll have appointed somebody in my place already, I expect. At the same time, you can tell my wife not to worry, they won't put me in jail because of my age. They'll just give me a dishonorable discharge, and I'll lose my officer's pension. Well, fuck it!" At this, he slapped a card down on the table: "What a fucking system it is. You serve all your life, like a dog, then one thing goes wrong and the boot goes up your ass— no pension even."

Yesterday, if anybody had said anything like that about our Soviet system in the presence of KGB Major Shatunov, I have no doubt that person would have spent the remainder of his life in places far away from central heating and other comforts of civilization. But today Shatunov didn't raise an eyebrow. He played his next card. "Jack of spades."

I began to feel sorry for them, both Zotov and Shatunov, sitting there together, putting on airs, drinking cognac and playing cards. In fact, if Bogomyatov himself and the head of the KGB had designated Shatunov and Zotov as being responsible for all that had occurred in the tundra, the matter would not rest with discharge and loss of pensions. But why should I speak to them about that and make their already miserable mood even worse?

"Men," I said with affected carelessness. "Have you had any breakfast yet? Or have you been living on brandy all night?"

Zotov coughed. "We're . . . not hungry."

Well, it was clear enough: for all their old-soldier manner, they couldn't go to the officers' canteen for breakfast. So there they were, sitting in their room eating herrings and brandy.

"Stop lying! Not hungry!" I teased them. "Just say what you want brought from the canteen. I saw macaroni navy style there, reindeer goulash, and millet porridge. And tell me, please, if you've seen Hudya Benokan today?"

"I believe I did," said Zotov. "Yes, he dropped in an hour or so ago. But there's all this army business going on here. So if you need him, better look for him at the local CID."

I went downstairs to the restaurant and it was only when I was coming back with two portions each of macaroni and goulash (honestly, even under a microscope, you couldn't tell the difference) that a new idea occurred to me and brought me to a halt. Of course! Why hadn't I thought of it before? If Shatunov and Zotov were put on trial, one of the first questions put to Zotov would be: "And who did you send to Camp RS-549 to ascertain the circumstances of the breakout? Investigator Anna Kovina, of course? Splendid! And why, Comrade Kovina, on your arrival at Camp RS-549 at two in the afternoon did you not interrogate the roommates of the escapees the same day and didn't even interrogate them the following morning? Surely you must have realized that a group escape, especially on the eve of the official pipeline opening, was an unusual occurrence? What were you doing in the camp all that evening, night, and following morning?''

I was already involved; I was already ''on the list'' as Zotov had put it. They'd put more pressure on. I know our judicial system all right. It's one thing when you're inside the machine and do as you like in its name—then, minor peccadilloes are forgivable, they turn a blind eye. It's quite another matter when the machine starts working against you. The night I had spent at Hudya's would simply be put down as ''corruption while carrying out official duties''; and as for the night spent with Orudjev in the meeting room at Camp RS-549—! These two facts were more than enough for the judicial findings to say, ''The Urengoi and Salekhard CID operatives have been wallowing in debauchery, which explains their absence of professional and party vigilance with regard to the anti-Soviet mood of the population of the Yamal-Nenets District.'' And if, in addition, they found anti-Soviet literature in Hudya's apartment . . .

I went cold inside. Doubtless Hudya, like me—known throughout the territory as the ''Urengoi Alsatian,'' a sniffer-out of pornography, narcotics, and anti-Soviet writings—had confiscated the books from local dissidents. He had not handed them over immediately to the KGB, however; he'd concealed them. But if there was an anti-Soviet uprising in the district, how could Hudya prove that he had not disseminated anti-Soviet literature among the young Nentsi? And that was an official offense, Article 118 of the Criminal Code, point three: use of official position for the subversion of Soviet power—minimum sentence ten years' strict regime—in practice, the uranium mines in the

Pamirs, where no one survives more than three months.

My first thought was to run over to Hudya's place, break in, and burn the books in the Dutch stove.

But with all that was whirling around in my head in these minutes, I realized that to break down the door of what was, after all, someone else's apartment, in broad daylight, wasn't a wise thing to do.

54

The whole ground floor of the Salekhard CID was crammed with arrested Nentsi. The entire town seemed to have been combed through, along with the encampments on the outskirts. While waiting their turn to be questioned, they sat on the floor, which was the standard brick-brown color to hide the occasional bloodstain. Guards stood over them having a smoke. Still higher, on the walls of the corridor, were photographs of the escaped convicts from Camp RS-549 with the thick inscription WANTED CRIMINALS, and a decorative poster with the full text of the moral code of a builder of Communism. Behind the doors of the interrogation rooms, investigators brought in from Moscow and Tyumen were conducting their ceaseless questioning. Their main object was to find out who was the leader of the Nenets rebellion, who had spread the rumor of the return of Vauli Piettomin across the tundra, and who had set fire to the drilling rigs.

Stepping across the legs of the seated Nentsi, I glanced into all the ground-floor offices. No Hudya. In an office on the second floor, the directorate secretary tore herself away from the continual ringing of the telephone to look at me, harassed. Hudya? He flew to Urengoi half an hour ago.

"Why?"

"Well, who knows? In this madhouse, everybody does what he wants!"

Odd, I thought. Hudya flies to Urengoi and leaves me that stupid note: "Good-bye. And, please, go back to Russia." Why should I up and go to Russia for no reason at all, and why "good-bye," if I live and work in Urengoi and that's exactly where he's gone?

I walked, puzzled, along the second-floor corridor. It was quieter here, with few detainees. I had already reached the staircase when the door of the nearest office opened and out came Ayuni Ladukai—the girl who had led the boys of Boarding School No. 3 in raping me the previous night.

We both froze. I was on the landing preventing her escape; she was in the corridor. The radiant smile slowly left her face—she'd obviously been set free after questioning.

My first desire was to pull out my pistol and shoot the bitch on the spot. My hand reached for the holster automatically. But it was then I recalled the words she had hurled at Hudya when he broke into the school and interrupted the violence. Glancing swiftly around at the Moscow investigators and guards, I quickly seized Ayuni's elbow and, with my trained hand, twisted her arm in a painful hold so that she could neither run nor resist.

"Come with me," I said in a low voice.

All the offices were occupied by crowds of investigators, but I had to interview this little cunt as soon as possible, alone and in secret. So I pushed her roughly into the ladies' room, so quickly that no one paid any attention.

There were only two cubicles and both were dirty; still, they were empty. I pushed Ayuni into one of them and closed the door behind me. It seemed the girl could feel the iron grip of my fingers even through the sleeve of her *malitsa,* and I twisted her arm to a point where the pain stops anyone from even contemplating resistance. Most probably the bitch never thought of resistance anyway, but last night she had shown no pity toward me—why in hell should I feel sorry for her today?

Raising the arm behind her back, I forced Ayuni's face almost into the toilet bowl, yellow from old urine and excrement, and only then released her.

"Who is Okka?" I asked.

The girl was silent. She wore a fine *malitsa* and was of middling height, shorter than me but strong boned. I didn't expect her to talk right away. Zotov had told us that under interrogation Nentsi are secretive and reticent; interviewing them was like getting blood out of a stone. But yesterday, in the school, she had been taking her part in the general boys' chorus of: *"Nut i shar!* Death to the Russian occupiers!"

"Who is Okka, damn you! Or I'll break your arm." I jerked her elbow upward so hard that her face splashed into the toilet bowl. But I forced her up again. "Well?"

All of a sudden, with an adroit movement, she twisted her whole body and I felt her elbow slipping out of my grasp, leaving me with just the empty sleeve of her *malitsa*. This they hadn't taught us in police school—jujitsu grips when your opponent is wearing a *malitsa* made of slippery reindeer fur. Another fraction of a second and she would have broken free altogether. But she'd chosen the wrong one this time!

Using my free hand, I gave her a powerful backhander across the nape of the neck. I followed it up by gripping her wrist in both hands and forcing it so far up her back that I heard the crunch of her shoulder joint quite clearly. The girl gave a suppressed scream. Not only had the little bitch organized a line of rapists for me the night before, now she was forcing me to torture her in earnest.

But I had no time for niceties. I pushed her face still

deeper into the toilet and held her under till she gurgled and tried to say something, her whole body writhing. Then I released her contorted limbs and allowed her to straighten up and draw breath. I kept standing behind her and so couldn't see her dirty face, smelling of urine, but I could guess how the beat of her suffocating heart must be deafening now and how she was gulping in air with her wet, gaping mouth. Well, the previous night they had tortured me worse—till I lost consciousness. Now she and I were almost even, but I still needed to know about the Okka for whom I had been raped. After all I had been through, I had the right to know that!

"Well! Will you say who Okka is? Or . . ." I began to squeeze her arm again, letting her understand that nothing would stop me from drowning her.

We were alone in the washroom and—I don't know, perhaps in that moment of bitterness, I really could have killed her and left her there.

She suddenly spoke.

"I'll talk . . . I'll tell you."

I kept her bent over the bowl.

"Talk!"

"Okka is Hudya Benokan's sister."

"What!" I released her hands in my astonishment, and she turned on me her dirty wet face, in which her narrow eyes shone with hatred.

"Okka—is Hudya Benokan's sister," she said with a crooked smile. "Five years ago, she died, however. She choked on Ryazanov's sperm, however."

"How do you know that?"

"I saw it myself, however. I was eleven years old, she was twelve. Hotko was the senior doctor in charge of our schools and he took Okka and me out of school, saying we were going to the hospital. He brought us to a drinking party at Ryazanov's, however. There were Ryazanov, Voropayev, and some American. They filled Okka and me up with alcohol and fucked us. Ryazanov, Hotko, and Voropayev fucked me but Okka had taken the American's fancy and he didn't let them fuck her. But in the morning, he flew away to Moscow, however. Then all of them started fucking Okka together. From behind, in front and in the mouth at once, however. When they stopped, they found that Okka had choked to death on Ryazanov's sperm. Nothing happened to them. They sent me home to the tundra immediately. Now the tundra spirits have taken revenge on them; it's only right. Only the spirits can't reach the American. Pity, however."

"When did all this happen?"

"I told you: five years ago, May, before the end of the school term."

"You mean you think the tundra spirits killed Ryazanov, Voropayev, and Hotko because of Okka?"

"Who else then?" She smiled bitterly, washing herself in the sink. "Not Hudya Benokan, was it? If he'd wanted to kill them, he'd have done it five years ago, however. But he went to Moscow to study, the shameful son of a dog."

"Why did the spirits wait five years, then?" I smiled.

"They were shut up in the ground, however. And now your drills have let them out, they've taken over the convicts and the convicts have started ripping up our enemies. This is only the beginning, however. Well, can I go?"

"Wait a minute," I said, thinking. "What was that American's name?"

"Siegfried they called him."

"Siegfried Shertz?" I said, recalling the surname of the American VIP the paras had captured at the Bright Way fur farm.

"Don't remember. Perhaps, however," she said indifferently and for lack of a towel wiped her face on her *malitsa* sleeve, then spat contemptuously on the floor and went out.

I did not hold her back.

I remained alone and walked over to the window.

Along the dark Salekhard streets moved personnel carriers and army trucks filled with paratroopers, marines, and police. I could see patrolling soldiers with dogs on the icy pavements. The air was filled with the drone of military helicopters and airplanes.

Surely all this—the Nenets rising, the burning of the drilling installations, the occupation of the territory by KGB, police, and marines—surely all this couldn't be happening just because in May of 1978, Ryazanov, Voropayev, Hotko, and some visiting American had overdone their bit of fun with a couple of Nenochkas? Why did nobody, not even Shatunov, know about this story? He would certainly have connected the three murders with the death of this Okka long ago. And how had it happened that the avengers were convicts escaping from Camp RS-549? Tundra spirits taking them over was crazy, of course.

And suddenly—it was as if a bolt of electricity went through my head, lighting up the events of the past few days. Like a word turning up among a jumble of blocks, even if a letter or two were missing.

I remembered how five years ago, in the summer of 1978, the whole of Moscow University was agog over Hudya Benokan, who had practically galloped into Moscow from the tundra on a reindeer. He had joined the Law Faculty to become an investigator.

I remembered Major Orudjev had kicked the base of the electricity pylon in Camp RS-549 and explained that it had been Hudya Benokan who had said in front of the prisoners how escape from the camp was feasible—by using the power lines. After that, three convicts had indeed used that escape route, mysteriously disappeared in the tundra, survived a severe blizzard, and executed, one after another, the murderers of Hudya Benokan's sister.

And I remembered that the first investigator on the scene at the murders of Hotko and Ryazanov had been who? Hudya Benokan!

55

I was still unsure; I didn't allow myself to believe that Hudya was a murderer or an organizer of murders and the fomenter of the Nenets rebellion. Even on the way to the local registry office, I kept trying to find another explanation for what had happened, damping my feverish imaginings.

The registry office was two blocks away from the Salekhard CID and police station; in provincial towns like Salekhard, all the municipal institutions are located next door to one another in the center of town.

I went in practically at a run. It was empty and quiet here—these mad days nobody was registering marriages, births, divorces, or even deaths. However, the head of the office was on duty—the first sign of the return of law and order, people were going back to work. Another two or three days and this office would see life again. The youngsters would be registering marriages, divorces, babies; champagne corks would be smacking the ceiling on any pretext; cognac and vodka would be flowing generously onto the floor from overfilled glasses and crystal goblets smashing musically on the stone porch. The job of registrar required either a strict teetotaler to withstand the assault wave of liquor gifts, or someone with the constitution of a horse, to drink to the newlyweds every day.

The Salekhard incumbent clearly belonged to the

second category. A hale old man in a wolfskin jacket, he looked up at me with the frank thirst of the alcoholic as soon as I entered. Realizing I was an investigator and not a newlywed, however, the old man subsided and at my request produced, with a scuffling of felt boots, the Civil Status Register for April—May—June 1978. This book contains all births and deaths in the town.

I opened the book and at the page dated May 19, I found the entry:

> Benokan, Okka Nogovna, born 1966, died on the night of 17–18 May from an asthma attack. Buried in the Nenets cemetery. Based on: Medical Certificate No. 852/6, May 18, 1978.''

From an asthma attack! So that's how the three had covered up the murder. Even if you exhumed the corpse and conducted an autopsy—after more than five years!—you'd hardly find traces of Ryazanov's sperm or lung infection. But to dig down to the truth I had no need to drag the girl's remains from her tundra grave.

''I need the medical findings on her death,'' I said to the registrar.

The old man shuffled over to a tall cupboard with a card index. He fussed around for ages with the bar that locked all the drawers at the same time, but finally pulled one of them out and picked up a hefty folder bound with twine. On it was written thickly in ink: *1978 April—May—June*. He undid the twine, licked a grimy finger, and began to leaf through the sheaf of medical reports. It took him a minute, the longest minute of my life, to extract a piece of paper and hand it to me.

It was not a medical report.

It was the standard form of the Salekhard Police

Militia Directorate CID. On it was a short, typewritten note:

Declaration No. 774, July 2, 1983

I, Hudya Benokan, investigator CID Salekhard Police Directorate Declare:
For official purposes, the medical report No. 852/6 supplied May 18, 1978, by V. Hotko, senior physician at Salekhard Municipal Children's Hospital, has been removed from records.

H. Benokan

These few lines removed any lingering doubt. The twentieth of June is the traditional date for defending one's diploma thesis at Moscow University, the twenty-fifth sees the official award of the diploma, followed by a banquet in the evening. The train from Moscow to Salekhard takes three days. That meant, no later than June 29 or 30, 1983, Hudya returned from Moscow to Salekhard and took up his duties as an investigator with the Salekhard police force. And the first thing he did was extract the medical report on his sister's death, signed by one of her killers, from the registry. Was this not the reason why Ryazanov, Hotko, and Voropayev had not cried out or shouted for help when their murderer cut off their genitals and ears—was it not because the murderer held that fake medical certificate in front of their eyes?

I went over to the registrar's desk and picked up the telephone. "Operator? Give me the North Hotel, duty staff officer."

A second later a clipped voice came on. "Staff duty officer, Colonel Khropachov here."

"Comrade Colonel, this is CID Investigator Anna Kovina speaking. This morning your paratroopers captured an American called Siegfried Shertz at the

Nenets fur farm Bright Way. Do you know where he is being held?''

"Why is the CID after him again? I told your investigator this morning—he's been taken by the KGB to Urengoi. Doesn't your left hand know what the right one's doing, or something?"

"What investigator did you inform?" I asked, growing cold. "What was his name?"

"Who the fuck knows what his name was! Some Nenets name . . ."

I opened my mouth and gulped some air. There was only one investigator in Salekhard with a Nenets name. Hudya Benokan. Hudya, who, according to the secretary of CID, had left for Urengoi an hour earlier.

"Comrade Colonel," I said beseechingly. "Could you possibly get in touch immediately with Urengoi KGB and find out exactly where this Shertz is now?"

"It's a madhouse in Urengoi at the moment—they're getting ready for the government flying in for the pipeline opening. If you like, I can connect you with the Urengoi Gee Bee on our radio and you can ask them yourself."

"No thanks, no need," I said quickly. No KGB operative would tell me over the phone what they were doing with Shertz or where they were holding him. And to tell them that I suspected Hudya Benokan of intending to kill Shertz—no thanks, I hadn't come to that yet. "Comrade Colonel, when is your next plane to Urengoi?"

"Two planes are getting ready to leave right now; they'll be off in about twenty minutes."

"Comrade Colonel, dearest!" I tried to put all my feminine charm into my voice, plus a hint of flirtation. "Couldn't you just hold one up just for about ten minutes? I'm in the center of town, I need about half an hour to get to the airport."

"Hold up the aircraft?" The colonel was astounded. "Well, sweetheart, that's asking a bit too much! Do you know how many passengers there are—important people too!''

I didn't let him finish. I dropped the receiver and raced out into the street.

An armored personnel carrier was bowling along, probing the polar night with powerful headlights.

I ran into the middle of the road, practically under its tracks, and waved my arms.

The carrier stopped and a youthful, hook-nosed face poked out of the cabin and swore. ''What's the matter with you? Off your fucking rocker?''

I ran up to the cabin and thrust out my red police identity card.

''Dear heart, I'm a police investigator! I have to get to the airport, urgent!'' Without waiting for an answer, I crawled up on the track.

''What's up? You giving birth or something?'' asked the driver, stupefied.

''Almost! Drive on, step on it to the airport, sweetie!''

''A kiss then!'' said the driver and stared at me with cheerful insolence.

Without thinking, I kissed him on the lips and made him gasp for breath and shake his head. Eventually, he said admiringly, ''Well, shit! Never thought I'd ever kiss the police!'' And he pressed the gas pedal to the floor.

56

Government Telegram

Urgent, Secret
Government Special Service

TO SECRETARY CENTRAL COMMITTEE CPSU
MEMBER OF POLITBURO CENTRAL COMMITTEE CPSU

IN ACCORDANCE WITH GOVERNMENT ORDERS AND YOUR PERSONAL INSTRUCTIONS, JOINT FORCES OF THE ARMY, KGB, AND POLICE HAVE DURING THE LAST 24 HOURS OCCUPIED VIRTUALLY ALL MAJOR INHABITED POINTS, WORKER SETTLEMENTS, AND NENETS CAMPS IN THE TERRITORY OF THE YAMAL-NENETS NATIONAL DISTRICT AND PLACED UNDER GUARD ALL GAS PIPELINES AND ALL GAS AND OIL INSTALLATIONS ON THE YAMAL PENINSULA. SPECIAL MEASURES ARE BEING TAKEN TO EXTINGUISH EIGHT GAS FLARES BURNING IN THE TUNDRA. KGB AND MVD FORCES ARE CONDUCTING ACTIVE OPERATIONS TO BRING TO LIGHT THE FOMENTERS OF THE DISTUR-BANCES. THE SECURITY OF THE OFFICIAL OPENING OF THE SIBERIA–WESTERN EUROPE GAS PIPELINE IS GUARANTEED.

President of KGB USSR
Army General Chebrikov
First Secretary Tyumen Province
    Party Committee CPSU
Bogomyatov

57

It's to Urengoi we're going,
Tundra round us as we pass . . .

A freckle-faced lad was singing this on the plane to the tune of the old colonial song "It's to Uruguay we're going." He was accompanying himself on a guitar. The whole plane joined in the chorus:

Night complete with snowstorms blowing
Watches over Nenets gas.

There were none of the usual passenger seats in an An-twenty-four paratrooper transport aircraft. Instead, there was a row of aluminum benches along the sides and a sort of rail overhead for the parachutists to secure their straps on. Now the entire plane was crammed full of people who in two days' time were going to stand around the government rostrum in Urengoi as heroes and guests of honor. Here were the drillers from Baku, Ufa, and Kishinyov who had bored the first exploratory and the first industrial wells on the Yamal a few years back. Here the first welders and pipe layers were playing cards and dominoes. The builders of the first tundra settlements, specialists in capping oil gushers, shift workers, who had been stuck for a few days at the airports in Siktivkar and Naryan-

Mar—all were singing, drinking, and eating as they sat on the aluminum benches, on suitcases, or on the floor. Here also, along with all the others, were five Georgians in enormous cloth caps, with cases of oranges and flowers. How the black marketeers had managed to get onto a military aircraft, what bribe had been required, God only knew, but after all, Georgian black marketeers had also done their bit toward the building of the pipeline. As one of them said, "Without our vegetables and fruit, you'd have been on a prison diet here!"

> *It's to Urengoi we're going,*
> *Silent night, like ammonal . . .*

Yes, everything was returning to normal—life with its gaiety, noise, songs, silly jokes, and Caucasian oranges was rolling back aboard military transport aircraft into the Yamal tundra, so that in a few days all the deaths, the explosions, the whole Nenets revolt would be forgotten as if they had never been. Along the whole five-thousand-kilometer length of the gas pipeline from Urengoi to West Germany and France, adjuster engineers were checking the readiness of compressor stations to receive the first of the Yamal gas. In Moscow members of the government delegation and foreign guests were already packing their suitcases no doubt, making sure to include three pairs of warm woolen underwear.

> *Just be careful, friend,*
> *Because nobody's ever yet been—*
> *In that mysterious land, that's called Yamal.*

The guitar twanged.

I was sitting in a festive atmosphere but I was on tenterhooks, checking my watch every minute. I tried to imagine what Hudya was doing right now in Urengoi. Surely he wouldn't risk penetrating the KGB to finish off this Siegfried Shertz! Damn it! We had gone chasing after the escaped convicts thinking up the most unlikely scenarios about how they'd managed to kill Ryazanov, Hotko, and Voropayev—Zotov had even brought Voropayev's sweaty underwear from Yaku-Tur! And all the time Hudya had been next to us, leading us by the nose, even tossing us Zaloyev's glove to keep us on the false scent. But who really did the killing? Hudya himself! Or did he just help the prisoners escape on condition they commit the murders?

We were coming in to land at Urengoi. Beneath us lay the tundra gas installations, the frosted filaments of the pipelines, and the Urengoi Main Compressor Station, the working heart of the pipeline. Just as blood in the body flows to the heart and is pumped out in massive surges to all parts of the organism, so this station collects gas from all over the Yamal and in two days, with its gigantic, superpowerful turbines, will begin sending it along the eightfold pipeline into Europe. Deep in the polar night, lying on the white dish of the tundra, the station resembled an extraterrestrial building put up by some superior civilization, centuries ahead of humankind.

The aircraft banked to the left and came down toward the Urengoi landing strip, swept clear by the ground wind. I was literally feverish with anxiety. What was waiting for me in Urengoi? News of the arrest of Hudya Benokan while attempting to get through to Siegfried Shertz? Or—if Hudya had succeeded in duping the Gee Bees—Shertz's corpse with ears and cock severed?

58

There were no taxis at Urengoi Airport, but calling for an official car from CID would mean losing at least forty minutes. That left the bus.

The Urengoi streets were thronged with people, despite the thirty-degree frost and a gusty wind. It was the first time in several days that people had come out in numbers without fear, to line up in the stores. In advance of the official opening, just as in Salekhard, scarce goods had appeared, real milk even, not the sour acidophilus stuff. People were in a hurry to buy, not just for the celebration of the opening of the pipeline but to stock up for the New Year's party. There was even a line at the hairdresser's, and I had the fleeting thought that, good heavens, it really was the holiday in two days, and when on earth could I get my hair done?

The crowds on the streets slowed the bus up though, and I grew more anxious with each minute—well, come on, come on! Why the hell are we waiting for that old biddy running with two heavy string bags?

At last we came to the square in front of the town party committee building and the government rostrum. This was draped in red calico and decorated with pine branches and government portraits—Andropov, Chernenko, Ustinov, Gorbachev, Gromyko. Carpenters were swarming around the rostrum tacking up an enormous placard: TO YOU, HOMELAND, SIBERIAN GAS! The Moscow architect was also fussing around here.

I jumped out of the bus and crossed the square at a run to the white two-story building that housed the local KGB. Before the door I took a moment to catch my breath, get ahold of myself, appear calm and collected. I pushed the door on its heavy spring; behind it, of course, was the checkpoint with its armed guard.

"Who do you want?"

I thrust out my police investigation identity card.

"I want to see Major Gromov."

The guard picked up the phone. The Urengoi KGB's a bit different from Salekhard; the building's new, and they even have an internal telephone.

A minute later they let me through, and I ran up to the first floor, noting on the way how the Gee Bees had tarted themselves up for the celebrations—red carpet strips along the corridors, red placards: KGB— SHIELD AND SWORD OF SOVIET POWER, and, of course, Andropov's portrait, festooned with red ribbons. Why shouldn't they decorate him, he raised their pay, didn't he? And all around, the KGB's now virtually the supreme authority in the country. The dirty work gets done by us, the police militia.

Now the office of Major Gromov, the deputy chief of the directorate. Behind the door, the peck of a typewriter. I straightened my fur jacket and hat and knocked briefly.

Major Gromov, seated at his desk, typing; next to him a tape recorder.

I spoke formally. "Comrade Major, permission to speak. Investigator Kovina from CID . . ."

"OK, Anechka." He smiled. "At ease. Take a seat. What can I do for you?"

"Oleg Borisovich," I said, to show that we in the police know their first names too, "I'm looking for Siegfried Shertz, the American picked up by the paras at Bright Way. The duty staff officer in Salekhard said you had him.''

Gromov said nothing, smiled faintly, but even his cocky little smile made me relieved—at least Shertz was alive; otherwise Gromov wouldn't be smiling. Naturally, Gromov wanted to know what the hell this American was to me, but he wanted to demonstrate his shrewdness, so he asked a typical man's question. ''Good looking, is he?'' Gromov lit a cigarette; his voice even held a note of jealousy.

OK, I thought, we'll play it your way, you asked for it.

''Not bad, considering.'' I spoke evasively, never having seen the man. ''Have you still got him?''

''You mean you've flown here from Salekhard to defend this Siegfried?''

Defend! Did Gromov know everything already? But I continued the game and asked, ''Why defend? Has he done anything?''

Gromov burst out laughing—frank, open laughter.

''You're wonderful! Armed reconnaissance! Brilliant! All right, relax. He has done something, of course, but not here; in Udmurtia. He made a monkey of the Udmurt KGB chief—took his car for a ride. Want to hear?''

Gromov pressed the rewind button on his tape recorder and ran the tape back a little way. While he was thus occupied, his face bore, how shall I put it?—a certain satisfaction that some American had outwitted the chief of the Udmurt KGB. Gromov stopped the tape and pressed the play button. He seemed to know the tape by heart (he wasn't transcribing it, was he?), for he knew the exact spot.

''If Comrade Khanov had told me he was chief of the KGB . . .'' A masculine voice came from the recorder. I marveled at how well this American spoke Russian. ''But judge for yourself, Comrade Major! That Kolesova, the interpreter, tells me that a snowstorm has covered the whole of Siberia for three days, then she introduces me to this guy, an Udmurt, and they cart me off to some hideaway in the taiga and start to get me drunk. It struck me as suspicious from the very start. You hear stories like that every day in the West: bandits kidnap millionaires and demand a ransom. You've heard of Heineken beer? Well, not long ago, Heineken himself was kidnapped in Holland.

"Well, when I heard on the radio that there wasn't any blizzard in Siberia, I decided right away that they'd kidnapped me—Kolesova and this Udmurt. I'm a millionaire as well, you know. Not as rich as Heineken, but still . . . Well, I got up in the middle of the night and quietly escaped. I drove the car away, but bear in mind, I didn't run off to Moscow to our embassy, I didn't call up any Western newspaper correspondents. I flew on here to Urengoi, to tell you and Comrade Bogomyatov the whole story. As regards material damage, the punctured tires and the telephone wire I cut, I'll pay for them. How much do I owe? Three hundred rubles? Four hundred? . . ."

Gromov switched off the recorder.

"Did you follow all that?" he asked me, smiling. My face obviously registered total blankness, so he condescended to clarify.

"General Chebrikov ordered the Udmurt, Colonel Khanov, to delay this Shertz of yours and amuse him while we sorted things out here. But Khanov got plastered, so much so that"—he pointed at the recorder—"he'll be fired." He raised his eyes to me and at once became serious. "So, Anya. You very well know that we don't encourage contacts with foreigners. However, I'm prepared to turn a blind eye on your affair with this Shertz, if you'll do me a favor. Find out from him, little by little, what he saw when he was with the Nentsi. He tried to tell me here that he saw nothing, no rebellion, but . . ." Gromov again smiled grimly. "I'm not Khanov, am I?"

"Where is he now?" I asked, ignoring the filthy talk of an affair with Shertz. "You've got him, haven't you?"

"We can't hold foreign subjects," Gromov smiled. "He's in the Polar Hotel catching up on his sleep."

"How long has he been there?" I moved impatiently toward the door. This self-satisfied idiot had let Shertz go to a hotel, alone, without protection!

"Well, not so long . . . About three hours ago . . . You understand what I asked you to do?"

I didn't hear him. I rushed out of his office, though there was still one more question I was dying to ask: had the Salekhard investigator Hudya Benokan shown any interest in Shertz? But maybe after all that was now a purely academic question!

It was only three blocks from the KGB to the spanking new Polar Hotel, and I set off at a run.

59

If I'd had the time to complete an interrogation statement from the duty manager of the Polar Hotel, it would have looked like this:

Duty manager of the Polar Hotel, Comrade
B. Mironov, stated:
At approximately 12 noon, on the instructions of KGB Major Comrade Gromov, Siegfried Shertz, a U.S. citizen, was accommodated in deluxe apartment No. 29 on the second floor of the hotel. Mr. Shertz was brought to the hotel in an official KGB car. He was wearing Nenets clothing—*malitsa* and *kisi*. He looked very tired and unshaven and smelled like Nentsi do. On receiving his key, he stated that he was going to bed and did not wish to be disturbed. He expressed an interest in when we were expecting the arrival of foreign journalists. Since this information is not secret, I told him that today and tomorrow the government delegation would be coming and the journalists tomorrow and the day after. Mr. Shertz said that he hadn't slept for three days and would probably sleep through till tomorrow. He therefore asked me to allow no phone calls and no visitors. After that, he went to his room. After about two and a half hours, that is, at three in the afternoon, a CID investigator from Salekhard

came to me. I have forgotten his name, unfortunately, although he did show me his official identification. This investigator, a Nenets in appearance, asked me the number of Mr. Shertz's room. I told him that Mr. Shertz did not wish to be disturbed for any reason whatsoever. The investigator told me that he had urgent official business with Mr. Shertz. Ten minutes later, the investigator and Mr. Shertz left the hotel together, got into an official police car, and went off, in which direction I do not know. I noticed nothing suspicious in their behavior. The car they left in was a Gazik with MILITIA written on it, I don't remember the license number.

I repeat—I kept no official record of my conversation with the hotel administrator. No time for that! I looked at my watch. Hudya had taken Shertz out of the hotel thirty-eight minutes before. I raced out and hurtled into our police directorate. In thirty-eight minutes, I thought on the way, the American could have been taken out onto the tundra and had everything cut off!

Near our directorate building stood an official Volga. I didn't go into the directorate to find out from the duty officer what pretext Hudya had used to get a police car. I didn't care whether Hudya had given him an official requisition for automobile transport or a couple of sturgeon.

I tore open the Volga door. Sergeant-driver Krylov was sitting there—the same "Uncle Kolya" who had taken me to Urengoi Airport on December 9 on my assignment to Camp RS-549. In the four years of my work with the Urengoi police, I had ridden often enough with Uncle Kolya to dispense with the niceties. Anyway, I was in Urengoi, wasn't I? My own backyard!

"Hi, Uncle Kolya! Go and report to the duty officer that I've taken the car for twenty minutes. Don't ask me anything; it's urgent and I'll take the responsibility! Well, move it, move it!'' I pushed him bodily out of the car, took his place at the wheel, and stepped on the gas. It was warm in the car—Uncle Kolya never turned the engine or the heater off. On the radio one of the policemen out on patrol was calling for first aid in Workingmen's Hostel No. 7. Usual drinking party and brawl, I thought briefly, as I turned the corner at full speed and almost rammed a municipal bus. One more turn and I was in the local schoolyard. The second-shift pupils were already in their classrooms and the yard was empty—just what I needed.

I picked up the mike. It was really because of the radio that I had tossed Uncle Kolya out of the car. Now for the main business. The flight from Salekhard to Urengoi, the talk with Major Gromov at KGB, and the questioning of the Polar manager—all of that had been simple. I took a deep breath, as if about to jump into water. Then I pressed the switch on the mike, put the radio onto transmit, and spoke, ''Hudya! Hudya! It's Anna! It's Anna! Hudya! It's Anna! I'm in Urengoi! Come in, I implore you! Over.''

Instead of Hudya in the crackling ether, there came the indignant voice of the duty officer, Captain Shevtsov: ''Kovina, what's all this? Why have you taken the car? Who's this Hudya you're after?''

''Boris Markovich, dear, get off the air. It's a life and death matter!'' I spoke pleadingly into the mike, secretly overjoyed that Shevtsov had come on. Hudya's car had a similar radio, and he'd most likely have it switched on to find out what the police were up to and whether he was being sought. Now he knew that I was in Urengoi, that I knew almost everything, and that all the police cars in the town were listening in. If Shertz was still alive, this might restrain Hudya from killing him. ''Boris Markovich, clear the channel. Hudya! Hudya! It's Anna! It's Anna! I know everything! Now, please come in! Hudya, dear, come in! Over!''

I can imagine the "duty" and the other police cars pricking up their ears hearing that *dear*. What did I care?

I switched over to receive and froze in anticipation. After a pause a calm voice sounded. "Anna, Hudya here. Over.

"Huddy, dear, sweet, darling! Is he still alive? Is he still alive? Over!"

"Do you want to talk to him? Over."

"Yes, I do! Of course I do! Over."

Lord, that meant Hudya hadn't killed the American yet! Now I heard the same masculine voice I had heard in Gromov's office. "Hello, over."

"Are you Mr. Shertz? Over." Well, I thought, go for broke, nothing else to do. "Mr. Shertz, I am CID investigator Anna Kovina. I am charging you on two counts. First, five years ago, in May 1978, you took part in the group debauchery of a twelve-year-old Nenets girl named Okka and an eleven-year-old named Ayuni Ladukai. As a result of the orgy at the villa of Pyotr Ryazanov, chief geologist of Yamal Oil and Gas Exploration Trust, Okka died. What have you got to say on the matter? Over."

I'd never preferred charges by radio before, and to a foreign subject, at that! I could imagine Captain Shevtsov and the rest going crazy. I wondered if it would occur to Shevtsov to switch on the tape recorder.

The calm voice of Siegfried Shertz came on again. "I would like to hear the second charge. Over."

Dammit, this American had nerves of steel. Or did Hudya have a gun on him and was it he dictating the questions?

"Certainly," I said. "At Ryazanov's villa, you, Ryazanov, Hotko, and Voropayev took part in the debauching of Nenets girls. The other three men have been killed over recent days. You must have connected the circumstances of their deaths with that orgy and

Okka's death. The Nentsi didn't know the real reasons for the murders of Ryazanov, Hotko, and Voropayev; they took it for the tundra spirits, a signal for an uprising. But you *did* know the truth! However, you concealed that truth from the police and even the KGB, although you were with KGB Major Gromov only three hours ago. In our country nondisclosure is equivalent to committing a crime. Especially in a situation like this. I accuse you of withholding information of importance to the state. Over.''

It seemed to me that even the atmospherics had died out. At any rate, neither Captain Shevtsov nor anyone else butted in.

''The business of the tundra spirits killing Russians and cutting off their genitals,'' said the unhurried, almost deliberately slowed voice of Siegfried Shertz, ''I heard while I was still in Siktivkar, at the airport. But it was just a rumor, a joke; nobody believed it there. That it was Ryazanov, Hotko, and Voropayev who had been killed I only found out this morning. Mr. Geizenrikh told me; you can check with him. Yes, I did connect their murders with that evening at Ryazanov's dacha. Moreover, I thought that I was in danger myself. But it wasn't so easy to give evidence against myself. At any rate, it isn't done in America. The main point is, I didn't seduce Okka. Yes, there was a party, my send-off to be exact. I was flying out of Salekhard the next morning.

''Ryazanov had brought the girl Okka to me a week earlier. He brought her to me at the hotel and she herself, of her own free will, stayed in my room, you may believe it or not. She wasn't a virgin; in fact, she was already . . . how can I put this . . . an adult, even passionate woman. I am trying to explain this to investigator Benokan, but he hasn't read Nabokov's *Lolita,* so I can't explain to him what sort of a girl Okka was. She was a depraved Nenets Lolita. She came to me in the hotel herself all that week, every evening, and stayed the night—you can check that with the staff at the North in Salekhard. I think her sexual education had been expertly supervised before me, by Ryazanov, Hotko, or Voropayev, maybe all three, I don't know.

"That evening you and Investigator Benokan are talking about, when Ryazanov organized my send-off, Dr. Hotko brought another little girl, I don't know what her name was, maybe it was the one you mentioned. She was just as depraved as Okka, though it seems she was even younger. They wanted to organize group sex immediately—two girls to four men. And, by the way, both Okka and the other girl were agreeable, to say the least. . . . But I didn't agree. You may believe this or not, but I was in love with this Okka. Honestly. She was a beautiful little girl, and I didn't give her to them. I mean I didn't give her to them for group sex. In the morning they took me to the airport and I flew to Moscow and later to the United States. It was only a year later when I was back in Salekhard that Ryazanov told me that my Okka had died of asthma. That's all I know. Over."

"Hudya! Hudya! Now listen carefully. EVERYTHING HE SAID IS THE TRUTH," I said into the microphone, putting my soul into it. My main job, after all, wasn't to interrogate Shertz or make accusations against him—what in hell did I want with Shertz? No, the main thing was to keep Hudya from committing a fourth murder. "Hudya, can you hear me? I interrogated Ayuni Ladukai. She was the second girl that evening. She confirms that when Shertz left for the airport, Okka was still alive. It all happened after that, when the three men had intercourse with Ayuni and Okka, all three at the same time. Can you hear me, Hudya? Over."

"I hear you." Hudya's reply was muffled. "Have you finished questioning Shertz? Over."

"No! I haven't finished! Hudya, please, dear, don't switch off! Mr. Shertz, one more question: do you know the surname of that girl—Okka? Do you know her surname? Over!''

I wanted to know where they were, Hudya and Shertz. But not I, or Captain Shevtsov, or even the local KGB could pinpoint their position in Hudya's car. We just didn't have the equipment. Maybe the paras had; in fact, they were sure to have. But it would hardly occur to Captain Shevtsov to get in touch with them.

"No, Anya, he doesn't know Okka's surname yet. Over." Hudya's voice came dryly through the radio. I realized he had taken over the microphone from Shertz.

"Hudya, where are you? I'll come to you right away! Dear, tell me where you are, over!''

"Anya, did you read the note I left you on the door?''

"Yes, I read it, Hudya. Over!''

"If you *immediately* do what was written on it, you will have the chance of speaking to me again. That's all. Transmission ends.''

"Hudya! Hud-ya! I don't understand! Hud-ya!'' I yelled into the microphone, but the only response was a faint crackle of interference. Hudya had switched off his radio.

I slumped dully behind the wheel. All around was the blackness of the polar night; the Volga's headlights still probed into the snow-laden wind.

The urgent voice of the police duty officer, Captain Shevtsov, jerked me out of my trance. "Kovina, what's going on? Can you explain? Over!''

"Just all of you fuck off!'' I said to the microphone, tossed it onto the mat, and began to swing the car around. The sense of Hudya's last reply began to trickle through to me. "Good-bye. And, please, go back to Russia''—that's what the note said. There's no railway in Urengoi. That meant I could only go to Russia from the airport. If so, Hudya had made an appointment to see me there. "Immediately," he had said.

I shot the car out of the schoolyard, switched on the siren, and sped off toward the airport.

The siren scared away the oncoming traffic and the people shopping; even the paras' armored personnel carriers gave me the right of way.

After about ten minutes I saw that two blue police Volgas were on my tail and a black one with no markings—Gee Bees. I didn't care; I paid no attention.

We raced out of Urengoi onto the airport road. Because of the government delegation arriving from Moscow, the road had been meticulously cleared; machines had raked up walls of snow on both sides. On some stretches bulldozers were still chugging along.

I gunned the engine, hanging grimly onto the wheel. Captain Shevtsov's voice broke in over the radio. "Kovina! Go easy, Kovina! Have you gone crazy? Kovina! I'm ordering you—reduce speed! You'll kill your fucking self!"

In the rearview mirror I saw that one of the blue police Volgas had skidded off at a sharp bend and buried itself up to the windshield in a snowdrift.

Just then, the cortege of black limousines and Volgas of the town party committee came into view in front of me. It was the local party and military chiefs on their way to the airport to meet the government delegation from Moscow. Hearing my siren the limousine drivers pulled over as I rocketed past. Out of the corner of my eye, I glimpsed the astonished, bewildered faces of Bogomyatov and Salakhov, and the gray astrakhan hats of KGB General Chebrikov and the paratroop commander, General Grinko.

60

As I tore up to the airport terminal, my headlights picked out a figure in a *militsa* standing by the entrance.

There was no sign of any police car or Hudya. I left the car and ran into the terminal. The Nenets by the entrance barred my way. "Are you Anna Kovina?"

"Yes, I . . ." I made to run off.

But the Nenets grabbed me by the arm.

"I'm Siegfried Shertz."

"You?"

It was only then I remembered that the Polar Hotel manager had described Shertz as being dressed in Nenets national clothing. "But where's Hudya?"

"Stop. He's gone."

"Where?"

"I don't know. He dropped me off here and asked me to give you this." Shertz handed me a sheet of paper, torn out of a notebook.

In the light pouring through the terminal windows, I read:

Anya,

I'm leaving him alive—for your sake, however. Good-bye. I am not a coward. The rest you will hear on the radio.

Hudya.

The police and Gee Bee Volgas came to a halt next to us and Captain Shevtsov, Major Gromov, and a number of other officers spilled out. Gromov grabbed Hudya's note out of my hand, and read it. "What does all this mean?"

"You heard my conversation with Hudya Benokan on the radio?" I asked.

"Not the beginning, but Captain Shevtsov patched me in at the most interesting part. Well?"

"The surname of the Nenets girl Ryazanov gave to Mr. Shertz five years ago was Benokan. Okka Benokan. She was Hudya's sister."

You have to give Major Gromov his due; it didn't take him more than a second to see the essentials.

"You mean the murder of Ryazanov, Hotko, and Voropayev was his work?" He didn't even wait for my answer. He nodded to his Gee Bees. "Into the car, the radio!"

The heavy drone of aircraft drowned out his last words. Above us in the dark polar skies, a Tu-104, with the government delegation on board, was coming in to land.

The motorcade of VIP limousines and Volgas was approaching the airport.

One of the KGB officers of Gromov's group dived into the Gee Bee Volga, while Gromov himself got into the one I had driven to the airport. He issued his orders. "Call him up! Your Benokan!"

I obeyed reluctantly. Siegfried Shertz seated himself in the rear without asking permission.

"Hudya!" I said into the microphone. "Hudya, it's me, Anna! We're at the airport. Over!"

The extraneous conversation of the police patrol still in the hostel kept breaking in.

". . . no need to secure him. He's drunk as a skunk as it is . . ."

Gromov smiled unpleasantly.

"We," he mimicked. "Are you informing him

you're not alone?'' He took the microphone from me and spoke into it himself: ''All radios off the air! All off the air! Benokan! Benokan! This is Major Gromov, state security. I'm asking you not to do anything else stupid. No more nonsense! If you give yourself up, we'll look into all the circumstances of the case.'' He followed the Tu-104 with his eyes as it descended toward the illuminated landing strip. ''Give yourself up, Benokan; we'll look into all the circumstances of the case, favorably! I promise! The word of an officer! Over!''

The Tu-104 touched down on its skis, raising a snow tornado behind it. After taxiing a short distance, it swung around and approached the terminal building. The gangway was hurried out to the aircraft, followed by the motorcade of limousines and black Volgas containing the town party committee and the military chiefs.

''This is Hudya Benokan,'' came through the radio. ''There will be no official opening of the gas pipeline. Do you hear me? Over.''

''I can hear, Benokan. Don't be a fool. I've told you: I guarantee a favorable review of the case. Over!'' Gromov glanced toward the neighboring Gee Bee Volga, where his officers were talking to somebody on their own radio.

''This is Hudya Benokan'' came over our radio. ''Five years ago, Ryazanov, Hotko, Voropayev, and Shertz killed my sister. I swore then that I would become an investigator and bring them to court in a show trial. I was a boy, a provincial member of the subarctic Komsomol. I believed in your slogans and your Soviet legality.'' Hudya spoke in a calm, even voice, as if dictating his will. ''But five years at Moscow University and practice in your Russian courts showed me what your Soviet legality is. If I had instituted proceedings against those four men, you would have expelled me from the force, however. Nobody would touch VIPs like Ryazanov, laureates all of them, on account of one little Nenets girl! You want to know how I killed them? No, I didn't kill them—I arranged a show trial for the whole tundra, as is the way of my people.

"Yes, I organized the escape of the three convicts from Camp RS-549. Every camp has at least one prisoner ready to escape; the swan waits for spring and the convict waits for freedom. I noted convicts like that in Camp RS-549; the rest was a technical matter as the Russians say. Tolmachov, Shimansky, and Zaloyev agreed to make a break during the first snowstorm. At night I waited for them outside the compound with a team of good reindeer, food, and warm clothing. I gave them a compass, and they went off into the storm, beyond the Urals, however. I think they are now on a sunny beach by the Black Sea. The rest you can imagine. It was I, instead of the convicts, who went to Yaku-Tur on the dogsled, and from there to Salekhard. Voropayev was the first. I dragged him drunk out of the choom of that Nenets slut, I dragged him out because it is our Nenets custom not to kill one's enemies in their chooms."

The door of the Tu-104 opened, and the Moscow visitors stepped onto the gangway. They all wore deerskin and astrakhan hats, warm overcoats with astrakhan collars. Their faces were—ministerial. The head of the government delegation, secretary to the central committee of the CPSU, Mikhail Gorbachev, gave a firm handshake to the party bosses and the joint chiefs of staff of the army, KGB, and police, who had so effectively restored order to the district.

Gromov, meanwhile, took a swift look at his Gee Bees in the next car. They nodded in confirmation.

"I tied Voropayev up and dragged him across the tundra," Hudya was continuing, as calmly as if he was simply testifying as a witness. "That's why you found bruises on his wrist and shoulder, Anya. . . . Then came Hotko and Ryazanov. *Nut i shar!* I organized a show trial for them—but I was just fulfilling my vow. I didn't know that my people would take it as the tundra spirits' summons to revolt. Still, you've taken everything from us Nentsi—rivers, land, sky, and even the gas under the earth. You have killed us; you have killed my people and bred a few hundred 'exemplary' Nentsi. And I was one of them, however. Think of that! The first Nenets investigator in the CID! Our own trained Nenets, however, yes? No, not true, however. The swan awaits the spring! I avenged my sister, but I was thinking of my daughter too, who would fall, in ten years' time, into the hands of your Ryazanovs and the rest. Just as Okka did, and my wife and Ayuni Ladukai and hundreds more. It helped me to grip the knife firmly . . ."

I couldn't understand why Gromov didn't say anything. Nor did I understand why Hudya was speaking so calmly and for so long. Gromov's silence was explained a minute later—two military helicopters suddenly flew over us, low, almost touching the car roofs. They flew off ahead of us across the airfield in the direction of the compressor station. Gromov started up his car and shot away after the helicopters. Only now did I realize why Gromov hadn't interrupted. On Gromov's orders, the paratroop radio operators had located the spot from where Hudya was broadcasting, and now two helicopters, with probably hundreds of soldiers on board, were on their way there. And so were we, two Volgas with police and Gee Bees. Toward us came the motorcade of black government cars. In one was the puzzled face of Salakhov, in another, Bogomyatov and Gorbachev.

And Hudya went on talking calmly, as if he'd been wound up, not suspecting that any minute he would be taken.

"But my people misunderstood me. They made a new Vauli Piettomin out of me, though none of the

Nentsi knows yet that the new Vauli Piettomin is plain Hudya Benokan. But I, I know. That's important, however . . ."

I couldn't sit quiet any longer; I twitched toward the microphone to shout to Hudya about the helicopters, that his position was known. But Gromov jabbed the barrel of his pistol in my side.

"Sit still! Take it easy! Let him talk." He smiled grimly, gripping the wheel with one hand, his eyes glued to the helicopters up ahead. This time, his smile was quite different from when he had flirted with me in the CID corridor. This was an evil smile, steely.

We sped across the airfield. Ahead of us, in the tundra, was the compressor station.

Still, Hudya went on, and his voice got louder, higher pitched. "When a man is driven to the wall, even a coward bites back, however. My people have been driven to the wall, you Russians have driven them there. And they have made a Vauli Piettomin out of me. And now I know that the death of that boy who blew up your armored vehicle is on my conscience. Even the hooligan behavior of those young people at the boarding school is on my conscience, Anya! I brought about this revolt, I alone. Of course, we cannot overcome your Russians. We're illiterate, backward, and sick. There are few of us, thirty thousand in all! Even a very large people like the Poles can't defeat you yet. But the time will come, however! There will be other times. The swan waits for spring and the convict waits for freedom. Small and big, sick and well, literate and illiterate—all the peoples you have robbed of oil and diamonds, rivers and mountains, life and liberty will rise up against you! They will all rise, you hear, Anna? And woe will come upon your people, woe, however. As is said in our old songs, *Nut i shar*, the bear's my witness, I can see the glow of fires. I can see the glow of fires and you will also see it, now, this moment. You will not get the gas of Yamal.

That's what little Vauli wanted, who died in Salekhard. That's what those boys wanted, those you shot in the tundra. And I, Hudya Benokan, will do what I must do. You remember, Anna, I told you about the sea gull . . ."

We had almost crashed against the wire fence of the compressor station. Close by, the two helicopters were hovering over a police car, Hudya's car. A para officer was running toward us from the car.

Gromov leapt out, I followed him, and both of us raced toward the car, but the para stopped us.

"It's empty. There's a tape-recorder running."

We still ran on to the abandoned car. On the front seat, an old reel-to-reel tape recorder lay next to the microphone; the spools were turning and Hudya's voice spoke straight into the radio mike. ". . . Sea gulls choose their own way to die. I also. Good-bye, Anna. And, please, go back to Russia."

Frustrated, Gromov looked around him.

"We need dogs! He can't have got far."

So that was why Hudya had spoken so calmly, so evenly. We had been listening to a tape.

I drew breath with a kind of inner relief. Hudya had gone away. Into the night of the tundra, the ground-hugging wind.

But Gromov was already shouting into the radio mike. "Dog handler and tracker dogs! Dog handler and tracker dogs! Call out the compressor station guard—red alert! Call out . . ."

An explosion at the far end of the compressor station interrupted him. The blast rocked me where I stood, and even the cars and helicopters swayed from the shock wave.

A pillar of fire rose over the compressor station, bathing in orange light that triumph of Russian, French, and German technology—six square kilometers, crammed with rectifier columns, turbine section housings, cooling substations, and its electronic control room.

The enormous spherical compressed gas holder had blown up, or rather, Hudya Benokan had blown it up.

There were twelve such gas holders towering above the compressor area, thousands of cubic meters of gas under pressure, and after the explosion two more began to sag toward the ground on their silver-steel supports.

The fire was spreading; it was already licking along the pipeline and along the earth itself toward the control room and the turbine units.

Another blast shook the air as a second gas holder sagged to the fire and detonated at a touch. A minute later the heat was breathing in our faces, a fleeting breath that melted the tundra earth beneath yet another gas holder; it collapsed. A third explosion . . .

The compressor station was blazing; fire hummed across the entire area, a fire from which no one could be saved, including, of course, Hudya.

The helicopters rose from the tundra into the sky. Gromov jumped into the Gee Bee Volga and backed away from the fire. Shertz and I leapt into Hudya's abandoned car and tore off, suffocated by the heat and smoke, into the tundra.

Away to one side of us, halfway between the airport and Urengoi, the motorcade of black government Volgas had halted. The Moscow and Tyumen VIPs had got out, and all of them, including Gorbachev, Chebrikov, Bogomyatov, Grinko, and Salakhov, stood in awe, staring at this tundra fireworks display, put on in honor of the pipeline opening not by the Moscow architect but by Hudya Benokan.

Yet farther off, in Urengoi, people were spilling out of their houses, gazing at the fire tearing into the black polar sky above the main compressor station. In the tongues of that fire, it seemed the tundra spirits were dancing.

I stopped the car and fell limply forward onto the steering wheel. I had no tears. There was an emptiness inside, an overwhelming emptiness. Ahead lay the Yamal tundra, dark and silent; behind lay the burning compressor station. And for some reason, relevant or not, the nagging jingle swam into my mind.

> *It's to Urengoi we're going*
> *Tundra round us as we pass*
> *Night complete with snowstorms blowing*
> *Watches over Nenets gas.*

The light gusts of the tundra blew oblique strands of white snow through the beams of my car headlights. It always does that when a blizzard is on the way.

EPILOGUE

*From AP, UPI, and Reuters News Agencies
and accredited Western correspondents in Moscow*

Moscow, January 11, 1984
On the 15th of December 1983 a fire occurred in the region of the Urengoi gas-fields, as a result of which, important electronic equipment was destroyed, and the delivery of Siberian gas via the new pipeline to Western Europe has had to be postponed for a considerable period. The *Washington Post*, quoting informed circles in Washington and Paris, says that the fire destroyed the Compressor Station in Urengoi. Moscow representatives of Western companies supplying equipment for the pipeline have declined to comment officially on this though they have confirmed that the Trans-Siberian gas pipeline will become operational only after many months.

Moscow, January 12, 1984
Soviet information and propaganda services are attempting to rebut stories of a fire and explosions on the Siberian pipeline. The official Soviet information agency Tass has published an interview with the Soviet gas industry minister Vasili Dynkov, who stated that "rumors put about by bourgeois mass-media are false and have no foundation in reality." Dynkov denies that there has been an explosion on the Siberia-

Western Europe gas pipeline, admitting, however, that a fire did take place at the Urengoi Compressor Station. He attempted to minimize the scale of this fire and stated that the equipment damaged as a result of the fire would be replaced in the immediate future.

In the opinion of Western diplomats in Moscow, the damage to the pipeline caused by the fire is more significant than the Soviet minister has admitted. In view of the prestige of this installation, however, and the passions aroused by it, the Soviet Union does not wish to disclose the true facts.

Has a Fire Stalled Moscow's Natural Gas Pipeline? For the Soviet Union, the building of a 2,759-mile natural gas pipeline from Siberia to Western Europe has become a test of technological prowess and a national crusade. Over the past two years, the Soviets have raced to finish the $18 billion project on schedule and prove that U.S. economic sanctions aimed at delaying the pipeline have had no impact. . . . With an air of satisfaction and triumph, Moscow announced two weeks ago that Siberian gas had started to flow into France on Jan. 1.

But even as the Soviets were proclaiming their success, reports were swirling in Moscow that the undertaking had suffered a setback. Western experts contend that the fire at the Urengoi station, the largest of 41 planned compressor units, will delay the project. . . .

Even the trickle of Soviet gas shipments to France this month may be a sham. Some Western businessmen in Moscow doubt that the pipeline will be completed before the end of 1985.

Time

January 23, 1984

In Paris, white synthetic fir trees shook their tiny Christmas lights on the Champs-Élysées, the Moulin

Rouge was a blaze of neon ads, and in the neighboring streets and alleys Palestinians dressed as Santa Claus enticed passersby into nightclubs and brothels.

Siegfried Shertz sat in a noisy bistro on Montmartre, occasionally turning unseeing eyes to look through the veranda window at the street swept by a damp wind, before lowering his eyes again to his tiny table. On it was a cup of coffee and the letter he had spent days of agony writing:

USSR, Urengoi, Yamal-Nenets District
CID Directorate
Investigator Anna Kovina

Dear Anna,
 In the hustle and bustle of the last few days I was in Urengoi, I did not manage to, or, more exactly, could not take the plunge and thank you for saving my life! Forgive me—and thank you! I do not think I shall be visiting the USSR again after all I went through during our short acquaintance. I was particularly struck by my last conversation with Mr. Chebrikov when, because of a number of circumstances you can probably guess, I was obliged to take a vow of silence concerning everything that had taken place in Urengoi before my eyes and yours. Of course, I will have to keep my promise and hold to my word as a businessman. But memory is not subject to blackmail and the orders of generals, even KGB generals. I remember you, I remember your friend Benokan, and even Ani-Opoi.
 Anna! If you ever find yourself in the West on business or as a tourist, I beg you to call me collect from any place in the Western world. My secretary will find me wherever I may be, and within hours I can be anywhere you name.

That letter had no chance of reaching its addressee even if by some miracle it had got through the inspection of foreign correspondence at the USSR Ministry of Communications. The simple fact was that on the day Shertz dropped his letter in a Paris mailbox, Anna Kovina was traveling south by train across Siberia, toward Voronezh. In her briefcase was a notice on a CID Directorate form:

> *For resourcefulness and effective action displayed during the rescue of the American citizen S. Shertz, CID Investigator Lieutenant Anna Kovina is posted to training at the Voronezh Advanced Police Academy.*

Kovina lay on the upper berth, gazing through the window at the snow-laden Siberian forests, but, like Shertz in Paris, she saw nothing. She was going to the Voronezh Academy with an empty heart. It seemed to her that the snowstorm outside still smelled of burning.

And up there on the Yamal, where the usual blizzard was, in fact, bearing the burning ash of the Urengoi Compressor Station out over the tundra along with the smoke of the gas flares, there in the polar night, in a swaying reindeer-skin choom, a two-year-old toddler was crawling out from under the hides that made a bed for him, his sisters, and his father. He tottered on his little bare feet to the entrance flap, stepping over the sleeping dogs, and went outside. The storm rocked the little boy, and the needle-sharp wind drove frozen snow into his face, but he stood his ground. Holding his *khote* in one little hand, he began to pee in the dark, fierce face of the blizzard.

"Hudya!" shouted Melkune from the choom. "Close the flap, it's drafty, cold!"

"Not cold, however," said the little boy, the youngest son of Ani-Opoi.

About the Author

Edward Topol knows intimately the people and the territory he depicts so magnificently. He was a prominent screenwriter and novelist in the Soviet Union—some of his work won awards, some of it was banned—before he emigrated. He is the author of *Submarine U-137*, *Red Square*, and *Deadly Games*. He lives now in Ontario, Canada, and Florida.